G R A P H I S   D E S I G N   9 4

# GRAPHIS DESIGN 94

The International Annual of Design and Illustration

Das internationale Jahrbuch über Design und Illustration

Le Répertoire International du Design et de l'Illustration

Edited by · Herausgegeben von · Edité par:

B. Martin Pedersen

Publisher and Creative Director: B. Martin Pedersen

Editors: Heinke Jenssen, Annette Crandall

Art Directors: B. Martin Pedersen, Tom Lewis

Photographer: Walter Zuber

Graphis Press Corp. Zürich (Switzerland)

Opposite Page: Carl-W. Röhrig · Page 6: Braldt Bralds · Last Page: Gidon Avraham

## GRAPHIS PUBLICATIONS

**GRAPHIS**, THE INTERNATIONAL BI-MONTHLY JOURNAL OF VISUAL COMMUNICATION

**GRAPHIS DESIGN**, THE INTERNATIONAL ANNUAL OF DESIGN AND ILLUSTRATION

**GRAPHIS PHOTO**, THE INTERNATIONAL ANNUAL OF PHOTOGRAPHY

**GRAPHIS POSTER**, THE INTERNATIONAL ANNUAL OF POSTER ART

**GRAPHIS NUDES**, A COLLECTION OF CAREFULLY SELECTED SOPHISTICATED IMAGES

**GRAPHIS PACKAGING**, AN INTERNATIONAL SURVEY OF PACKAGING DESIGN

**GRAPHIS LETTERHEAD**, AN INTERNATIONAL SURVEY OF LETTERHEAD DESIGN

**GRAPHIS DIAGRAM**, THE GRAPHIC VISUALIZATION OF ABSTRACT, TECHNICAL AND STATISTICAL FACTS AND FUNCTIONS

**GRAPHIS LOGO**, AN INTERNATIONAL SURVEY OF LOGOS

**GRAPHIS PUBLICATION**, AN INTERNATIONAL SURVEY OF THE BEST IN MAGAZINE DESIGN

**GRAPHIS ANNUAL REPORTS**, AN INTERNATIONAL COMPILATION OF THE BEST DESIGNED ANNUAL REPORTS

**GRAPHIS CORPORATE IDENTITY**, AN INTERNATIONAL COMPILATION OF THE BEST IN CORPORATE IDENTITY DESIGN

**ART FOR SURVIVAL: THE ILLUSTRATOR AND THE ENVIRONMENT**, A DOCUMENT OF ART IN THE SERVICE OF MAN.

**THE GRAPHIC DESIGNER'S GREEN BOOK**, ENVIRONMENTAL RESOURCES FOR THE DESIGN AND PRINT INDUSTRIES


## GRAPHIS PUBLIKATIONEN

**GRAPHIS**, DIE INTERNATIONALE ZWEIMONATSZEITSCHRIFT DER VISUELLEN KOMMUNIKATION

**GRAPHIS DESIGN**, DAS INTERNATIONALE JAHRBUCH ÜBER DESIGN UND ILLUSTRATION

**GRAPHIS PHOTO**, DAS INTERNATIONALE JAHRBUCH DER PHOTOGRAPHIE

**GRAPHIS POSTER**, DAS INTERNATIONALE JAHRBUCH DER PLAKATKUNST

**GRAPHIS NUDES**, EINE SAMMLUNG SORGFÄLTIG AUSGEWÄHLTER AKTPHOTOGRAPHIE

**GRAPHIS PACKAGING**, EIN INTERNATIONALER ÜBERBLICK ÜBER DIE PACKUNGSGESTALTUNG

**GRAPHIS LETTERHEAD**, EIN INTERNATIONALER ÜBERBLICK ÜBER BRIEFPAPIERGESTALTUNG

**GRAPHIS DIAGRAM**, DIE GRAPHISCHE DARSTELLUNG ABSTRAKTER TECHNISCHER UND STATISTISCHER DATEN UND FAKTEN

**GRAPHIS LOGO**, EINE INTERNATIONALE AUSWAHL VON FIRMEN-LOGOS

**GRAPHIS MAGAZINDESIGN**, EINE INTERNATIONALE ZUSAMMENSTELLUNG DES BESTEN ZEITSCHRIFTEN-DESIGNS

**GRAPHIS ANNUAL REPORTS**, EIN INTERNATIONALER ÜBERBLICK ÜBER DIE GESTALTUNG VON JAHRESBERICHTEN

**GRAPHIS CORPORATE IDENTITY**, EINE INTERNATIONALE AUSWAHL DES BESTEN CORPORATE IDENTITY DESIGNS

**ART FOR SURVIVAL: THE ILLUSTRATOR AND THE ENVIRONMENT**, EIN DOKUMENT ÜBER DIE KUNST IM DIENSTE DES MENSCHEN

**THE GRAPHIC DESIGNER'S GREEN BOOK**, UMWELTKONZEPTE DER DESIGN- UND DRUCKINDUSTRIE


## PUBLICATIONS GRAPHIS

**GRAPHIS**, LA REVUE BIMESTRIELLE INTERNATIONALE DE LA COMMUNICATION VISUELLE

**GRAPHIS DESIGN**, LE RÉPERTOIRE INTERNATIONAL DE LA COMMUNICATION VISUELLE

**GRAPHIS PHOTO**, LE RÉPERTOIRE INTERNATIONAL DE LA PHOTOGRAPHIE

**GRAPHIS POSTER**, LE RÉPERTOIRE INTERNATIONAL DE L'AFFICHE

**GRAPHIS NUDES**, UN FLORILEGE DE LA PHOTOGRAPHIE DE NUS

**GRAPHIS PACKAGING**, LE RÉPERTOIRE INTERNATIONAL DE LA CRÉATION D'EMBALLAGES

**GRAPHIS LETTERHEAD**, LE RÉPERTOIRE INTERNATIONAL DU DESIGN DE PAPIER À LETTRES

**GRAPHIS DIAGRAM**, LE RÉPERTOIRE GRAPHIQUE DE FAITS ET DONNÉES ABSTRAITS, TECHNIQUES ET STATISTIQUES

**GRAPHIS LOGO**, LE RÉPERTOIRE INTERNATIONAL DU LOGO

**GRAPHIS PUBLICATION**, LE RÉPERTOIRE INTERNATIONAL DU DESIGN DE PÉRIODIQUES

**GRAPHIS ANNUAL REPORTS**, PANORAMA INTERNATIONAL DU MEILLEUR DESIGN DE RAPPORTS ANNUELS D'ENTREPRISES

**GRAPHIS CORPORATE IDENTITY**, PANORAMA INTERNATIONAL DU MEILLEUR DESIGN D'IDENTITÉ CORPORATE

**ART FOR SURVIVAL: THE ILLUSTRATOR AND THE ENVIRONMENT**, L'ART AU SERVICE DE LA SURVIE

**THE GRAPHIC DESIGNER'S GREEN BOOK**, L'ÉCOLOGIE APPLIQUÉE AU DESIGN ET À L'INDUSTRIE GRAPHIQUE

PUBLICATION NO. 226 (ISBN 3-85709-194.0)

© COPYRIGHT UNDER UNIVERSAL COPYRIGHT CONVENTION

COPYRIGHT © 1993 BY GRAPHIS PRESS CORP., DUFOURSTRASSE 107, 8008 ZURICH, SWITZERLAND

JACKET AND BOOK DESIGN COPYRIGHT © 1993 BY PEDERSEN DESIGN

141 LEXINGTON AVENUE, NEW YORK, N.Y. 10016 USA

PRINTED IN JAPAN BY TOPPAN PRINTING CO., LTD.

# CONTENTS · INHALT · SOMMAIRE

## REMARKS

WE EXTEND OUR HEARTFELT THANKS TO CONTRIBUTORS THROUGHOUT THE WORLD WHO HAVE MADE IT POSSIBLE TO PUBLISH A WIDE AND INTERNATIONAL SPECTRUM OF THE BEST WORK IN THIS FIELD.

ENTRY INSTRUCTIONS MAY BE REQUESTED AT:
GRAPHIS PRESS CORP.,
DUFOURSTRASSE 107,
8008 ZÜRICH, SWITZERLAND

## ANMERKUNGEN

UNSER DANK GILT DEN EINSENDERN AUS ALLER WELT, DIE ES UNS DURCH IHRE BEI- TRÄGE ERMÖGLICHT HABEN, EIN BREITES, INTERNATIONALES SPEKTRUM DER BESTEN ARBEITEN ZU VERÖFFENTLICHEN.

TEILNAHMEBEDINGUNGEN:
GRAPHIS VERLAG AG,
DUFOURSTRASSE 107,
8008 ZÜRICH, SCHWEIZ

## ANNOTATIONS

TOUTE NOTRE RECONNAISSANCE VA AUX DESIGNERS DU MONDE ENTIER DONT LES ENVOIS NOUS ONT PERMIS DE CONSTITUER UN VASTE PANORAMA INTERNATIONAL DES MEILLEURES CRÉATIONS.

MODALITÉS D'ENVOI DE TRAVAUX:
EDITIONS GRAPHIS,
DUFOURSTRASSE 107,
8008 ZÜRICH, SUISSE

COMMENTARIES


KOMMENTARE


COMMENTAIRES

# REMEMBERING WHAT IT MEANS TO BE HUMAN

People are angry, confused, and afraid. The old order is disappearing. Boundaries and identities are in flux, or non-existent. The rules have failed. □ Perhaps the most striking thing about such statements is how applicable they have become to so many aspects of modern society. One could easily discuss conditions in Russia, the American corporate culture, or the international design community without changing a word in the paragraph above; a rather sobering thought in itself. □ Five years ago, if somebody had told me the day was coming when design firms would not only compete against each other for clients, but with advertising agencies, production houses, computer engineering firms, and industrial design groups, I'm not sure how I would have reacted, or if a reaction would have even been possible. There must be a context in order for any reaction to occur, and five years ago the context for competition of this nature didn't exist. Now it's just part of doing business. □ Investigating the collective identity crisis for an entire profession becomes especially difficult, when you consider that practically every other major profession is undergoing a similar crisis and the aftershocks affect us all. Design is not a discreet commodity, it is a piece of the big picture, the big network. When the sum of the parts comes into question, then inevitably the way the parts fit together must change as well. Of course, the 500 pound gorilla creating all this havoc may simply be change itself. Change happens, requiring that we change our thinking, adapt our behavior, and remind ourselves on occasion that we are only human. □ Among the many ideas being questioned by business big and small is the notion of "owning expertise." Specific problem solving would have entailed, in the not too distant past, the creation of a specific in-house department, charged with the task at hand and any others that vaguely resembled it. Companies tried to win markets by controlling the cost of bringing products to those markets and it worked, especially when markets were stable or mature. In accelerated markets, or markets undergoing massive fragmentation, the idea of owning expertise is about as feasible as an accurate map of what used to be Yugoslavia. To compensate, corporations are recreating themselves in a phenomena known as the "virtual corporation." Expertise in the virtual corporation is resident outside the corporate enclave, and appears only when and as needed. In this way, companies can respond quickly to a wide range of challenges, tapping the very best resources for the job, while neatly sidestepping the costs of a large, unwieldy superstructure. It's the epitome of the lean, mean, strategic alliance machine. □ Yesterday's monolithic corporations have died and come back as chameleons who are expert at blending in with target markets, or resembling perceived benefits. Hallmark, for instance, has exchanged its time honored identity as a greeting card company for the fuzzy plurality of the personal greeting business. Why limit yourself to just one delivery medium when you can be all of them? Success in the past is no longer the foundation for success in the future, as evidenced by IBM's struggles and constant restructuring over the last decade. Accounting firms like KMPG and Cooper's & Lybrand have expanded their identity to include strategic consulting. It's almost as though business people were searching for the new Esperanto, the right syntax for a broader interpretation of expertise and specialization. □ How we sell products is changing radically, too. Who needs sophisticated retail packaging when you can move 8,000 units an hour just by pointing a camcorder at your product and distributing the image to millions of consumers via a home shopping channel? Who needs retail outlets, when an interactive, self-contained kiosk strategically placed at the mall can serve as an electronic catalog, a customer service agent, and order facilitator? Before long, we may be asking ourselves who needs paper, when there is electricity? □ Anyone looking for a safe haven from these kind of developments can stop right now, because there are no safe havens. Change can assume many forms. It can even

**CLEMENT MOK** BEGAN HIS CAREER IN NEW YORK WHERE HE DEVELOPED PRINT, ON-AIR BROADCAST GRAPHICS, AND THREE-DIMENSIONAL DESIGN PROJECTS FOR CLIENTS SUCH AS ROCKEFELLER CENTER, REPUBLIC NATIONAL BANK, AND CBS. PRIOR TO FORMING HIS OWN AGENCY, HE SPENT FIVE YEARS AS A CREATIVE DIRECTOR AT APPLE COMPUTER, WHERE HE DIRECTED A MYRIAD OF PROJECTS. CLEMENT'S WORK HAS BEEN PUBLISHED INTERNATIONALLY AND HAS RECEIVED OVER 100 AWARDS FROM PROFESSIONAL ORGANIZATIONS AND PUBLICATIONS. HIS DESIGNS HAVE ALSO BEEN EXHIBITED IN MUSEUMS AND GALLERIES IN EUROPE AND JAPAN.

(THIS PAGE LEFT): A SCREEN SHOT FROM APPLE'S QUICKTIME CLIPS FEATURING ILLUSTRATIONS BY CLEMENT MOK. (MIDDLE): A SHOT OF THE 3COM BOOTH (RIGHT) GO CORPORATION PRODUCT/DEMO SHOT.□ (FACING PAGE TOP): MACROMEDIA PACKAGING SYSTEM (MIDDLE) MIRAGE LOGO (BOTTOM) REVO 1993 "3 HEAD" POSTER.■

masquerade as progress, or innovation, when actually it is much deeper than that. The computer, or the act of computing, began as a benign means to an end for most of us—a typography tool, a faster way to produce mechanicals, en electronic "sketch pad"—only to become the desired end product, the driving force behind the reinvention of our profession. □ Part of the problem lies in the general misconception that to own a computer is to be a designer. The tangible things that used to differentiate us from other professionals have turned into common commodities. Brochures, illustrations, photographs, fact sheets and catalogs are being created on the desktop by people with no design experience. The friendly, neighborhood "printing-while-you-wait" shop usually harbors a self-proclaimed expert on publication design, who is more willing to give advice. The computer has placed the "craft" of design into the hands of the untrained, and unskilled, allowing anybody to develop things that, on the surface, look and smell like design, the pressure on real designers intensifies. The question arises: why does client "A" need design firm "B" when client "A" has computer "C" and a desktop publishing specialist fresh out of college and raring to go? It's not enough any more to say that we solve communications problems—so does a telephone operator. □ Adding to the confusion is the failure of language to establish or solidify meaning. Designers are struggling with words and definitions like never before. Is a graphic artist someone who arranges graphics on a piece of paper, a computer screen or for MTV? What is an artist? Someone who originates one-of-a-kind designs or who creates mass producible templates? Words like "content" have been granted special powers and meaning. It can refer to the message, or the executional components of the message seemingly at the whim

of the speaker. Old words have been pressed into service as "repurposed solutions," while new words like "multimedia" are sprouting up like weeds. If you think it's hopelessly confusing to people within the design community, imagine how it must be to outsiders. □ Where else but on the computer do we have the ability to "undo" our mistakes in life? Technology has outstripped our ability to comprehend, or even fully appreciate the powers it bestows. It terrifies and allures. It dangles the carrot of god-like perfection before our eyes, and we reach out our hands, because we are human. □ Just as the collapse of the Soviet Union became the context for strife in the Balkans, the spreading imprint of technology is the new context for design. Design is going beyond the "look" and "feel" of things. It is asking deeper, more important questions. As our technical capacities grow, ultimately designers will employ their skills and judgment to define and redefine the human element, framing an appropriate response to so much power and chaos. □ In the near future, designers will be asked to convert the tangible into the intangible; to convey lasting messages through ephemeral electronic medias. Don't be too quick to judge what is good or bad, because the rules may be different. With each new medium, an aesthetic will follow that takes into consideration the strengths and limitations of the medium. Illustrations in the digital world are mathematical formulas defined by vector pints. Measurements are not in inches or picas on the computer screen, they are in tiny specks of light called pixels. Realities of this kind need to be assimilated, before judgments are passed. □ A new generation of designers are wading into a sea of data—available as text, video, graphic images, high resolution photography, illustration, animation and audio—and returning with templates for

Mirage

See what you've been missing.    RĒVO
SUNGLASS COLLECTIONS

new ways of communicating, learning and experiencing information. One of the templates may detail the user interface. Another might diagram the levels and scenarios for user interaction. Do such activities still fall under the rubric of design? Of course they do. The computer hasn't limited design or rendered it impotent, it has expanded our aware- ness of what constitutes design, and focused our attention on what creates design of lasting value. In the face of overwhelming change, the primary concern of design hasn't changed. It continues to probe and examine the fundamental art of being human. It is a constant reminder that ultimately we decide what is possible and what is not. ∎

Die Menschen sind wütend, verwirrt, und sie fürchten sich. Die alte Ordnung verschwindet. Grenzen und Identitäten sind in Fluss geraten oder nicht-existent. Die Regeln haben versagt. □ Das überraschendste an solchen Statements ist vielleicht, wie gut sie sich auf viele Aspekte der modernen Gesellschaft anwenden lassen. Man könnte ohne weiteres über die Zustände in Russland, die amerikanische Firmen- kultur oder die internationale Designbranche diskutieren, ohne ein Wort dieses Statements zu ändern. □ Wenn mir vor fünf Jahren jemand gesagt hätte, dass der Tag kommt, an dem Designfirmen es nicht nur mit der Konkurrenz aus der eigenen Branche zu tun haben, sondern es auch mit Werbe- agenturen, Produktionsfirmen, Computerproduzenten und Produktdesigngruppen aufnehmen müssen, weiss ich nicht, wie ich reagiert hätte, wenn eine Reaktion überhaupt mög- lich gewesen wäre. Jede Reaktion setzt bestimmte Umstän- de voraus, und vor fünf Jahren waren sie für diese Art des Konkurrenzkampfes nicht gegeben. Jetzt gehört es ganz einfach zum Geschäft. □ Die kollektive Identitätskrise für einen ganzen Berufszweig zu untersuchen wird besonders schwierig, wenn man bedenkt, dass praktisch jede andere Branche eine ähnliche Krise durchmacht, und wir alle sind vom nachträglichen Schock betroffen. Design ist keine diskrete Ware, es ist Teil des grossen Bildes, des grossen Netzwerks. Wenn die Summe der Teile in Frage gestellt wird, dann muss sich auch die Art der Zusammensetzung der Teile ändern. Natürlich könnte der ungefähr 200 kg schwere Gorilla, der all diesen verheerenden Schaden anrichtet, schlicht eine Veränderung bedeuten. Verän- derungen gibt es. Sie verlangen, dass wir unsere Denk- weise ändern, unser Verhalten anpassen und uns gelegent- lich daran erinnern, dass wir nur Menschen sind. □ Unter den vielen Dingen, die von kleinen und grossen Unter- nehmen in Frage gestellt werden, ist die Vorstellung, «Fachwissen zu besitzen». In nicht allzu ferner Vergan- genheit wäre für die Lösung spezieller Probleme eine be- sondere firmeninterne Abteilung gegründet worden, mit dem Auftrag, die anstehende Aufgabe und andere, die irgendwie damit vergleichbar waren, zu lösen. Firmen versuchten, Märkte zu gewinnen, indem sie die Kosten für die Versor- gung dieser Märkte mit ihren Produkten niedrig hielten. Das klappte, besonders wenn die Märkte stabil oder reif waren. Bei Märkten, die sich schnell verändern oder in viele Kom- ponenten zersplittern, ist die Vorstellung, Fachwissen zu besitzen, ungefähr so glaubhaft wie eine genaue Landkarte der Gebiete des ehemaligen Jugoslawien. Um dem entge- genzuwirken, erfinden sich Firmen neu. Das Phänomen ist als «virtual corporation» bekannt. Fachwissen ist bei einer solchen Firma ausserhalb zu suchen, und es wird nur einge- setzt, wenn es gebraucht wird. Auf diese Weise können Firmen schnell auf breitgefächerte Anforderungen reagie- ren. Sie nutzen die allerbesten Kräfte für den Job und ver- meiden damit ganz klar die Kosten eines grossen, unbe- holfenen Überbaus. Es ist der Inbegriff der mageren, strate- gischen Allianz-Maschine. □ Die gigantischen Unternehmen von gestern sind gestorben und als Chamäleons zurück- gekommen, Experten darin, sich Zielmärkten anzupassen oder Vorzüge zu signalisieren. Die amerikanische Firma Hallmark z.B. hat ihre ehrwürdige Identität als Grusskar- tenfirma gegen die verschwommene Bezeichnung «perso- nal greeting business» eingetauscht. Warum soll man sich auf nur ein Medium beschränken, wenn man alle haben kann? Erfolg in der Vergangenheit ist nicht mehr die Grund- lage für Erfolg in der Zukunft, wie IBMs verzweifeltes Ringen und ständiges Umstrukturieren in den vergangenen zehn Jahren zeigt. Steuerberatungsfirmen wie z.B. KMPG und Cooper's & Lybrand haben ihre Tätigkeit auf strategische Beratungen ausgedehnt. Es ist fast so, als suchten Ge- schäftsleute nach einem neuen Esperanto, die richtige Syntax für eine breitere Interpretationsmöglichkeit von Expertise und Spezialisierung. □ Die Art, wie wir Produkte verkaufen, verändert sich ebenfalls radikal. Wer braucht anspruchsvolle Verpackungen für den Einzelhandel, wenn man 8000 Einheiten per Stunde absetzen kann, indem man einfach via Home-Shopping-TV-Kanal ein Bild davon zu Millionen von Konsumenten schickt. Wer braucht Läden, wenn ein interaktiver, unabhängiger Kiosk, gut plaziert in einem Einkaufszentrum, als elektronischer Katalog, Kundendienst und Auftragsempfänger dienen kann? Bald werden wir uns fragen: Wer braucht Papier, wenn es Elektrizität gibt? □ Wer einen Hafen sucht, in dem er vor diesen Entwicklungen sicher ist, muss auf der Stelle aufhören, denn einen solchen gibt es nicht. Veränderung kann verschiedene Formen haben. Sie kann auch als Fortschritt verkleidet daherkommen, als Innovation, während sie tatsächlich viel tiefgreifender ist. Der Computer oder der Umgang damit war für die meisten von uns ein willkommenes Werkzeug für bestimmte Zwecke – Satzherstellung, schnellere Produktion von Druckvorlagen, ein elektronischer Skizzenblock. Daraus wurde dann das, was er heute ist: die treibende Kraft hinter der Neuerfindung unseres Berufes. □ Ein Teil des Problems liegt in dem allgemeinen Irrtum, der Besitz eines Computers bedeute, dass man ein Designer sei. Die greifbaren Dinge, die den Unterschied zwischen uns und anderen Berufsgruppen ausmachten, sind Allgemeingut geworden. Broschüren, Illustrationen, Photos, Tabellen und Aufstellungen sind per Desktop von Leuten ohne Designerfahrung hergestellt. In dem netten Laden in der Nachbarschaft, der «für Sie druckt, während Sie warten», sitzt normalerweise ein selbsternannter Experte im Publication Design, jederzeit bereit, Ratschläge zu erteilen. Der Computer hat das «Handwerk» in die Hände von unausgebildeten Leuten gelegt, so dass jeder Sachen machen kann, die oberflächlich betrachtet wie Design aussehen. Wenn Kunden anfangen, Dinge zu produzieren, die nach Design aussehen, geraten die wirklichen Designer noch mehr unter Druck. Es stellt sich die Frage: Warum braucht der Kunde «A» die Designfirma «B» wenn der Kunde «A» einen Computer «C» und einen Desktop-Spezialisten frisch vom College hat? Es genügt nicht mehr zu sagen, dass wir Kommunikationsprobleme lösen – das macht eine Telephonistin auch. □ Die Verwirrung wird noch grösser durch das Versagen der Sprache, Bedeutung zu etablieren bzw. festzulegen. Designer kämpfen wie nie zuvor mit Worten und Definitionen. Ist jemand, der Graphik auf einem Stück Papier, auf dem Bildschirm oder für MTV arrangiert ein Designer? Was ist ein Künstler? Jemand, der Einzelstücke herstellt oder Vorlagen für die Massenproduktion liefert? Worten wie «Inhalt» wurden besondere Kraft und Bedeutung beige-

messen. Das kann sich auf die scheinbar dem Sprecher überlassene Botschaft oder auf Komponenten ihrer Umsetzung beziehen. Alte Worte, die früher eine bestimmte Bedeutung hatten, werden heute neuen Zwecken angepasst. Gleichzeitig schiessen neue Worte wie zum Beispiel «Multimedia» wie Pilze aus dem Boden. Wenn das für Leute in der Designbranche hoffnungslos verwirrend ist, wie muss es erst auf Aussenstehende wirken? □ Wo sonst als auf dem Computer können wir unsere Fehler mit einer «undo»-Taste ungeschehen machen? Technologie hat unsere Fähigkeit, die uns von ihr gebotenen Möglichkeiten zu verstehen oder richtig einzuschätzen, überholt. Sie macht Angst und zieht an. Sie gaukelt uns gottähnliche Perfektion vor, und wir strecken unsere Hände aus, weil wir Menschen sind. Wie das Zusammenbrechen der Sowjetunion das Umfeld für die Umwälzungen auf dem Balkan liefert, so ist die sich ausbreitende Technologie der neue Kontext für Design. Design geht über die Wirkung der Dinge auf Augen und Tastsinn hinaus. Das heisst, tiefergehende, wichtigere Fragen sind zu stellen. Während unsere technischen Möglichkeiten wachsen, werden die Designer schliesslich ihr Können und ihre Urteilskraft so einsetzen, dass die menschliche Komponente definiert bzw. redefiniert wird. Damit wäre eine angemessene Antwort auf so viel Macht und Chaos gegeben. □ In naher Zukunft wird man von Designern verlangen, das Greifbare in Nicht-Greifbares umzuwandeln; wichtige Botschaften durch ephemere elektronische Medien mitzuteilen. Seien Sie mit Ihrem Urteil über gut oder schlecht nicht zu schnell, weil die Regeln anders aussehen können. Mit jedem neuen Medium wird eine Ästhetik folgen, die den Stärken und Grenzen des Mediums gerecht wird. Illustrationen in der digitalen Welt sind mathematische Formeln, in Vektor-Punkten definiert. Masse erscheinen nicht in Inches oder Punkten auf dem Computerbildschirm, es sind kleine Lichtsprenkel, die man Pixel nennt. Man muss sich Realitäten dieser Art anpassen, bevor man urteilt. □ Eine neue Designergeneration watet durch ein Meer von Daten – verfügbar als Text, Video, graphische Bilder, Hochauflösungsphotographie, Illustration, Animation und Ton – sie kommen mit Vorlagen für neue Wege der Kommunikation, des Lernens und der Aufnahme von Informationen zurück. Eine der Schablonen mag sich mit

CLEMENT MOK BEGANN SEINE KARRIERE IN NEW YORK, WO ER DRUCK- UND TV-GRAPHIK SOWIE DREIDIMENSIONALE PROJEKTE FÜR KUNDEN WIE DAS ROCKEFELLER CENTER, DIE REPUBLIC NATIONAL BANK UND CBS MACHTE. BEVOR ER EINE EIGENE AGENTUR ERÖFFNETE, WAR ER FÜNF JAHRE CREATIVE DIRECTOR BEI APPLE COMPUTER. DANK SEINER ERFAHRUNG UND EXPERTISE IN DIESEM NEUEN MEDIUM BERÄT ER EINERSEITS ZAHLREICHE COMPUTERFIRMEN, UND ANDERERSEITS SPIELT ER EINE AKTIVE ROLLE BEI DER AUSBILDUNG DER DESIGNER IN DIESEM BEREICH. SEINE ARBEITEN WURDEN IN MUSEEN UND GALERIEN IN EUROPA UND JAPAN AUSGESTELLT.

Verbraucher-Interface befassen. Eine andere mit Ebenen und Szenarios von Interaktion der Verwender. Fällt so etwas noch unter die Rubrik Design? Natürlich. Der Computer hat Design nicht beschränkt oder zur Ohnmacht verurteilt, er hat lediglich die technischen Möglichkeiten erweitert, ohne das

anzutasten, was Design von bleibendem Wert schafft. Trotz überwältigender Veränderungen hat sich die Hauptaufgabe des Designs nicht verändert, nämlich eine menschliche Umwelt zu erforschen und zu gestalten. Denn schliesslich sind wir es, die entscheiden, was möglich ist und was nicht. ∎

Les gens sont en colère, ils sont effrayés et déconcertés. L'ancien ordre s'effondre. Les règles sont caduques, repères et identités, quand ils existent encore, sont fluctuants. ☐ Le plus frappant s'agissant de ce type de déclarations, c'est qu'elles ont fini par s'appliquer de façon adéquate à bien des aspects de la société moderne. On pourrait discuter sans problème de la réalité russe, de la culture d'entreprise américaine ou de la communauté internationale des designers, sans ajouter ni retrancher un seul mot au paragraphe ci-dessus; un constat qui donne à réfléchir. ☐ Si on m'avait dit il y a cinq ans qu'un jour les bureaux de design ne se feraient plus seulement de concurrence entre eux, mais auraient également à compter avec la concurrence des agences de publicité, des maisons de production, des entreprises d'informatique et des groupes de design industriel, je ne sais pas comment j'aurais réagi ou s'il y avait seulement un moyen de réagir. Toute réaction est tributaire du contexte dans lequel elle se produit, or, il y a cinq ans, le contexte ne permettait pas de supposer une concurrence de cette nature. Aujourd'hui, c'est simplement une des données du business. ☐ Tenir compte, pour un secteur professionnel, de cette crise d'identité collective pose des difficultés croissantes, puisque cette crise affecte toutes les professions et que ses effets rejaillissent sur l'ensemble de la société. Le design ne fait pas exception, il appartient comme tout produit à un réseau d'influences, il est une pièce du puzzle. C'est pourquoi, lorsque tout est remis en question, le rapport des différentes parties qui composent le tout devra nécessairement être remis en question. Bien sûr, on trouve peut-être tout bonnement à l'origine de ce tohu-bohu le changement , mais lorsque vient le temps du changement, il nous faut réviser notre façon de penser, adapter notre comportement et nous souvenir qu'après tout, nous sommes humains. ☐ Parmi les nombreuses idées que le grand comme le petit commerce ont remis en question, se trouve la notion de «savoir-faire interne». Le besoin de répondre à des problèmes spécifiques aurait abouti dans un passé récent à la mise sur pied d'un département interne directement chargé de ce problème et d'autres tâches similaires. Les compagnies tentèrent de gagner des marchés en contrôlant le prix d'acheminement des produits sur ces marchés, ce qui aboutit

à des résultats satisfaisants, notamment dans le cas des marchés stables ou ayant atteint leur phase de maturité. En ce qui concerne les marchés évoluant rapidement ou les marchés soumis à une forte segmentation, l'idée d'un savoir-faire interne n'est pas plus crédible qu'une carte précise de la Yougoslavie. Pour compenser, les sociétés réalisent des projections connues sous le nom de «sociétés virtuelles». Dans le cas des sociétés virtuelles, le savoir-faire n'est plus interne, mais externe. De cette façon, les entreprises peuvent faire face rapidement à un large éventail de défis en faisant appel pour chaque projet aux ressources les mieux appropriées, tout en faisant l'économie d'une infrastructure trop importante, donc encombrante. ☐ Les sociétés monolithiques d'hier sont devenues des caméléons, expertes dans l'art de s'adapter à des marchés ciblés ou alors de suggérer des rentrées de bénéfice.Hallmark, par exemple, a troqué son identité de fabricants de cartes de vœux réputé contre celle diversifiée et floue de «société de vœux personnalisés». Pourquoi se limiter à un seul medium de distribution, lorsqu'on peut les représenter tous? Les succès remportés par le passé ne sont plus la clef des succès futurs comme l'ont démontré les combats et les continuelles restructurations qu'a connus IBM au cours des dix dernières années. Des fiduciaires comme KMPG ou Cooper's & Lybrand ont élargi leur identité en y ajoutant des prestations en matière de consulting stratégique. ☐ Notre manière de vendre les produits, elle aussi, change de façon radicale. Qui a encore besoin d'un emballage détaillé et sophistiqué quand vous pouvez en écouler 8000 unités par heure tout simplement en diffusant une image vidéo par le biais d'un programme d'achat à domicile? Qui a encore besoin de magasins, quand un kiosque interactif indépendant placé stratégiquement dans une galerie marchande peut faire office de catalogue électronique, de service à la clientèle et de preneur de commandes? Bref, qui a besoin de papier alors qu'il y a de l'électricité? ☐ Toute personne cherchant à se protéger contre ce type de développements doit renoncer séance tenante, car il n'existe pas de moyen de protection sûr. Le changement peut prendre bien des formes. Il peut même passer sous couvert de progrès ou d'innovation, alors qu' il s'agit en fait de quelque chose de beaucoup plus profond.

L'ordinateur, ou le recours à l'ordinateur, d'abord considéré comme un simple moyen, un outil du typographie, un engin permettant de produire rapidement des machines, un bloc-note électronique, est aujourd'hui tout bonnement devenu le moteur de la rénovation de notre profession. □ Une grande part du problème est due à cette idée fausse qui veut que posséder un ordinateur, c'est être designer. Les choses tangibles qui nous distinguaient des autres professionnels sont devenues des moyens banals. Brochures, illustrations, photographies, tableaux et catalogues sont réalisés sur des consoles par des gens dépourvus d'expérience graphique. Le sympathique «copy-quick» du coin cache souvent un expert en PAO auto-proclamé, qui n'hésitera pas à vous conseiller. Avec l'ordinateur, le «métier» du designer a abouti entre les mains de personnes inexpertes, permettant à tout un chacun de développer des produits qui, superficiellement, offrent l'apparence et le fini du design. Quand les clients commencent à produire des choses qui ont l'apparence et le fini du design, les vrais designers doivent satisfaire un niveau d'exigence plus élevé. La question qui se pose est: pourquoi le client A a-t-il besoin du bureau de design B quand ce même client possède un ordinateur, ainsi qu'un spécialiste en PAO fraîchement émoulu d'une école spécialisée et hyper-motivé. □ Il ne suffit plus de déclarer que nous résolvons des problèmes de communication -la téléphoniste aussi. □ L'incapacité du langage à fixer ou affirmer le sens ajoute encore à la confusion. Plus que jamais, les designers se battent avec les mots et les définitions. Un artiste graphiste est-il quelqu'un qui dessine des graphiques sur une feuille de papier, sur un écran ordinateur ou pour MTV? Qu'est-ce qu'un artiste? Celui qui est à l'origine d'un design unique ou celui qui crée les modèles des produits de série? On a attribué à des termes comme "contenu" des pouvoirs et des sens particuliers. Ce terme peut ainsi se référer au message ou à sa transcription selon l'émetteur. D'anciens termes ont connu une deuxième jeunesse, tandis que de nouveaux termes comme "multimédia" prolifèrent. Quand on sait que cet état de choses porte la communauté des designers à la confusion, imaginez ce qu'il en est des profanes. □ Où a-t-on l'occasion, mis à part sur l'ordinateur, de revenir sur nos erreurs? La technologie défie toute évaluation exhaustive des pouvoirs qu'elle met à notre portée, elle devance l'entendement. Elle fascine et terrifie, elle fait miroiter à nos yeux l'illusion d'une perfection absolue que nous cherchons à saisir parce que nous sommes humains. □ De même que l'effondrement de l'Union Soviétique donne sa véritable dimension au conflit des Balkans, l'influence croissante de la technologie donne une nouvelle dimension au design. Le design va bien au-delà de l'apparence et du toucher. Il pose des questions plus importantes, plus profondes. A mesure que progressent nos capacités techniques, les designers mettent leurs compétences et leur jugement au service d'une redéfinition de l'élément humain, ils donnent forme à ces nouveaux pouvoirs et au chaos qu'ils impliquent. □ Dans un futur proche, on exigera des designers qu'ils fassent de l'intangible à partir du tangible, qu'ils transmettent des messages durables au moyen d'éphémères médias électroniques. Ne jugez pas trop vite ce qui est bon et ce qui est mauvais, car les règles pourraient avoir changé. De chaque nouveau medium s'ensuivra une esthétique qui tiendra compte des forces et des limites de ce medium. Dans le monde digital, les illustrations sont des formules mathématiques définies par des points vectoriels. Sur l'écran ordinateur, les dimensions ne se mesurent pas en centimètres ou en picas, mais en minuscules taches de lumière nommées pixels. Ce sont des connaissances de ce type dont il faut tenir compte avant d'émettre un jugement. □ Une nouvelle génération de designers pénètre dans la jungle des données professionnelles - textes, vidéos, images graphiques, photographies à haute définition, illustrations, son et animation - et en retire les paradigmes d'une nouvelle forme de communication, de formation et d'assimilation de l'information.L'un des paradigmes expose en détail l'interface avec le consommateur. Un autre servira à dresser un synopsis des niveaux et situations de l'interaction avec l'utilisateur. Est-ce que de telles activités relèvent encore du design? Sans aucun doute. L'ordinateur n'a ni limité, ni stérilisé le design, il a élargi notre définition du design et centré notre attention sur ce qui fait du design durable. Malgré les menaces que fait peser le changement sur le design,le but premier de celui-ci est resté le même. Il continue d'explorer l'art fondamental qui consiste à être humain. Il nous rappelle sans cesse que c'est à nous que revient la tâche de définir ce qui est possible et ce qui ne l'est pas. ■

. . . . . . . . . . . . . . . . . . . . . . . . . . . . . . . . . . . . . . . . . . . . . . . . . . . . . . . . .
**CLEMENT MOK** A COMMENCÉ SA CARRIÈRRE À NEW YORK, OÙ IL A RÉALISÉ DES TRAVAUX POUR L'ÉDITION ET POUR LA TÉLÉVISION, AINSI QUE DES PROJETS EN TROIS DIMENSIONS POUR DES CLIENTS COMME LE ROCKEFELLER CENTER, LA REPUBLIC NATIONAL BANK ET CBS. AVANT D'OUVRIR SA PROPRE AGENCE, IL A ÉTÉ DURANT CINQ ANS DIRECTEUR EN CRÉATION CHEZ APPLE COMPUTER. GRÂCE À L'EXPÉRIENCE ET À LA COMPÉTENCE ACQUISE DANS CE DOMAINE, IL CONSEILLE DORÉNAVANT DE NOMBREUSES ENTREPRISES DE PROGRAMMATION INFORMATIQUE, TOUT EN FORMAT ÉGALEMENT DES GRAPHISTES À L'UTILISATION DE CE NOUVEL INSTRUMENT.

## GOODBY, BERLIN & SILVERSTEIN

*In* a recent survey, 88% of men and 90% of women employed in advertising said they were "pleased with their jobs." □ We're happy for them. We just wonder what sort of standards they apply to their work. □ At Goodby, Berlin & Silverstein, morale should be totally off the chart. Because, compared to ordinary agencies, GBS is nirvana. □ They are an explosively growing, sensationally successful agency. The agency reeks of success. □ How can the good guys at Goodby Silverstein actually win in this mean, tough business? □ At a time when the clients are supposedly so difficult to handle and so hostile to creativity, how can this San Francisco agency manage to sustain their outstanding creative standards? □ One reason: They worked for Hal Riney. □ Riney's a tough hombre...tough enough to stand nose-to-nose with Julio Gallo and the General Motors metal-benders. A mentor like Riney teaches you how to stand for the creative you believe in. □ Jeff Goodby, the copy side of the creative leadership, is soft spoken, but he's got some hidden assets. Like the Harvard education he gently minimizes. □ "We think of ourselves as a kind of idea factory that reinterprets pieces of culture, like movies, books, our entire pop-culture...we're not interested in aping ideas from other advertising campaigns." □ "Our people are given time to free-associate...to do things that may not pay off in an ad the same afternoon, but will fertilize in their brains and turn into something special and unique some time in the future.." □ The payoff for this enlightened management is superb work. □ The way the agency handles its work is the way Cartier handles its diamonds. □ Their print work sparkles like precious jewels. Their reel is alive...funny, clever, fast. □ The quality of all their print advertising is exceptional, and shows a sensitivity to the printed piece that's not always true with ad agencies. □ Understandably, agency art directors are preoccupied with the selling prices...and design considerations therefore usually always play a secondary role to The

Concept. □ This is why so many art directors skimp on the design side of their craft. There's even the pernicious idea floating around that ad world that "dumb design" or "absence of design" even the active stripping out of anything smacking of design somehow makes better advertising. □ Designers, if they are any good, never stray far from the desire to arrange things beautifully. So while an art director may quit when an ad works on a selling level, designers never stop there. □ This creates an interesting tension between the two disciplines. □ Refreshingly, no such barriers exist at Goodby, Berlin & Silverstein. □ Richard Silverstein, the art part of the team, is a perpetually pumped-up, electric personality. Richard is no computer geek. Instead he does a lot of his concept development on a xerox machine. A xerox that expands or reduces images. With this amazing low-tech tool, Richard is able to mess around to his heart's content, orchestrating visuals and type, until he achieves an optimal balance between his message and his masses. At Graphis, we have the unparalleled opportunity to review the finest work from agencies and designers from all over the world. This is different from judging awards shows, where we usually see only a fraction of an agency's work, and then only the few things agencies wish to submit to the show. □ It's when we get the agency's entire reel and a whole bagful of print ads, that the agency truly bares its creative soul to us. □ And when you see the entire body of their work, that's when GBS truly stands out from the crowd. They refuse to embrace any sort of "house style"; instead, they purposefully seek to develop campaigns that are specifically derived from their client's special opportunities. □ Their print ads are printed on super-heavy stock, meticulously reproduce, and appear more like limited edition fine-art prints than mere ad reprints. □ But being meticulous and detailed does not inhibit their drive to be creative and astonishing. □ Consider the bizarre graphic

**DICK CALDERHEAD** BEGAN HIS CAREER WITH Y&R NEW YORK AFTER GRADUATING FROM SAN DIEGO STATE UNIVERSITY. HE MOVED TO Y&R'S OFFICE IN FRANKFURT, GERMANY AND LATER TO DDB IN DUSSELDORF. UPON HIS RETURN TO THE US, DICK BECAME THE EXECUTIVE CREATIVE DIRECTOR OF CAMPBELL EWALD NY. AFTER TOURS AT A COUPLE OF AGENCIES, HE FOUNDED HIS OWN, CALDERHEAD JACKSON, WHICH LEAD TO HIS CURRENT AGENCY, CALDERHEAD & PHIN LTD. DICK HAS GOLD MEDALS IN BOTH ART AND COPY AND HAS TAUGHT ADVERTISING AT SYRACUSE UNIVERSITY GRAD. SCHOOL, THE NEW SCHOOL FOR SOCIAL RESEARCH, AND THE SCHOOL OF VISUAL ARTS.

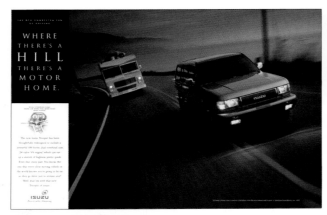

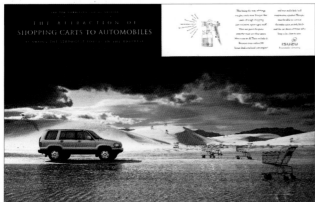

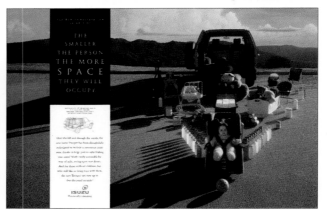

(OPENING SPREAD) CAMPAIGN FOR UNUM, A LIFE INSURANCE COMPANY THAT APPEARED IN SPORTS ILLUSTRATED. (FIRST): Creative Director: DAVE O'HARE Art director: JEREMY POSTAER copywriter: HARRY COCCIOLO Photographer: GALEN ROWELL Designer: BOB PULLUM Illustrator: BRUCE HUTCHISON. (SECOND): Creative Director: DAVE O'HARE Art Director: ERICH JOINER copywriter: STEVE SIMPSON Photographer: GILES HANCOCK Designer: BOB PULLUM Illustrator: BRUCE HUTCHISON. (THIRD): Creative Director: DAVE O'HARE Art director: MIKE FAZENDE Copywriter: DAVE O'HARE Photographer: HEIMO Designer: BOB PULLUM Illustrator: BRUCE HUTCHISON. (FOURTH): Creative Director: DAVE O'HARE ART DIRECTOR: MIKE FAZENDE Copywriter: DAVE O'HARE Photographer: MICHELE CLEMENT Designer: BOB PULLUM Illustrator: BRUCE HUTCHISON. ■ (THIS PAGE ALL IMAGES): ADVERTISING CAMPAIGN FOR AMERICAN ISUZU MOTORS, INC. (TOP LEFT, RIGHT AND BOTTOM RIGHT): Art Director: DAVID PAGE Copywriter: DAVE O'HARE Photographer: DUNCAN SIM Illustrator: ALAN DANIELS. (BOTTOM LEFT): Art Director: ERICH JOINER Copywriter: SCOTT BURNS Photographer: DUNCAN SIM Illustrator: ALAN DANIELS. ■ (FACING PAGE ALL IMAGES): CAMPAIGN FOR THE NEW YORKER MAGAZINE. Creative Director: JEREMY POSTAER Copywriter: STEVE SIMPSON (TOP): Illustrator: ANN RHONEY (MIDDLE); Photographer: DAN ESCOBAR (BOTTOM) Photographer: BRUCE DAVIDSON. ■

of the well-shod fly in the Clarks shoe ad. The arresting visual was first conjured up for a trade ad. □ The agency loved it so much that they sweet-talked Colossal Film Studios into doing an animated version on spec; they trusted their client to ultimately buy the concept and pay for the full-scale production The client did buy it and they got their fabulous spot on the air. □ That, boys and girls, is what creative is all about. □ GBS is based in beautiful San Francisco, surely one of the most enviable places to live in the entire U.S. □ Unfortunately, that makes it a town with too many agencies and too little business. This doesn't faze GBS: They'll go anywhere for the right account. □ They handle *The New Yorker*. With 1,000 agencies in New York to pick from, can you believe this magazine found it necessary to go all the way to San Francisco for a great campaign? □ They did, and they got their great campaign. □ Finlandia, icy-cool, with superb, original graphics, has been growing at an astonishing 30% rate! (Creativity Sells). □ It's still too soon to see the new work for Porsche, but based on everything else they do, this will blow your socks off, too. It is a pleasure to review the work of that rare handful of agencies like GBS, who defy the mediocre norms, and choose instead to perform at the leading edge of the creative envelope. We note with pleasure the resulting sales increases these out-standing advertising campaign produce. □ Jeff Goodby and Richard Silverstein manage their agency with heart as well as spirit. □ "It's crucial that we manage this company so that our people have cues that help them focus their careers. We don't want our people working for their book...we want them working to build their careers." □ Success. It's great to know it need not come at the price of selling out. ■

The sorts of looks that people in the nineteenth century considered ravishing (Lillian Russell's, Lillie Langtry's) for the most part leave us indifferent today. That our taste in faces and bodies changes from one era to the next is clear; that it changes for the better, however, is not.

**THE NEW YORKER**
WHEN YOU READ IT, YOU'LL SEE

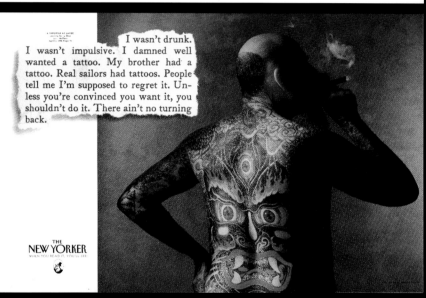

I wasn't drunk. I wasn't impulsive. I damned well wanted a tattoo. My brother had a tattoo. Real sailors had tattoos. People tell me I'm supposed to regret it. Unless you're convinced you want it, you shouldn't do it. There ain't no turning back.

**THE NEW YORKER**
WHEN YOU READ IT, YOU'LL SEE

"Actually, Lou, I think it was more than just my being in the right place at the right time. I think it was my being the right race, the right religion, the right sex, the right socioeconomic group, having the right accent, the right clothes, going to the right schools..."

**THE NEW YORKER**
WHEN YOU READ IT, YOU'LL SEE

(THIS PAGE, BOTH IMAGES): ADVERTISEMENTS FOR FINNISH NATIONAL DISTILLERS, INC. CREATIVE DIRECTORS: RICH SILVERSTEIN, JEFF GOODBY ART DIRECTOR: JEREMY POSTAER COPYWRITER (RIGHT): ROB BAGOT, (LEFT) ROB BAGOT,

Gemäss einer kürzlich veröffentlichten Studie sind 88 Prozent der Männer und 90 Prozent der Frauen, die in der Werbebranche arbeiten, «mit ihren Jobs sehr zufrieden». ☐ Das freut uns für sie. Wir fragen uns nur, welchen Massstab sie dabei anlegen. ☐ Bei der Werbeagentur Goodby, Berlin & Silverstein in San Francisco, müsste die Begeisterung der Angestellten alles übertreffen, denn verglichen mit den üblichen Agenturen ist Goodby, Berlin & Silverstein ein Paradies. ☐ Es ist eine rasant wachsende, sensationell erfolgreiche Agentur. Sie stinkt förmlich nach Erfolg. ☐ Wie schaffen es die 'good guys' bei GBS in diesem gemeinen, harten Geschäft die Gewinner zu sein? In einer Zeit, in der der Umgang mit den Kunden angeblich schwierig ist, fragt man sich, wie es der Agentur gelingt, ihr hohes kreatives Niveau beizubehalten. ☐ Ein Grund: Sie arbeiten für Hal Riney. Riney ist ein harter Typ, der es mit jedem aufnimmt. Ein Mentor wie Riney lehrt einen, für die kreative Arbeit, die man gut findet, geradezustehen. ☐ Jeff Goodby, die Textseite der kreativen Führung, ist zurückhaltend und bescheiden. Dinge wie seine Harvard-Ausbildung spielt er herunter. ☐ «Wir betrachten uns als eine Art Ideenfabrik, die Teile der Kultur neu interpretiert, zum Beispiel Filme, Bücher, die gesamte Pop-Kultur. Ideen anderer Werbekampagnen nachzuahmen interessiert uns nicht.» ☐ «Unsere Leute haben die Zeit, sich mit Dingen zu befassen, die sich vielleicht nicht am selben Nachmittag auszahlen, aber zu fruchtbaren Ideen führen, so dass irgendwann einmal etwas ganz Spezielles und Einzigartiges entsteht.» ☐ Dieses weitsichtige Management wird mit hervorragender Arbeit belohnt. Die Agentur geht mit ihrer Arbeit um wie die Juweliere bei Cartier mit Brillanten. ☐ Ihre Anzeigen sind wahre Juwelen. Ihre TV-Werbung lebt... ist lustig, clever, spritzig. ☐ Richard Silverstein, der die Kunst in diesem Team vertritt, ist energiegeladen und ständig in Hochform. Richard ist kein Computerfanatiker. Er macht viele seiner Konzepte mit dem Photokopierer – einem, der Bilder vergrössern und verkleinern kann. Mit diesem relativ einfachen Instrument schafft er es, sein Innerstes nach aussen zu kehren, und Bilder und Schrift so zu verbinden, dass er eine optimale Balance erreicht. ☐ Bei Graphis haben wir die einmalige Gelegenheit, die besten Arbeiten von Agenturen und Designern aus aller Welt zu Gesicht zu bekommen. Es ist anders als bei der Jurierung von Wettbewerben, bei der wir oft nur einen Bruchteil der Arbeit einer Agentur sehen und dann nur von den wenigen Agenturen, die mitmachen. ☐ Wenn wir die gesamte TV- und Druckwerbung einer Agentur zu sehen bekommen, dann wird uns die kreative Seele der Agentur wirklich offenbart. ☐ Und wenn man alle Arbeiten anschaut, hebt sich Goodby, Berlin & Silverstein wirklich von der Masse ab. Sie wehren sich gegen jede Art von Haus-Stil; stattdessen bemühen sie sich, Kampagnen zu schaffen, die ganz auf das, was der Kunde anzubieten hat, zugeschnitten sind. ☐ Ihre Druckanzeigen werden auf besonders dickem Papier mit grösster Sorgfalt gedruckt, so dass sie wie Kunstdrucke in limitierter Auflage und nicht wie Anzeigen wirken. ☐ Die Sorgfalt und Liebe zum Detail

DICK CALDERHEAD STUDIERTE AN DER SAN DIEGO STATE UNIVERSITY UND BEGANN SEINE KARRIERE BEI YOUNG & RUBICAM IN NEW YORK. DANN ARBEITETE ER BEI Y&R FRANKFURT UND DDB DÜSSELDORF UND WURDE NACH SEINER RÜCKKEHR IN DIE USA EXECUTIVE CREATIVE DIRECTOR BEI CAMPBELL EWALD. NACHDEM ER BEI VERSCHIEDENEN AGENTUREN GEARBEITET HATTE, GRÜNDETE ER SEINE EIGENE, CALDERHEAD JACKSON, DIE HEUTIGE CALDERHEAD & PHIN LTD. DICKS ARBEIT WURDE MIT MEHREREN GOLDMEDAILLEN AUSGEZEICHNET. ER UNTERRICHTET WERBUNG AN DER SYRACUSE UNIVERSITY, DER NEW SCHOOL FOR SOCIAL RESEARCH UND AN DER SCHOOL OF VISUAL ARTS.

BOB KERSTETTER, PHOTOGRAPHER: DUNCAN SIM ■ (THIS PAGE, BOTH IMAGES) ADVERTISEMENTS FOR NORWE-
GIAN CRUISE LINES ART DIRECTOR: STEVE STONE PHOTOGRAPHER: DAN ESCOBAR COPYWRITER: BOB KERSTETTER.■

hindert sie keinesfalls in ihrer Kreativität. □ Man denke an die bizarre Darstellung der Fliege in der Anzeige für Clarks-Schuhe. Das kreative Team von Goodby, Berlin & Silverstein hatte diese unheimlich wirkungsvolle Graphik zuerst für ein Fachzeitschrifteninserat vorgesehen. □ Sie waren so begeistert, dass sie Colossal Film Studios überredeten, auf Verdacht hin eine TV-Version davon zu machen; sie waren überzeugt, dass ihr Kunde das Konzept akzeptieren und für die gesamte Produktion bezahlen würde. Er tat es und ihr wunderbarer Spot lief über die Bildschirme. □ Das nenne ich Kreativität. □ San Francisco ist zweifellos einer der beneidenswertesten Orte zum Arbeiten und Leben in den USA. Leider gibt es dadurch in der Stadt zu viele Agenturen und zu wenig Auftraggeber. Das allerdings berührt GBS wenig: Sie würden für den richtigen Auftrag überall hinfliegen. □ Sie betreuen die Zeitschrift *The New Yorker*. Können Sie sich vorstellen, dass eine Zeitschrift es bei 1000 New Yorker Werbeagenturen, die zur Auswahl stehen, nötig fand, ihre Fühler ganz bis nach San Francisco auszustrek-

ken, um eine grossartige Kampagne zu bekommen? Sie taten es und bekamen ihre grossartige Kampagne. Finlandia-Schnaps, eiskalt, hervorragend präsentiert, konte eine Umsatzsteigerung von 30% verzeichnen. (Kreativität verkauft.) □ Über die neue Arbeit für Porsche kann man noch nichts sagen, aber angesichts der bisher abgelieferten Arbeiten, kann man sicher sein, dass auch diese umwerfend sein wird. □ Es ist ein Vergnügen, Arbeiten von Agenturen des GBS-Kalibers anzusehen, von den wenigen also, für die Mittelmässigkeit nicht in Frage kommt, die in Punkto Kreativität an der Spitze stehen. □ Mit Freude nehmen wir von Verkaufssteigerungen als Resultat so hervorragender Werbekampagnen Kenntnis. Jeff Goodby und Richard Silverstein führen ihre Agentur mit Herz und Verstand. □ «Ausschlaggebend ist, dass wir diese Firma so führen, dass wir unseren Leuten helfen, eine Karriere aufzubauen. Sie sollen nicht fürs Papier, sondern an ihrer Weiterentwicklung arbeiten.» □ Es ist gut zu wissen, dass Erfolg nicht unbedingt etwas mit faulen Kompromissen zu tun haben muss. ■

. . . . . . . . . . . . . . . . . . . . . . . . . . . . . . . . . . . . . . . . . . . . . . . . . . . . . . . . . . . . . . . . . . . . . . . . . . . . .

Un sondage récent révèle que 88% des hommes et 90 % des femmes employés dans la publicité sont «satisfaits de leur travail». □ Si nous sommes de tout cœur avec eux, nous ne pouvons toutefois nous empêcher de nous demander sur quels critères repose cette opinion. □ Chez Goodby, Berlin & Silverstein, dans tous les cas, cet enthousiasme devrait même être exorbitant puisque, comparé aux agences ordinaires, GBS, c'est le nirvana. □ L'agence est en pleine croissance et remporte un succès sensationnel; on peut même dire de cette agence qu'elle est l'image même du succès. □ On se demande alors tout naturellement comment les collaborateurs de Goodby Silverstein peuvent bien réussir dans

un business où la compétition est aussi âpre qu'exigeante. Surtout à un moment où il est apparemment si difficile de traiter avec les clients et où ceux-ci se montrent particulièrement hostiles envers la créativité. Comment cette agence de San Francisco parvient-elle à maintenir un niveau de créativité aussi remarquable? □ A cette question, une seule réponse: les collaborateurs de GBS ont tous travaillé pour Hal Riney. □ Riney est un gars qui a les reins assez solides pour parler d'égal à égal avec Julio Gallo ou les industriels de fer de la General Motors. Riney a la carrure d'un mentor qui vous enseigne à défendre vos intérêts de créateur. □ Jeff Goodby, le copywriter en chef, joue la discrétion, bien qu'il possède plus d'un talent caché, à commencer par ses études à Harvard qu'il passe sous silence par modestie. □ «Nous sommes une sorte de fabrique d'idées qui réinterprète des éléments culturels comme les films, les livres ou, plus généralement, tout ce qui relève de la culture populaire; nous ne cherchons pas à singer d'autres campagnes publicitaires.» □ «Nos collaborateurs ont le temps de se consacrer à la libre association, de s'intéresser à des choses qui ne se concrétisent pas immédiatement sous forme d'annonce, mais qui à terme déboucheront peut-être sur un résultat nouveau et original.» □ Cette gestion clairvoyante trouve sa récompense dans un travail d'une qualité irréprochable: l'agence peaufine son travail comme Cartier ses diamants. □ Les travaux d'imprimerie que réalise l'agence brillent comme des pierres précieuses. Et les spots publicitaires pour la télévision sont vivants, pleins d'humour, subtils et directs. □ Richard Silverstein, l'artiste de l'équipe, est un homme hyperactif au tempérament bouillonnant. Pourtant, il n'a rien de commun avec un fanatique de l'ordinateur. En effet, il développe la plupart de ses concepts au moyen d'un appareil Xerox qui réduit ou agrandit les images. Doté de cette boîte à outils rudimentaire, Richard fait la chasse aux idées et harmonise l'image et la typographie jusqu'à ce que son message corresponde parfaitement au public visé. □ Chez Graphis, nous avons le privilège de passer en revue les meilleurs travaux des agences et designers du monde entier. Une situation sans rapport avec celle des concours-expositions où les jugements ne sont émis que sur la base d'un échantillon restreint de productions, celles que l'agence met en compétition. □ Or, ce n'est qu'en ayant accès à la production complète d'une agence et à l'ensemble de ses annonces publicitaires qu'on peut estimer que celle-ci a dévoilé sa véritable identité créatrice. □ C'est alors précisément qu'on est forcé de reconnaître que GBS sort du lot. Si l'agence refuse d'adopter un style «maison», c'est parce qu'elle tient à réaliser ses campagnes en accord avec les besoins spécifiques de ses clients. □ Les annonces publicitaires de GBS sont réalisées sur du papier très épais et reproduites avec un tel soin qu'elles ressemblent plus à des œuvres d'art à tirage limité qu'à de simples épreuves. □ Mais l'amour du détail ne les empêche pas d'être créatifs et sur-

prenants. □ Prenez le graphisme surprenant de la mouche dans l'annonce pour les chaussures Clarks. L'équipe de création avait d'abord développé ce graphisme tape-à-l'œil pour une publicité destinée au commerce. Mais ils en furent si contents qu'ils entreprirent, sait-on jamais, de convaincre Colossal Films Studio d'en tirer une version animée. Ils étaient prêts à parier que leur client achèterait le concept dans son intégralité et payerait pour l'ensemble de la production, ce qu'il fit, permettant du coup la création d'un spot extraordinaire. □ Un bel exemple de création! □ L'agence GBS est installée à San Francisco, probablement l'un des endroits où l'on vit le mieux dans tous les Etats-Unis. Malheureusement, pour cette même raison, les agences y sont trop nombreuses et, en conséquence, le volume d'affaires insuffisant. Pourtant, cela n'a pas découragé GBS, qui irait jusqu'au bout du monde quand il s'agit de décrocher un bon contrat. □ C'est ainsi que l'agence compte parmi ses clients *The New Yorker*. Qui aurait pensé qu'avec plus de 1000 agences à New York, ce magazine éprouverait le besoin de faire réaliser sa campagne de publicité par une agence de San Francisco? C'est pourtant ce qu'il fit, sans avoir à le regretter vu la formidable campagne qui en résulta. □ La campagne pour l'eau-de-vie glacée Finlandia, au graphisme aussi original que splendide, s'est soldée par une étonnante augmentation des ventes de l'ordre de 30%. (Comme quoi, la créativité fait vendre.) □ Il est encore trop tôt pour parler de la campagne effectuée pour Porsche, mais s'ils demeurent fidèles à leur standing actuel, cela risque d'être vraiment décoiffant. □ C'est un réel plaisir de présenter le travail de ces très rares agences comme GBS qui défient la norme de la médiocrité et choisissent de se situer d'emblée à la pointe de la créativité. □ D'autre part, nous relevons avec plaisir l'augmentation des ventes suite aux campagnes menées par cette agence remarquable. □ Jeff Goodby et Richard Silverstein dirigent leur entreprise avec autant de cœur que d'esprit. □ «Il est essentiel que nous dirigions cette compagnie de façon à ce que nos collaborateurs puissent se concentrer sur leur carrière. Nous ne voulons pas qu'ils travaillent pour se faire une carte de visite, nous voulons qu'ils mènent leur carrière avec nous.» □ Bref, un franc succès qui, de surcroît, ne résulte d'aucun compromis. ∎

**DICK CALDERHEAD** A COMMENCÉ SA CARRIÈRE CHEZ Y&R À NEW YORK APRÈS AVOIR TERMINÉ SES ÉTUDES À L'UNIVERSITÉ DE SAN DIEGO. IL FUT ENSUITE TRANSFÉRÉ CHEZ Y&R FRANCFORT, PUIS TRAVAILLA CHEZ DDB À DÜSSELDORF. DE RETOUR AUX ÉTATS-UNIS, IL DEVIENT DIRECTEUR EN CRÉATION CHEZ CAMPBELL EWALD. APRÈS AVOIR COLLABORÉ AVEC DIVERSES AGENCES, IL CRÉE LA SIENNE, CALDERHEAD JACKSON, ACTUELLEMENT DEVENUE CALDERHEAD & PHIN. DICK A OBTENU DES MÉDAILLES D'OR AUSSI BIEN POUR SES IMAGES QUE POUR SES TEXTES. IL A ÉGALEMENT ENSEIGNÉ LA PUBLICITÉ À L'UNIVERSITÉ DE SYRACUSE, AINSI QU'À.LA SCHOOL OF VISUAL ARTS.

ADVERTISING

WERBUNG

PUBLICITÉ

■ **1** CREATIVE DIRECTOR/COPYWRITER: TOSHIHIRO KIUCHI ART DIRECTOR: KAZUHIRO SEKI DESIGNERS: KAZUHIRO SEKI, MITSUE MURAKAMI PHOTOGRAPHER: SAKAE TAKAHASHI AGENCY: OSAKA YOMIURI ADVERTISING INC. CLIENT: HANKYU FIVE COUNTRY: JAPAN ■ **1** THE COPY OF THIS AD FOR A DEPARTMENT STORE SAYS (APPROXIMATELY): "WE LEARNED MANY THINGS IN SCHOOL. WE ARE STILL LEARNING NOW: FROM THE EARTH, THE BIRDS, THE FLOWERS. AND WE WILL NEVER STOP LEARNING." SHOWN IS A CLASSROOM OF A JAPANESE PRIMARY SCHOOL. ● **1** DER TEXT DIESER ANZEIGE FÜR EIN KAUFHAUS LAUTET (UNGEFÄHR): «WIR HABEN VIELE DINGE IN DER SCHULE GELERNT, UND WIR LERNEN IMMER NOCH: VON DER ERDE, DEN VÖGELN, DEN BLUMEN. SO WERDEN WIR NIE AUFHÖREN ZU LERNEN.» GEZEIGT IST EIN KLASSENRAUM EINER JAPANISCHEN SCHULE. ▲ **1** LE TEXTE DE CETTE ANNONCE POUR UN MAGASIN DIT À PEU PRÈS CECI: «NOUS AVONS APPRIS BEAUCOUP DE CHOSES À L'ÉCOLE. LA TERRE, LES OISEAUX ET LES FLEURS NOUS EN APPRENNENT CHAQUE JOUR DAVANTAGE; ET NOUS NE FINIRONS JAMAIS D'APPRENDRE.»

■ **2-5** ART DIRECTOR: HAKKI MISIRLIOGLU PHOTOGRAPHER: EYÜP GÖRGÜLER COPYWRITER: ALPER UYGUR AGENCY: AJANS ULTRA CLIENT: GÖN COUNTRY: TURKEY ■ **2-5** "THERE IS SOMETHING THAT WE HAVE IN COMMON." CAMPAIGN FOR LEATHER GOODS. ● **2-5** «ES GIBT ETWAS, DAS UNS VERBINDET.» KAMPAGNE FÜR LEDERWAREN. ▲ **2-5** «NOUS AVONS QUELQUE CHOSE EN COMMUN». POUR LES ARTICLES DE MAROQUINERIE GÖN.

1

■ (FOLLOWING SPREAD) **6-8** ART DIRECTOR/DESIGNER: BILL THORBURN PHOTOGRAPHER: DEBRA TERBERVILLE AGENCY: DAYTON'S HUDSON'S, MARSHALL FIELD'S CLIENTS: DAYTON'S OVAL ROOM, MARSHALL FIELD'S 28 SHOP COUNTRY: USA ■ **6-8** THE IDEA BEHIND THIS CAMPAIGN FOR DESIGNER FASHIONS SOLD IN DEPARTMENT STORES WAS TO PUT IT IN CONTEXT OF ITS CREATION. IT WAS PHOTOGRAPHED IN AN ARTIST'S STUDIO. ● (NÄCHSTE DOPPELSEITE) **6-8** BEI DIESER KAMPAGNE FÜR DESIGNER-MODE GEHT ES UM DEN BEZUG ZUM SCHÖPFERISCHEN. DIE KLEIDER WURDEN IM ATELIER EINES KÜNSTLERS AUFGENOMMEN. ▲ (DOUBLE PAGE SUIVANTE) **6-8** L'IDÉE DE FOND DE CETTE CAMPAGNE POUR LA MODE DES COUTURIERS ÉTAIT DE PRÉSENTER CES VÊTEMENTS DANS UN CONTEXTE CRÉATIF. ILS ONT ÉTÉ PHOTOGRAPHIÉS DANS L'ATELIER D'UN ARTISTE.

■ (FOLLOWING SPREAD) **9-11** ART DIRECTOR: BARBARA WAIBEL PHOTOGRAPHER: HANS HANSEN COPYWRITER: UWE SCHNEIDER AGENCY: SCHNEIDER UND WAIBEL, FEUERBACHER CLIENT: LAUTON MODEN GMBH & CO. COUNTRY: GERMANY ■ **9-11** LAUTON'S IS CASHMERE. AND ONLY THAT. MADE IN ITALY. AND ONLY THERE—LAUTON'S IS CASHMERE. SOMETHING PRECIOUS TREATED IRREVERENTLY, BUT WELL. UNDERSTATEMENT GUARANTEED. BUT THAT, LUXURIOSLY—LAUTON'S IS CASHMERE. TO BE SEEN AT VARIOUS TRADE FAIRS. (A LISTING OF FASHION FAIRS IN GERMANY FOLLOWS). ● (NÄCHSTE DOPPELSEITE) **9-11** UNDERSTATEMENT IST DAS MOTTO DIESER KAMPAGNE. ▲ (DOUBLE PAGE SUIVANTE) **9-11** «LAUTON'S, C'EST LE CACHEMIRE. ET RIEN QUE CELA. FABRIQUÉ EN ITALIE. ET RIEN QUE LÀ.» LA MARQUE ET L'EMBALLAGE SEULS SUFFISENT À ÉVOQUER CET ARTICLE HAUT DE GAMME PRÉSENTÉ DANS DIVERSES FOIRES DU TEXTILE EN ALLEMAGNE (LEUR LISTE EST FOURNIE ICI).

2

3

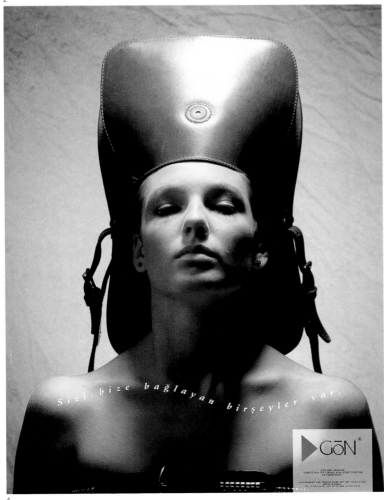

4

5

Chanel Boutique *
Dayton's Oval Room
Minneapolis

6

Yves Saint Laurent
rive gauche

Dayton's Oval Room, Minneapolis

7

Marshall Field's 28 Shop
State Street

8

LAUTON'S ist Cashmere. Und nur das. Made in Italy. Und nur dort.

LAUTON'S ist Cashmere. Edles wird respektlos behandelt,

das aber gut. Understatement garantiert. Das aber üppig.

LAUTON'S ist Cashmere. Zu sehen während der CPD (1. - 4. 2. 92)

und IGEDO (7. - 11. 3. 92) in der Düsseldorf Gallery, Class 1 Club.

Oder in München, Park Hilton, Zi. 617 (16. - 18. 2. 92). Oder in

Hamburg, Interconti, Suite 600 (Ordertage: 9. - 12. 2. 92, Modetage:

1. - 4. 3. 92). Wir freuen uns hier wie dort auf Ihren Besuch.

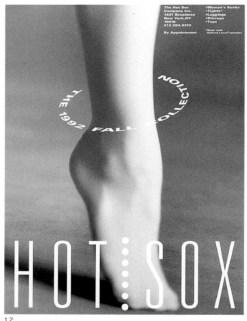

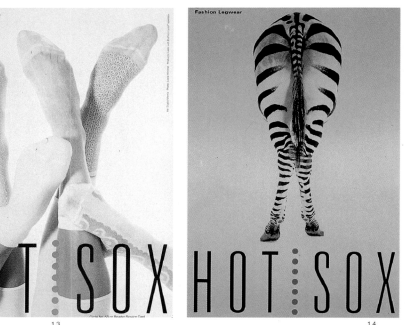

12
13
14

15
16
17

18
19
20

21

LEVI'S 501 JEANS. THE MORE YOU WASH THEM. THE BETTER THEY GET

■ **12-14** ART DIRECTOR/DESIGNER: JEFFREY MORRIS PHOTOGRAPHERS: JAIME PHILIPS (12), LIZZIE HIMMEL (13, 14) ILLUSTRATOR: JAIME VINAS (TYPE) AGENCY: STUDIO MORRIS CLIENT: HOT SOX COUNTRY: USA ■ **12-14** CAMPAIGN FOR HOT SOX. THE AD/POSTER FEATURING THE ZEBRA IS FOR THE NEW COLLECTION OF ANIMAL PATTERN LEGWEAR. ● **12-14** KAMPAGNE FÜR HOT SOX. DIE ANZEIGE MIT DEM ZEBRA (AUCH ALS PLAKAT ERSCHIENEN) IST FÜR DIE TIERMUSTER-STRUMPFKOLLEKTION. ▲ **12-14** CAMPAGNE POUR HOT SOX, UNE MARQUE DE CHAUSSETTES. L'ANNONCE AVEC LE ZÈBRE (QUI EST AUSSI PARUE SOUS FORME D'AFFICHE) A ÉTÉ CONÇUE POUR LA COLLECTION ORNÉ DE DÉCORS ANIMALIERS.

■ **15-17** ART DIRECTORS: THOMAS VASQUEZ, CHUCK JOHNSON DESIGNER: THOMAS VASQUEZ PHOTOGRAPHER: NEILL WHITLOCK COPYWRITERS: THOMAS VASQUEZ, CHUCK JOHNSON, KEN KOESTER AGENCY: BRAINSTORM INC. CLIENT: MARATHON SHOPPING CENTERS GROUP COUNTRY: USA ■ **15-17** A HUMOROUS CAMPAIGN FOR MARATHON'S 13 MALLS ACROSS THE SOUTHWESTERN UNITED STATES, STATING VARIOUS REASONS TO SHOP. ● **15-17** VERSCHIEDENE GRÜNDE, WARUM MAN (IN BESTIMMTEN SHOPPING MALLS) EINKAUFEN GEHT. GRUND NR. 1: WEIL MAN KEINEN GRUND BRAUCHT. NR. 8: WEIL EIN PAAR BRILLANTEN JEDERZEIT EIN HERZ GEWINNEN KÖNNEN. NR. 55: WENN DER SCHUH PASST, TRAG' IHN. ▲ **15-17** UNE CAMPAGNE PLEINE D'HUMOUR POUR MARATHON SHOPPING (MAGASINS DE CERTAINS CENTRES COMMERCIAUX DU SUD-OUEST DES ÉTATS-UNIS). ELLE ÉNUMÈRE UNE FOULE DE BONNES RAISONS D'ACHETER: 1° PARCE QU'ON A PAS BESOIN D'UNE SEULE RAISON, 8° PARCE QU'UNE PAIRE DE DIAMANTS PEUVENT VOUS FAIRE GAGNER UN CŒUR À TOUT MOMENT, 55° PARCE QUE QUAND UNE CHAUSSURE VOUS VA, IL FAUT LA PORTER.

■ **18-20** ART DIRECTORS/DESIGNERS: BABY IMPERIAL, DAMIEN ANNE PHOTOGRAPHER: PIERRE GAYTE STYLIST: CAROLINE CORNU COPYWRITER: STEPHANE TISSINIER AGENCY: DUFRESNE & CORRIGAN CLIENT: ARTHUR COUNTRY: FRANCE ■ **18-20** ENGLISH HUMOR AND FRENCH QUALITY. THESE ADS FOR A FRENCH MENSWEAR COMPANY SHALL EVOKE TRADITION, ELEGANCE, SOPHISTICATION AND QUALITY WHILE MAINTAINING AN ASPECT OF MODERNITY THROUGH THE HUMOROUS PRODUCT INTEGRATION. ● **18-20** ENGLISCHER HUMOR UND FRANZÖSISCHE QUALITÄT. IN DIESEN ANZEIGEN FÜR EINEN HERRENAUSSTATTER SOLL TRADITION, ELEGANZ, HOHER ANSPRUCH UND QUALITÄT ZUM AUSDRUCK KOMMEN, WÄHREND HUMORVOLLE EINBEZIEHUNG DER PRODUKTE FÜR DEN MODERNEN ANSTRICH SORGT. ▲ **18-20** CAMPAGNE IRRÉVÉRENCIEUSE POUR UNE MARQUE DE SOUS-VÊTEMENTS ET CHAUSSETTES POUR HOMMES. DANS CETTE ANNONCE, IL S'AGISSAIT D'EXPRIMER L'ÉLÉGANCE, LE RAFFINEMENT ET LA QUALITÉ DE CES PRODUITS. LES VISUELS PLEINS D'HUMOUR ONT PERMIS DE MODERNISER L'IMAGE DE CETTE MAISON.

■ **21** ART DIRECTOR: JOHN GORSE COPYWRITER: NICK WORTHINGTON AGENCY: BARTLE BOGLE HEGARTY CLIENT: LEVI'S COUNTRY: GREAT BRITAIN ■ **21** AN ANTI-GLAMOUR CAMPAIGN EMPHASIZING THE DURABILITY OF LEVI'S JEANS. ● **21** «LEVI'S 501 JEANS. JE ÖFTER MAN SIE WÄSCHT, UM SO BESSER WERDEN SIE.» EINE ANTI-GLAMOUR-KAMPAGNE, BEI DER ES UM DIE DAUERHAFTIGKEIT DIESER JEANS GEHT. ▲ **21** «JEANS LEVI'S 501. PLUS VOUS LES LAVEZ, PLUS ILS SONT BEAUX.» UNE CAMPAGNE QUI MET L'ACCENT SUR LA PRINCIPALE QUALITÉ DE CE JEANS: IL EST INUSABLE!

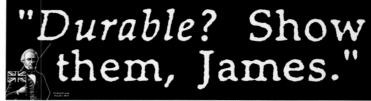

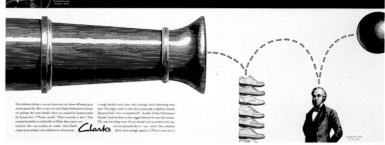

22

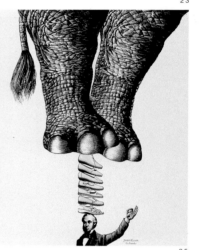

23

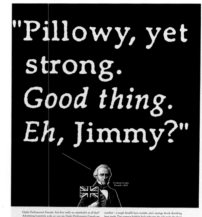

24

25

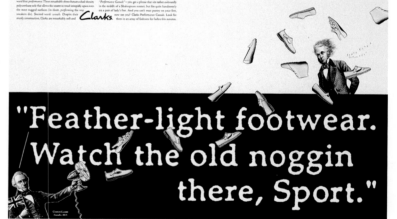

26

27

■ 22-24 Art Director: JOHN HEGARTY Photographer: ANDREW MACPHERSON Copywriter: CHARLES HENDLEY Agency: BARTLE BOGLE HEGARTY Client: ALFRED DUNHILL Country: GREAT BRITAIN ■ 22-24 CAMPAIGN FOR DUNHILL PRODUCTS, RANGING FROM CLOTHES AND LEATHER LUGGAGE TO VARIOUS ACCESSORIES. ON THE RIGHT, RECENTLY PUBLISHED ADS FROM THE *TIMES* REPRESENT THE SEARCH FOR OBJECTS (OR MISSING OBJECTS LIKE THE VALET) SHOWN ON THE LEFT. ● 22-24 IN DIESER KAMPAGNE WIRD RECHTS EIN INSERAT AUS DER *TIMES* GEZEIGT, IN DEM NACH DEM LINKS BEWORBENEN OBJEKT (BZW. DEM FEHLENDEN GEGENSTAND WIE DEM KLEIDERBOY) GESUCHT WIRD. ▲ 22-24 DANS CETTE CAMPAGNE POUR LES PRODUITS DUNHILL, LE VISUEL DE DROITE REPRÉSENTE UNE ANNONCE PARUE DANS LE *TIMES*. CELLE-CI DÉCRIT LE PRODUIT DONT ON FAIT LA PROMOTION SUR L'IMAGE DE GAUCHE (OU DONT ON SUGGÈRE L'UTILITÉ, COMME DANS LE CAS DU PORTE-MANTEAU).

■ 25-27 Art Director: STEVE STONE Illustrator: GREG DEARTH Copywriters: ROB BAGOT, STEVE SIMPSON Agency: GOODBY, BERLIN & SILVERSTEIN Client: CLARKS OF ENGLAND Country: USA ■ 25-27 A TRADE CAMPAIGN FOR CLARKS OF ENGLAND THAT PLAYS ON THE SPECIAL QUALITIES OF THEIR SHOES. ● 25-27 AUS EINER HÄNDLERKAMPAGNE FÜR CLARKS: «HALTBAR? ZEIG'S IHNEN, JAMES!»; «FEDERND, ABER STARK. GUTE SACHE, WAS JIMMY?»; «FEDERLEICHTES SCHUHWERK. PASS AUF DEINE BIRNE AUF.» ▲ 25-27 «RÉSISTANTS? MONTREZ-LEUR UN PEU, JAMES!»; «DU RESSORT, MAIS DU SOLIDE. PAS MAL HEIN, JIMMY?»; «DES CHAUSSURES LÉGÈRES COMME LA PLUME. FAITES GAFFE!»

AMERICA'S TOUGHEST FACES.

28

QUIRKS OF NATURE.

29

Levis. L'esprit de la couleur.

30

Levis. La vie a du pigment.

31

■ 28, 29 Art Director/Designer: TERRY SCHNEIDER Photographers: ED COOPER (SCENIC 28), STEVE TERRILL (SCENIC 29), PETE STONE (MODELS), DOUG PETTY (PRODUCTS) Copywriter: GREG EIDEN Agency: BORDERS, PERRIN & NORRANDER Client: COLUMBIA SPORTSWEAR Country: USA ■ 28, 29 CAMPAIGN FOR SPORTSWEAR. ● 28, 29 ANZEIGEN FÜR SPORTSBEKLEIDUNG. «AMERIKAS HÄRTESTE GESICHTER.» «NATUREREIGNISSE.» ▲ 28, 29 «LES VISAGES LES PLUS DURS DE L'AMÉRIQUE», «LES CATASTROPHES NATURELLES». CAMPAGNE POUR DES VÊTEMENTS DE SPORT.

■ 30, 31 Art Director: ANNE VAN DE VELDE Photographer: HANS KROESKAMP Copywriter: CARL HANSENNE Agency: LOWE TROOST Client: LEVIS Country: BELGIUM ■ 30, 31 "LEVIS. THE SPIRIT OF COLOR." "LEVIS. LIFE IS FULL OF COLOR." CAMPAIGN FOR A BELGIAN MANUFACTURER OF COLORS AND VARNISHES. ● 30, 31 «LEVIS. DER GEIST DER FARBE.» «LEVIS. DAS LEBEN IST VOLLER FARBE.» BEISPIELE AUS EINER KAMPAGNE FÜR FARBEN UND LACKE DER BELGISCHEN MARKE LEVIS. ▲ 30, 31 CAMPAGNE POUR UN FABRICANT BELGE DE COULEURS ET VERNIS.

As Jaemo Parñi peered out the window on the morning of his 50th birth-
day, his hopes for an impromptu party began to fade. His wife assured him
that not even the standard of friends could be expected to brave two
meters of fresh snow. Apparently she underestimated the loyalty of friends,
and the drawing power of Jaemo's well-known stockpile of Finlandia.

 Finlandia. Vodka From The Top Of The World.

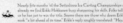

Nearly five months 'til the Svänjslivea Ice Curling Championships and
already we find Erkki Hokkanen busy sharpening his skills. Folks tell
us he has yet to win the title. Seems there are those who deem Erkki's
work "a bit ahead of its time." Erkki's reply roughly translated: "Hey,
it's not like the grand prize is a lifetime supply of Finlandia or anything."

 Finlandia. Vodka From The Top Of The World.

It is something of an annual block party every spring between the families
Okko and Kari. This year, the Okkos (seen below) are bringing fresh-
roasted tippulaiva across Lake Puula. This being the aard such get-
together (an other year) it is spread the Karis will supply the Finlandia.

 Finlandia. Vodka From The Top Of The World.

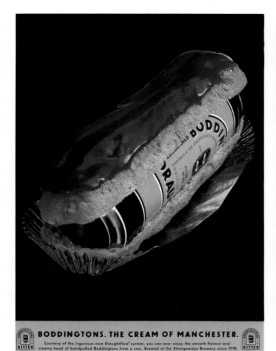

35

36

37

38

39

40

■ 32-34 ART DIRECTOR: JEREMY POSTAER PHOTOGRAPHER: DUNCAN SIM COPYWRITERS: ROB BAGOT (32, 34), BOB KERSTETTER (32-34) AGENCY: GOODBY, BERLIN & SILVERSTEIN CLIENT: FINNISH NATIONAL DISTILLERS COUNTRY: USA ■ 32-34 FINLANDIA VODKA PLAYS THE PROTAGONIST IN THESE STORIES FROM "THE TOP OF THE WORLD." ● 32-34 DOPPELSEITIGE ZEITSCHRIFTENANZEIGEN. FINLANDIA-WODKA IST DER PROTAGONIST DIESER GESCHICHTEN AUS DEM HOHEN NORDEN. ▲ 32-34 LA VODKA FINLANDIA EST LE PROTAGONISTE DE CES HISTOIRES DU GRAND NORD.

■ 35-40 ART DIRECTOR: MIKE WELLS PHOTOGRAPHER: TIF HUNTER RETOUCHING: TAPESTRY & MATEY ON PAINTBOX MODEL MAKER: GAVIN LINDSEY COPYWRITER: TOM HUDSON AGENCY: BARTLE BOGLE HEGARTY CLIENT: WHITBREAD BREWERY COUNTRY: GREAT BRITAIN ■ 35-40 VISUAL PUNS THAT ASSOCIATE BODDINGTONS WITH CREAM, THEREBY HIGHLIGHTING THE PARTICULAR SMOOTHNESS OF THIS BEER. ● 35-40 VISUELLE WORTSPIELE, IN DENEN BODDINGTONS IN VERBINDUNG MIT RAHM GEBRACHT WIRD, UM DIE CREMIGKEIT DES BIERS ZU PROPAGIEREN. ▲ 35-40 DES JEUX DE MOTS VISUELS QUI PEUVENT ÊTRE MIS EN RELATION AVEC LA CRÈME: IL S'AGISSAIT ICI DE SOULIGNER LA LÉGÈRETÉ D'UNE MARQUE DE BIÈRE.

**Wenn man
die Welt nicht ändern kann,
muß man eben
seinen Standpunkt
ändern.**

REINE GESCHMACKSSACHE.

41

# Urlaubsvertretung.

REINE GESCHMACKSSACHE.

42

# Denk mal.

REINE GESCHMACKSSACHE.

43

# Es bleibt alles anders.

REINE GESCHMACKSSACHE.

44

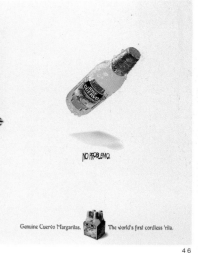

45

46

47

48

49

■ 41-44 ART DIRECTORS: HARRY SCHMITT, BETTINA HÖLZINGER, ANDREA SCHMIDT ILLUSTRATOR: RAINER DIEKERHOFF COPYWRITERS: S. STEPHAN, I. RAATZ, O. HESSE, K. SCHWARZ AGENCY: MCCANN ERICKSON CLIENT: R. J. REYNOLDS TOBACCO COUNTRY: GERMANY ■ 41-44 "IF YOU CANNOT CHANGE THE WORLD, YOU HAVE TO CHANGE YOUR STANDPOINT." "REPLACEMENT DURING VACATION". GERMAN PLAY ON WORDS: "DENKMAL" MEANS "STATUE"; WRITTEN IN TWO WORDS IT MEANS "THINK A BIT". "EVERYTHING REMAINS DIFFERENT." ● 41-44 IN DIESEN ANZEIGEN WIRD DIE CAMEL-PACKUNG EINMAL ANDERS GEZEIGT. ILLUSTRATION IN AIRBRUSH-TECHNIK; ACRYL AUF KARTON. ▲ 41-44 «SI VOUS NE POUVEZ PAS CHANGER LE MONDE, VOUS POUVEZ TOUJOURS CHANGER DE POINT DE VUE»; «REPRÉSENTANT PENDANT LES VACANCES»; UN JEU DE MOTS EN ALLEMAND: «DENKMAL» VEUT DIRE «MONUMENT»; ÉCRIT EN DEUX MOTS, IL SIGNIFIE «RÉFLÉCHIS UN PEU»; «TOUT RESTE DIFFÉRENT».

■ 45, 46 ART DIRECTOR: STEVE STONE PHOTOGRAPHER: DAN ESCOBAR AND STOCK ILLUSTRATOR: ANN RHONEY COPYWRITER: ROB BAGOT AGENCY: GOODBY, BERLIN & SILVERSTEIN CLIENT: JOSE CUERVO TEQUILA COUNTRY: USA ■ 45, 46 GENUINE CUERVO MARGARITAS: NO BLENDER RE-QUIRED. ● 45, 46 «KEIN MIXER? KEIN PROBLEM.» CUERVO MARGARITAS IST EIN FERTIGER COCKTAIL. BEISPIELE AUS EINER ANZEIGENKAMPAGNE UNTER DEM GLEICHEN SLOGAN. ▲ 45, 46 «PAS DE MIXER, PAS DE PROBLÈME». CUERVO MARGARITAS EST UN COCKTAIL PRÊT À CONSOMMER.

■ 47-49 ART DIRECTOR: EDITH KILGER PHOTOGRAPHER: CHRISTOPHER THOMAS COPYWRITER: OTWARD BUCHNER AGENCY: HEYE + PARTNER CLIENT: SECHSÄMTERTROPFEN G. VETTER COUNTRY: GERMANY ■ 47-49 "SOMETIMES THE JUNGLE IS VERY CLOSE..."; "ONE NIGHT, IN A BAR..."; "SOMEWHERE IN THE ASPHALT JUNGLE". THE JUNGLE ATMOSPHERE WAS CREATED IN THE STUDIO. ● 47-49 DIE DSCHUNGELATMOSPHÄRE IN DIESEN ANZEIGEN WURDE MIT EINFACHEN MITTELN IM STUDIO ERZEUGT. ▲ 47-49 L'ATMOSPHÈRE DE LA JUNGLE SUGGÉRÉE AVEC UN MINIMUM DE MOYENS: «PARFOIS, LA FORÊT VIERGE EST TOUTE PROCHE...», «UN SOIR DANS UN BAR...», «DANS LA JUNGLE DE LA GRANDE VILLE...»

■ 50-52 ART DIRECTORS: TOM HUDSON (50, 52), NICK WORTHINGTON (51) PHOTOGRAPHERS: GRAHAM HUGHES (50, 52), TONY EVANS (51)
COPYWRITERS: ROBERT JENSON (50, 52), JOHN GORSE (51) AGENCY: BARTLE BOGLE HEGARTY CLIENT: SPILLERS COUNTRY: GREAT BRITAIN ■ 50-
52 EACH ADVERTISEMENT OF THIS CAMPAIGN FEATURES A DOG DESCRIBING HOW HE WOULD GO AS FAR AS TO BECOME A CAT JUST TO BE
ABLE TO EAT NEW, IMPROVED CHOOSY. ● 50-52 «SEIT ICH VON CHOOSY GEHÖRT HABE, NENNE ICH MICH TIDDLES (KATZENNAME).» «WENN
ICH GROSS BIN, MÖCHTE ICH EINE KATZE SEIN.» «DAS LETZTE, DAS ICH SEIN WOLLTE, WAR EINE KATZE, BIS ICH VON CHOOSY HÖRTE.» ▲
50-52 «DEPUIS QUE J'AI ENTENDU PARLER DE CHOOSY, JE M'APPELLE TIDDLES» (UN NOM DE CHAT); «QUAND JE SERAI GRAND, JE VEUX
ÊTRE UN CHAT»; «ÊTRE UN CHAT, C'ÉTAIT BIEN LA DERNIÈRE CHOSE QUE JE VOULAIS, JUSQU'À CE QUE J'ENTENDE PARLER DE CHOOSY.»

■ 53-58 ART DIRECTOR: ROONEY CARRUTHERS PHOTOGRAPHERS: JEAN LOUP-SIEFF (53, 55-58), BARRY LATEGAN (54) COPYWRITER: LARRY BARKER
AGENCY: BARTLE BOGLE HEGARTY CLIENT: HÄAGEN-DAZS COUNTRY: GREAT BRITAIN ■ 53-58 HÄAGEN-DAZS, POSITIONED AS THE ICE-CREAM THAT
TITILATES THE SENSES. IN THE SECOND WAVE OF THE CAMPAIGN (SEE 54) THE PEOPLE USED WERE GENUINE COUPLES. ● 53-58 HÄAGEN-DAZS
– DAS SPEISEEIS, DAS MAN KAUFT, WENN ES UM SINNESFREUDEN GEHT. IN DER ZWEITEN PHASE DER KAMPAGNE (SIEHE ABBILDUNG 54) WUR-
DEN RICHTIGE PAARE ALS MODELLE EINGESETZT. ▲ 53-58 HÄAGEN-DAZS — DES GLACES SAVOUREUSES ET RAFFINÉES, POUR LE PLAISIR DES
SENS. DANS LA DEUXIÈME PHASE DE LA CAMPAGNE (VOIR ILLUSTRATION 54), DES COUPLES AUTHENTIQUES ONT POSÉ COMME MODÈLES.

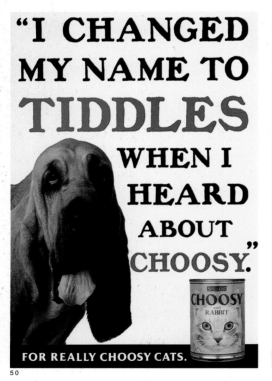

50                                         51                                         52

"I ALWAYS SAY
THAT HÄAGEN-DAZS IS THE

*delicate*

COMBINATION OF THE

WORLD'S FINEST INGREDIENTS

WITH JUST A

*touch*

OF INSPIRATION."

KEN SNIDER, DEVELOPMENT DIRECTOR

**Häagen-Dazs**

*Dedicated to pleasure.*

"to ensure our Belgian chocolates

*LOSE*

*none of their smoothness, we strictly*

*CONTROL*

*their temperature and humidity."*

**Häagen-Dazs**

*Dedicated to Pleasure.*

"Artificial flavours and colours have no part to

*PLAY*

in the Häagen-Dazs story. Consequently we spend much of our

*TIME*

searching for the finest ingredients"

**Häagen-Dazs**

DEDICATED TO PLEASURE

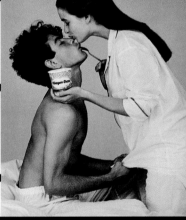

*In order to remain as*

**CLOSE**

*to perfection as humanly possible
only prime ingredients come into*

**CONTACT**

*with our ice cream.*

**Häagen-Dazs**

*Dedicated to Pleasure.*

"Before eating, always let Häagen-Dazs

*TEMPER*

or soften for ten minutes. Only when allowed to

*TEMPER*

can the full flavour be appreciated."

**Häagen-Dazs**

Dedicated to Pleasure.

"TO COMPLEMENT THE

*smooth*

CREAMY TEXTURE

OF HÄAGEN-DAZS WE

SELECT ONLY

*tender,*

RIPE OREGON STRAWBERRIES."

**Häagen-Dazs**

*Dedicated to pleasure.*

## Death by chocolate.

*4oz dark truffle chocolate ice-cream,
layered with creamy vanilla and
roasted almonds, ensconced in crisp
florentines and smothered with
continental chocolate.
Grudgingly serves one.*

59

## For those unfortunate wretches who have succumbed to a state of disgusting fitness through regular and sensible diet.

60

## Crisp, light, crunchy, served steaming from the waffle. And that's just the ice-cream cone.

61

## "I'll start with the lychee ice-cream with black grape sauce topped with cherries, followed by an apple strudel with a scoop of vanilla, and a fruit tart with fresh mango ice-cream."

## "What! No chocolate truffle monsieur?"

62

### IS IT POSSIBLE TO BOTTLE PURITY AND GOODNESS?

A seemingly impossible task. Such elusive qualities. Yet in its own way Mazola Corn Oil is truly the essence

of both purity and goodness. It is 100% pure, with no additives or preservatives. And Mazola's goodness is inherent

in its light, golden nature and its delicate, refined taste. With Mazola comes a sense of well-being because you can't offer

your family anything more precious than purity and goodness.
MAZOLA CORN OIL 100% PURE.

■ 59-62 ART DIRECTORS: URSHILA KERKAR, DHUN CORDO DESIGNER: HEMANT SHIRODKAR ILLUSTRATOR: RAHIM CHIKTEY AGENCY: GRAPHITECTURE CLIENT: PURE GOLD COUNTRY: INDIA ■ 59-62 PROMOTION FOR A NEW ICE-CREAM CHAIN. THE RED COLOR ALLUDES TO THE PURE RED PACKAGING OF THE PRODUCT. ● 59-62 FÜR EINE NEUE EISDIELENKETTE. DIE ROTE FARBE ENTSPRICHT DER ROTEN VERPACKUNG DER PRODUKTE. ▲ 59-62 PUBLICITÉ POUR LE LANCEMENT D'UNE NOUVELLE CHAÎNE DE GLACIERS. LE ROUGE EST CELUI DES EMBALLAGES DE GLACES MAISON.

■ 63 ART DIRECTOR: MICHAEL MC LAUGHLIN PHOTOGRAPHER: GEORGE SIMHONI COPYWRITER: STEPHEN CREET AGENCY: MACLAREN:LINDAS INC. CLIENT: BEST FOODS, MAZOLA COUNTRY: CANADA ■ 63 MAZOLA CORN OIL AND ITS GOLDEN COLOR, ASSOCIATED WITH PURITY AND GOOD OLD TIMES. ● 63 «KANN MAN REINHEIT UND GÜTE IN FLASCHEN ABFÜLLEN?» ▲ 63 «PEUT-ON METTRE EN BOUTEILLE LA PURETÉ ET LE GOÛT?»

■ 64, 65 ART DIRECTOR/DESIGNER: TIM PARKER PHOTOGRAPHER: STEVE BONINI COPYWRITER: DAVE NEWMAN AGENCY: BORDERS, PERRIN & NORRANDER CLIENT: OREGON DAIRY PRODUCTS COMMISSION COUNTRY: USA ■ 64, 65 CHEESE PRESENTED AT ITS MOST APPETIZING, INTENDED TO PROMOTE CONSUMPTION OF CHEESE. ● 64, 65 «GESCHMACK IN ORIGINALGRÖSSE.» «GROSSARTIG, NOCH EIN «KÄSIGES» (IM SLANG BEDEUTET «CHEESY» MIES) BILLBOARD.» BEISPIELE AUS EINER WERBEKAMPAGNE ZUR FÖRDERUNG DES KÄSEKONSUMS ▲ 64, 65 «LE GOÛT GRANDEUR NATURE»; «FANTASTIQUE! ENCORE UNE AFFICHE AU FROMAGE» (JEU DE MOTS: EN ARGOT «CHEESY» VOUDRAIT DIRE «MAUVAISE»).

66

67

Packaging reveals a lot more than it conceals. And as a way to make a real impact on interested parties, packaging is hard to beat. • That is why excitingly different products, like exclusive perfumes, have to be given maximum impact and appeal in their presentation. Which is exactly what you can achieve with the right packaging design and finish. • So when choosing your packaging material, remember, Invercote G has it covered. It feels good, looks great and it has all the properties needed to realise your creative designs; for embossing, cutting and creasing, foil blocking or lamination. Invercote G is available in grammages from 180–380 gm². • So get inspired! Ring us for more information on packaging and product samples, or send in the coupon below.

Invercote G

*For masterpieces in the making*

Packaging has a life and personality of its own. That's why you would expect the inside to be just as interesting and tempting as the outside. • The subtle mystery of a box of distinctively different chocolates is just one example of creating a uniquely appealing design that sells. • When manufacturers and designers are looking for packaging materials that will truly enhance their products they turn to Invercote G. It feels good, looks great and has all the properties needed to realise creative designs; for embossing and creasing, foil blocking or lamination. Invercote G is available in grammages from 180–380 g/m². • So get inspired! Ring us for more information on packaging and product samples, or send in the coupon below.

Invercote G

*For masterpieces in the making*

68

69

# Unlike

*An interview with Bert Schroeder, Producer of Batman Returns on Sega CD, Genesis and Game Gear*

## Bert's wife,

**How will the new Batman Returns games be different from the previous ones?**

## you'll appreciate

**What are your favorite parts of the game?**

## the long,

**How is the music on the CD version?**

## hard hours

**Were the games difficult to create?**

## he's spent at the office.

SEGA

# An attitude,

*An interview with two of the creators of Sonic The Hedgehog 2*

## tons of enemies,

**How was Sonic 2 be different from the original?**

## and a running

**Will there be more levels?**

## mate with the

**How do you get your ideas?**

## mind of a four-year-old.

**How do you go about creating a game?**

(No, it's not another presidential election.)

**Is there anything you'd like to say to Sonic 2 players?**

SEGA

70

71

■ **67** ART DIRECTOR: STEVE STONE PHOTOGRAPHER: BRETT FROOMER COPYWRITER: DAVID FOWLER AGENCY: AMMIRATI + PURIS CLIENT: NIKON INC. COUNTRY: USA ■ **67** VARIOUS CAMERA FUNCTIONS OF THE NIKON N8008S FOR PROFESSIONALS. ● **67** «WIR SAGTEN, ES GÄBE NICHTS ZU VERBESSERN. WIR MÜSSEN UNS KORRIGIEREN.» ▲ **67** «NOUS AVIONS DIT QU'IL N'Y AVAIT RIEN À AMÉLIORER. NOUS DEVONS NOUS CORRIGER.»

■ **68, 69** ART DIRECTOR: HÅKAN WIKANDER PHOTOGRAPHER: JÖRGEN REIMER COPYWRITER: NINA RADSTROM AGENCY: WELINDER CLIENT: IGGESUND PAPERBOARD COUNTRY: SWEDEN ■ **68, 69** THIS PROMOTIONAL CAMPAIGN IS AIMED AT PACKAGE DESIGNERS. ● **68, 69** «VERPACKUNG ZEIGT MEHR ALS SIE VERBIRGT.» «VERPACKUNG HAT EIN EIGENES LEBEN UND EINE EIGENE PERSÖNLICHKEIT.» ▲ **68, 69** «L'EMBALLAGE MONTRE PLUS QU'IL NE CACHE»; «L'EMBALLAGE A SA VIE ET SA PERSONNALITÉ PROPRE». PROMOTION S'ADRESSANT AUX CRÉATEURS DE PACKAGING.

■ **70, 71** ART DIRECTORS: JOHN BUTLER, MIKE SHINE PHOTOGRAPHERS: DAN ESCOBAR (70), JOHN GIPE (71) COPYWRITERS: MIKE SHINE, JOHN BUTLER AGENCY: GOODBY, BERLIN & SILVERSTEIN CLIENT: SEGA OF AMERICA, INC. COUNTRY: USA ■ **70, 71** A CAMPAIGN FOR SEGA VIDEO GAMES. ● **70, 71** «IM GEGENSATZ ZU BERTS (BERT SCHROEDER, PRODUZENT VON «BATMAN RETURNS») FRAU WERDEN SIE SICH ÜBER DIE VIELEN STUNDEN FREUEN, DIE ER IM BÜRO VERBRACHTE.» «EINE HALTUNG, MASSENHAFT FEINDE UND EIN MITSPIELER (IN DEN USA AUCH DER

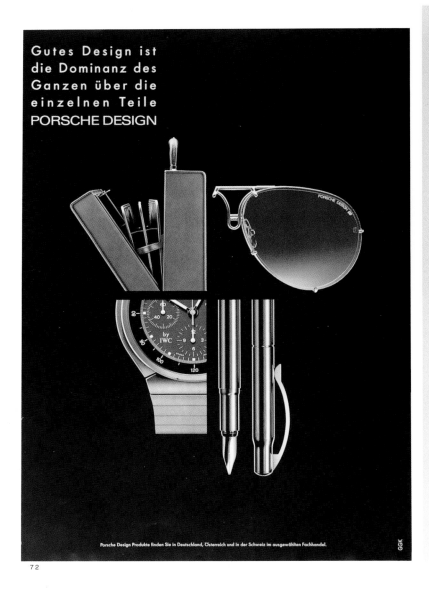

72                                                                                                                73

KANDIDAT FÜR DIE VIZEPRÄSIDENTSCHAFT) MIT DEM VERSTAND EINES VIERJÄHRIGEN. NEIN, ES GEHT NICHT UM EINE PRÄSIDENTSCHAFTSWAHL.» ▲ **70, 71** «AU CONTRAIRE DE LA FEMME DE BERT (BERT SCHROEDER, PRODUCTEUR DU FILM «LE RETOUR DE BATMAN»), VOUS VOUS RÉJOUIREZ QU'IL RESTE DE LONGUES HEURES AU BUREAU»; «UN COMPORTEMENT, UNE FOULE D'ENNEMIS ET UN COMPAGNON DE JEUX (LITTÉRALEMENT UN AUTRE CANDIDAT) AVEC LA MENTALITÉ D'UN GOSSE DE QUATRE ANS. NON, IL NE S'AGIT PAS D'UNE ÉLECTION PRÉSIDENTIELLE.»

■ **72** ART DIRECTORS/DESIGNERS: CHRISTIAN SATEK, THOM KAJABA PHOTOGRAPHER: HERB RITTS COPYWRITER: UNA WIENER AGENCY: GGK WIEN CLIENT: PORSCHE DESIGN COUNTRY: AUSTRIA ■ **72** "GOOD DESIGN MEANS DOMINANCE OF THE WHOLE OVER THE INDIVIDUAL PARTS." ● **72** DIE VIER PRODUKTGRUPPEN VON PORSCHE DESIGN. AUS EINER INTERNATIONALEN KAMPAGNE. ▲ **72** LES QUATRE TYPES DE PRODUITS DE PORSCHE DESIGN.

■ **73** ART DIRECTOR: MICHAEL MCLAUGHLIN PHOTOGRAPHERS: GRANT FAINT, BILL DRUMMOND COPYWRITER: STEVEN CREET AGENCY: MACLAREN:LINTAS CLIENT: LEVER BROTHERS COUNTRY: CANADA ■ **73** THE ENVIRONMENT AS CENTRAL ISSUE OF A CAMPAIGN FOR SUNLIGHT DISHWASHER DETERGENT. ● **73** «WIR FINDEN, DASS SICH 'KRISTALLKLAR' AUF MEHR ALS NUR GLÄSER UND GESCHIRR BEZIEHEN SOLLTE.» ▲ **73** «NOUS TROUVONS QUE LE TERME 'CLAIR COMME LE CRISTAL' DEVRAIT S'APPLIQUER À AUTRE CHOSE QU'À DES VERRES OU DE LA VAISSELLE.»

74

75

76

■ **74-76** ART DIRECTORS: ERICH JOINER (74), DAVID PAGE (75-77) PHOTOGRAPHER: DUNCAN SIM ILLUSTRATOR: ALAN DANIELS COPYWRITERS: SCOTT BURNS (74), DAVE O'HARE (75-77) AGENCY: GOODBY, BERLIN & SILVERSTEIN CLIENT: AMERICAN ISUZU MOTORS, INC. COUNTRY: USA ■ **74-76** THE UNWRITTEN LAWS OF DRIVING, AND THE ANSWER ISUZU CARS HAVE TO OFFER. ● **74-76** «DIE ANZIEHUNGSKRAFT, DIE EINKAUFSWAGEN AUF AUTOS AUSÜBEN, GEHÖRT ZU DEN STÄRKSTEN KRÄFTEN DES UNIVERSUMS.» «WO ES EINEN BERG GIBT, GIBT ES EINEN WOHNWAGEN.» «JE KLEINER DIE PERSON, DESTO MEHR PLATZ BRAUCHT SIE.» «WENN ES EIN LOCH IN DER STRASSE GIBT, WERDEN SIE ES TREFFEN.» ▲ **74-76** «LA FORCE D'ATTRACTION QU'EXERCENT LES CADDIES SUR LES AUTOMOBILES»; «LÀ OÙ IL Y A UNE COLLINE, IL Y A UNE VOITURE-CAMPING»; «PLUS LA PERSONNE EST PETITE ET PLUS DE PLACE ELLE OCCUPE»; «S'IL Y A UN TROU SUR LA ROUTE, VOUS TOMBEREZ DESSUS.»

# This Just Might Be The Tackiest Thing We've Ever Done.

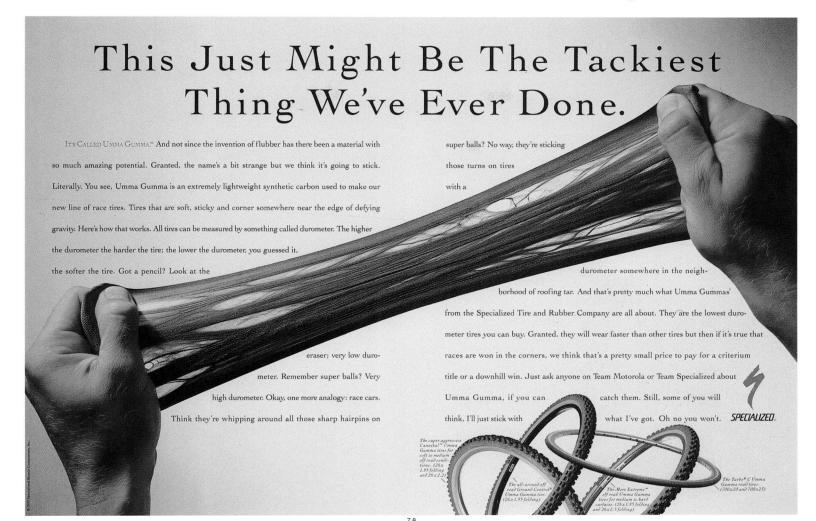

IT'S CALLED UMMA GUMMA.™ And not since the invention of flubber has there been a material with so much amazing potential. Granted, the name's a bit strange but we think it's going to stick. Literally. You see, Umma Gumma is an extremely lightweight synthetic carbon used to make our new line of race tires. Tires that are soft, sticky and corner somewhere near the edge of defying gravity. Here's how that works. All tires can be measured by something called durometer. The higher the durometer the harder the tire; the lower the durometer, you guessed it, the softer the tire. Got a pencil? Look at the eraser; very low durometer. Remember super balls? Very high durometer. Okay, one more analogy: race cars. Think they're whipping around all those sharp hairpins on super balls? No way, they're sticking those turns on tires with a durometer somewhere in the neighborhood of roofing tar. And that's pretty much what Umma Gummas' from the Specialized Tire and Rubber Company are all about. They are the lowest durometer tires you can buy. Granted, they will wear faster than other tires but then if it's true that races are won in the corners, we think that's a pretty small price to pay for a criterium title or a downhill win. Just ask anyone on Team Motorola or Team Specialized about Umma Gumma, if you can catch them. Still, some of you will think, I'll just stick with what I've got. Oh no you won't.

SPECIALIZED

*The super aggressive Cannibal™ Umma Gumma tires for soft to medium off road conditions. (26 x 1.95 folding and 26 x 2.2)*

*The all-around off road Ground Control® Umma Gumma tire. (26 x 1.95 folding)*

*The More Extreme™ off road Umma Gumma tires for medium to hard surfaces. (26 x 1.95 folding and 26 x 2.5 folding)*

*The Turbo® C Umma Gumma road tires. (700 x 20 and 700 x 23)*

78

---

## Welcome Back To The Future.

They say that what goes around comes around. And once upon a time, road bikes were crafted, not made, of steel, not poly-kevlarcarbonbondedspacegoop. Steel was out. And now, steel is back. Introducing the new Specialized Allez. A steel bike of such precise workmanship, such remarkable engineering, that the editors at *Bicycling* magazine summed it up thusly: "All you need is a USCF license and you're ready for the big time." And speaking of big time, check out the frame weight: 3.63 pounds. That's a full pound lighter than the old Allez.

Why this thing is so thinned out—in the tube walls, the lugs, everywhere—that it could easily be mistaken for a composite. But the ride is pure steel: stiff, rigid, powerful. Or as the *Bicycling* guys found out, "jump all you want but you won't get any wag from the rear wheel... or wimpiness from the frame, just forward thrust." It's the kind of exhilaration riders have been feeling on the flats of Bordeaux and up in the Gavia Pass for as long as anyone can remember. And it's the same kind of exhilaration we invite you to experience at your Specialized dealer on a time honored tradition called the Allez. And oh, by the way, welcome back.

*The new Allez steel frame Specialized bikes.*

79

---

## Thank God There Are People Who Stayed In The Science Club.

$$I = \frac{\pi}{4}(d_0^4 - d_i^4)$$

$$\dot{x} = -\left(\frac{3}{L}\right)\frac{c\sqrt{k}}{\sqrt{m}\sqrt{m}}\sqrt{k}\quad x - \left(\frac{c}{m}\right)x$$

$$K = \frac{nPA^2}{V_1}\left[\frac{1}{\frac{1}{V_1}}\right]^{n+1}$$

$$\ddot{x} = \frac{d^4 G}{8 D^3 N}$$

$$d_h = \frac{F_h l^3}{3 E I}$$

$F_h$

While you were learning how to french kiss, they were learning how to manipulate gravity. Introducing the S-Works FSR.™ The most thought out, dialed in, thoroughly tested, fully suspended mountain bike there is. See your nearest physicist (or your local S-Works™ dealer) for a thorough explanation.

80

---

*Featured—Office of certified psychologist Dr. Theodore P. Uecker PhD.

**$115**
AN HOUR*

WHILE WE'RE NOT SUGGESTING THAT YOU CAN PUT A PRICE ON SANITY, WE DO BELIEVE IT SHOULD AT LEAST BE ACCESSIBLE TO EVERYONE. WHICH IS WHY WE AT ISUZU CREATED THE RODEO. A BUTT-KICKING, 4-WHEEL DRIVE SPORT UTILITY VEHICLE

*Featured—3.1 liter, V6 Rodeo of fairly well-adjusted, non-dysfunctional person.

**$1.15**
A GALLON*

THAT COMES WITH A PRICE TAG YOU CAN ACTUALLY AFFORD. BECAUSE THE WAY WE SEE IT, WHAT GOOD IS A VEHICLE THAT TAKES YOU AWAY FROM IT ALL, IF THE PAYMENTS ARE DRIVING YOU NUTS IN THE MEANTIME?

**ISUZU**
*Practically/Amazing*

81

■ 81 ART DIRECTORS: JOHN BUTLER, MIKE SHINE PHOTOGRAPHER: HARRY DEZITTER COPYWRITERS: MIKE SHINE, JOHN BUTLER AGENCY: GOODBY, BERLIN & SILVERSTEIN CLIENT: AMERICAN ISUZU MOTORS, INC. COUNTRY: USA ■ 81 "WHAT GOOD IS A VEHICLE THAT TAKES YOU AWAY FROM IT ALL, IF THE PAYMENTS ARE DRIVING YOU NUTS IN THE MEANTIME?" THE CLAIM: ISUZU OFFERS 4-WHEEL SPORT UTILITY VEHICLES YOU CAN AFFORD. ● 81 «$115.- PRO STUNDE (BEIM PSYCHIATER), $ 1.15 PRO GALLONE (BENZIN).... WAS NÜTZT EIN AUTO, MIT DEM MAN DEM ALLTAG ENTKOMMT, WENN DIE KOSTEN EINEN WAHNSINNIG MACHEN?» ISUZU BIETET EINEN GÜNSTIGEN 4-RADANTRIEB-GELÄNDEWAGEN AN. ▲ 81 «115 DOLLARS DE L'HEURE (CHEZ LE PSYCHIATRE), 1.15 DOLLARS LE GALLON (D'ESSENCE). A QUOI SERT UNE VOITURE QUI VOUS PERMET D'ÉCHAP-PER AU TRAIN-TRAIN QUOTIDIEN SI LES COÛTS SONT EXCESSIFS?» ISUZU PROPOSE ICI UNE 4/4 TOUT TERRAIN À UN PRIX ABORDABLE.

■ 82-84 ART DIRECTORS: DAVID PAGE (82, 84), RICH SILVERSTEIN (83) PHOTOGRAPHERS: PAUL FRANZ-MOORE (82, 84), DAVE EPPERSON (83) COPYWRITER: DAVE O'HARE AGENCY: GOODBY, BERLIN & SILVERSTEIN CLIENT: SPECIALIZED BICYCLE COMPONENTS, INC. COUNTRY: USA ■ 82-84 EXAMPLES FROM A CAMPAIGN FOR BICYCLE COMPONENTS, SUCH AS SPECIAL HELMETS AND A NEW RIDER-ADJUSTED SUSPENSION FORK. ● 82-84 BEISPIELE AUS EINER WERBEKAMPAGNE FÜR FAHRRADZUBEHÖR WIE HELME UND EINE SPEZIELLE AUFHÄNGUNG. ▲ 82-84 EXEMPLES D'UNE CAMPAGNE DE PUBLICITÉ POUR LES ACCESSOIRES DE VÉLOS, PAR EXEMPLE DES CASQUES OU UN MODÈLE DE SUSPENSION PARTICULIER.

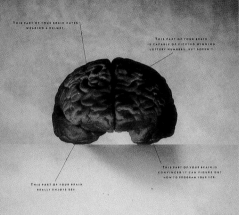

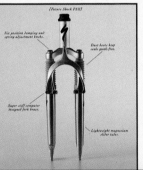

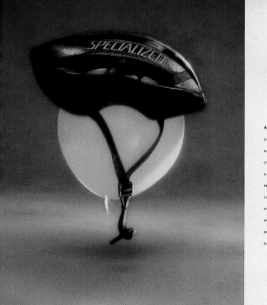

Why man learned to walk.

The new Sony Spy-Micro
cassette recorder.

Putting a CD multi-player
in our Mini Hi-Fi has made it
hundreds of feet shorter.

Sony's new HiBlack Trinitron will give
you the worst shave you've ever had.

If these two reds look the same,
then the new
HiBlack Trinitron's not for you.

Virtual reality?

First shoot your dog
then freeze it.

Sony's cordless headphones free
you from being tied to your hi-fi.

To see how big it is, cover up
the bottom fruit bowl.
To see how big it sounds,
cover up the top one.

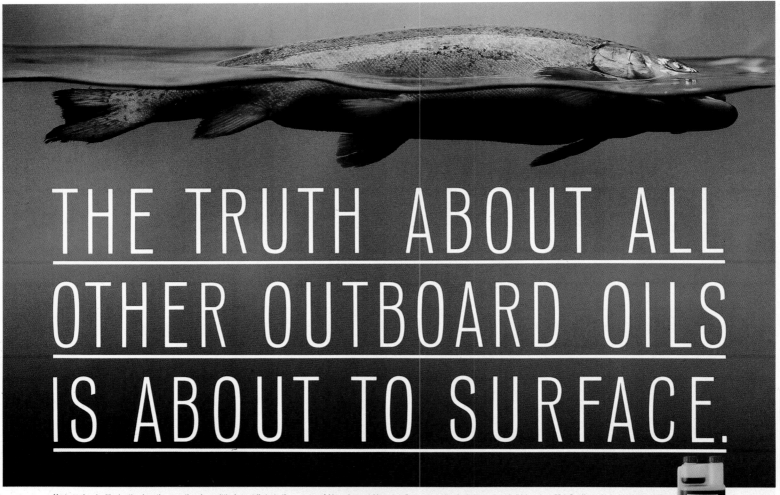

# THE TRUTH ABOUT ALL OTHER OUTBOARD OILS IS ABOUT TO SURFACE.

Most people who like boating love the environment. Unfortunately, while you enjoy yourself on the water, the marine life beneath you is slowly suffocating. That's because people using oils in their outboards unwittingly contribute to the pollution of our waterways. Which is why Castrol has developed an outboard oil that's more than 70% biodegradable. It's called BIOLUBE 100, and it has been so successful in environmental impact studies, it won the International Pollution Abatement Award, launched in the UK. But as well as being kind to the environment, BIOLUBE 100 provides the best possible protection for both pre-mix and oil-injected outboards. It's a high performance, fully synthetic product and is so effective, it can be used at ratios of up to 100:1, where other outboard oils are used at 50:1. But if you think all this sounds like a tall fisherman's tale, contact one of our boating lubricant specialists for more details about Castrol's advanced range of boating products and select stockists.

Oils ain't oils.

95

■ 95 ART DIRECTOR/COPYWRITER: PETER SUTHERLAND AGENCY: YOUNG & RUBICAM CLIENT: CASTROL COUNTRY: AUSTRALIA ■ 95 THIS OUTBOARD MOTOR OIL WON THE INTERNATIONAL POLLUTION ABATEMENT AWARD LAUNCHED IN THE UK. ● 95 «DIE WAHRHEIT ÜBER ALLE ANDEREN AUSSEN-BORDMOTORÖLE WIRD BALD AN DIE OBERFLÄCHE KOMMEN.» DIESES MOTORENÖL GEWANN IN GROSSBRITANNIEN EINEN INTERNATIONALEN UMWELTSCHUTZPREIS. ▲ 95 «LA VÉRITÉ SUR TOUTES LES AUTRES HUILES DE MOTEURS DE HORD-BORDS REMONTERA BIENTÔT À LA SURFACE.»

■ 96 ART DIRECTOR: GARY GOLDSMITH PHOTOGRAPHER: ILAN RUBIN COPYWRITER: GARY GOLDSMITH AGENCY: GOLDSMITH/JEFFREY CLIENTS: US, ROLLING STONE COUNTRY: USA ■ 96 PROMOTION FOR AD SPACE IN US AND ROLLING STONE MAGAZINES. ● 96 «NICHT JEDER INTERESSIERT SICH FÜR DIE NEUSTE AUDIO-TECHNIK. LETZTES JAHR GABEN JEDOCH DIE LESER VON US UND ROLLING STONE 1.9 MILLARDEN FÜR ELEKTRONIK AUS, 998 MILLIONEN DAVON FÜR STEREOGERÄTE.» ▲ 96 «TOUT LE MONDE NE S'INTÉRESSE PAS AUX DERNIÈRES PETITES MERVEILLES DE L'AUDIO-VISUEL. L'ANNÉE DERNIÈRE, LES LECTEURS DE US ET ROLLING STONE ONT POURTANT DÉPENSÉ 1,9 MILLIARDS EN ÉQUIPEMENTS STÉRÉOS.»

■ 97, 98 ART DIRECTOR: JEREMY POSTAER PHOTOGRAPHERS: STOCK PHOTO (97), DAN ESCOBAR (98) HAND TINTING: ANN RHONEY (97) COPYWRITER: STEVE SIMPSON AGENCY: GOODBY, BERLIN & SILVERSTEIN CLIENT: THE NEW YORKER COUNTRY: USA ■ 97, 98 EXCERPTS FROM FEATURES THAT APPEARED IN THE NEW YORKER: "WHEN YOU READ IT, YOU WILL SEE." ● 97, 98 AUSZÜGE AUS BEITRÄGEN IM THE NEW YORKER: «WENN SIE ES LESEN, WERDEN SIE ES WISSEN.» ▲ 97, 98 EXTRAITS D'ARTICLES DU MAGAZINE THE NEW YORKER: «SI VOUS LE LISEZ, VOUS LE SAUREZ.»

NOT EVERYONE IS INTERESTED IN THE LATEST SOUND TECHNOLOGY. HOWEVER, LAST YEAR READERS OF US AND *Rolling Stone* SPENT 1.9 BILLION ON CONSUMER ELECTRONICS, INCLUDING 998 MILLION ON NEW STEREOS.

Advertisers who buy matching space in both US and Rolling Stone will receive a 15% discount in both publications. For details call Mr. Leslie Zeifman at (212) 484-1495.

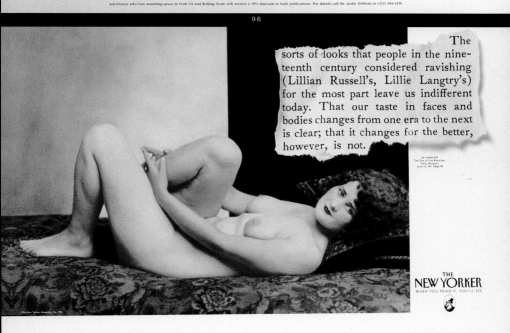

The sorts of looks that people in the nineteenth century considered ravishing (Lillian Russell's, Lillie Langtry's) for the most part leave us indifferent today. That our taste in faces and bodies changes from one era to the next is clear; that it changes for the better, however, is not.

THE NEW YORKER
WHEN YOU READ IT, YOU'LL SEE

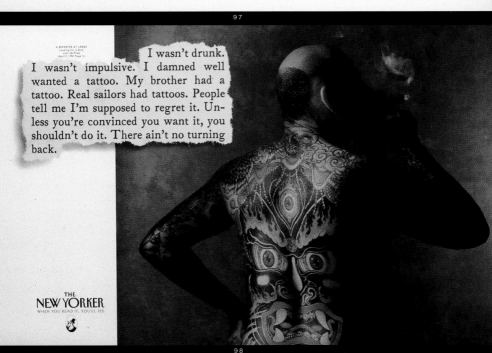

I wasn't drunk. I wasn't impulsive. I damned well wanted a tattoo. My brother had a tattoo. Real sailors had tattoos. People tell me I'm supposed to regret it. Unless you're convinced you want it, you shouldn't do it. There ain't no turning back.

THE NEW YORKER
WHEN YOU READ IT, YOU'LL SEE

99

100

# David Bowie: The House Tour

September's Architectural Digest features David Bowie's exotic Caribbean retreat. Stop by your local newsstand, or call 1-800-234-4378 to reserve a copy.

## Our September Issue On Sale This Week.

# Rudolph Valentino Really Knew How To Make An Entrance.

Valentino's entrance. Garbo's living room. Fonda's den. Cher's bedroom. They're all part of Architectural Digest's exclusive tour through the homes of past and present Oscar winners and nominees. Don't

miss this classic Academy Awards edition. Reserve your copy by calling 1-800-289-1214. Or stop by your local newsstand.

## Our 2nd Academy Awards Edition On Sale This Week.

# How The West Was Decorated.

From Liz Claiborne's ranch in Montana to Robert Redford's resort in Utah, Architectural Digest takes you on an exclusive tour through some of the most spectacular western abodes. Call 1-800-289-1214 for our June issue. Or, go to your local newsstand and round one up.

## Our Wild West Edition On Sale This Week.

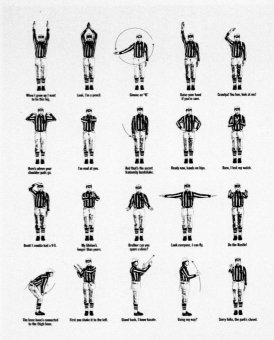

If this is your understanding of the game then the NFL Kickoff is probably not for you.

The NFL Kickoff is for die-hard fans. Fans who spew statistics. Fans who want in-depth analysis. Fans who just might need some in-depth analysis. Pull it from our sports section. **The Sunday Pioneer Press.**

*Words to live by.*

109

■ **105-107** ART DIRECTOR: STEVE DAVIS COPYWRITERS: LIZ PARADISE, JOHN RUSSO AGENCY: MCKINNEY & SILVER CLIENT: *ARCHITECTURAL DIGEST* COUNTRY: USA ■ **105-107** IN ORDER TO BUILD NEWSSTAND CIRCULATION OF THREE SPECIAL ISSUES OF *ARCHITECTURAL DIGEST*, THESE ADS FOCUS ON CELEBRITIES BY PROVIDING A PEEK AT THEIR HOMES AND THEIR PERSONAL LIVES. "RUDOLPH VALENTINO" GENERATED THE LARGEST NEWSSTAND SALES OF ANY ISSUE IN THE HISTORY OF THE MAGAZINE. ● **105-107** UM DEN EINZELVERKAUF VON DREI SONDERAUSGABEN VON *ARCHITECTURAL DIGEST* ZU STEIGERN WURDEN ANZEIGEN LANCIERT, DIE EINEN BLICK DAS PRIVATLEBEN VON PROMINENTEN VERSPRECHEN. DIE VALENTINO-AUSGABE ERZIELTE DIE HÖCHSTEN VERKÄUFE IN DER GESCHICHTE DES MAGAZINS. ▲ **105-107** AFIN DE FAIRE MONTER LES VENTES DE TROIS ÉDITIONS SPÉCIALES DU *ARCHITECTURAL DIGEST* DANS LES KIOSQUES, ON FIT PUBLIER CES ANNONCES QUI NE SE CONTENTAIENT PAS DE DONNER UNE IDÉE DES INTÉRIEURS DES CÉLÉBRITÉS, MAIS QUI PROMETTAIENT DES RÉVÉLATIONS SUR LEUR VIE PRIVÉE. LE NUMÉRO CONSACRÉ À RUDOLPH VALENTINO A BATTU TOUS LES RECORDS DE VENTE JAMAIS ENREGISTRÉS PAR CE MAGAZINE.

■ **108, 109** ART DIRECTOR: RANDY HUGHES PHOTOGRAPHER: CURTIS JOHNSON COPYWRITER: JOSH DENBERG AGENCY: CLARITY COVERDALE RUEFF CLIENT: ST. PAUL PIONEER PRESS COUNTRY: USA ■ **108, 109** PROMOTION FOR THE SPORTS SECTION OF THE PIONEER PRESS. THE NEWSPAPER AD TALKS TO DIE-HARD FOOTBALL FANS BY GRACEFULLY EXCLUDING THOSE NOT INTERESTED IN THE GAME. THE BILLBOARD WAS PLACED AT STREET LEVEL NEXT TO THE METRODROME. THE LOCATION USED TO BE NOTORIOUS FOR ILLEGAL TICKET SALES. ● **108, 109** WERBUNG FÜR DEN SPORTTEIL EINER ZEITUNG. DIE ANZEIGE RICHTET SICH AN FOOTBALL FANS, INDEM SIE DIE NICHT INTERESSIERTEN TAKTVOLL AUSSCHLIESST: «WENN SIE DAS SPIEL SO VERSTEHEN, IST DER NFL KICKOFF NICHTS FÜR SIE.» DAS BILLBOARD WURDE DIREKT VOR DEM STADION PLAZIERT. ▲ **108, 109** PUBLICITÉ POUR LA RUBRIQUE SPORTIVE D'UN JOURNAL. L'ANNONCE S'ADRESSE AUX FANS DE FOOTBALL, EXCLUANT D'EMBLÉE TOUS CEUX QUI NE S'INTÉRESSENT PAS À CE SPORT. «SI VOUS COMPRENEZ LE JEU COMME ÇA, LE NFL KICKOFF N'EST PAS FAIT POUR VOUS.»

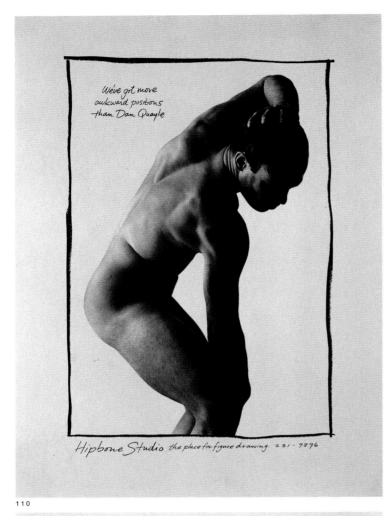

We've got more awkward positions than Dan Quayle.

Hipbone Studio the place for figure drawing. 231 - 7876

110

Contemplate someone else's navel.

Hipbone Studio the place for figure drawing. 231 - 7876

111

Beats the hell out of still lifes.

Hipbone Studio the place for figure drawing. 231 - 7876

112

Meanwhile, most of your friends will be home watching "Wheel of Fortune."

Hipbone Studio the place for figure drawing. 231 - 7876

113

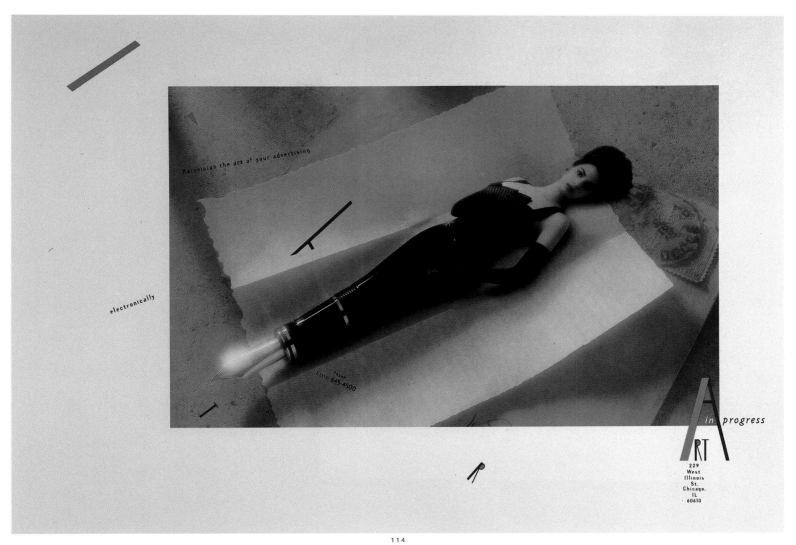

114

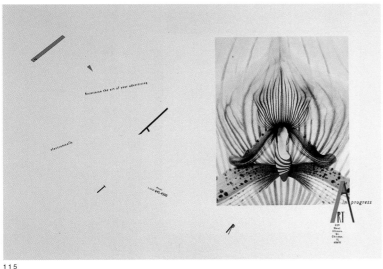

115

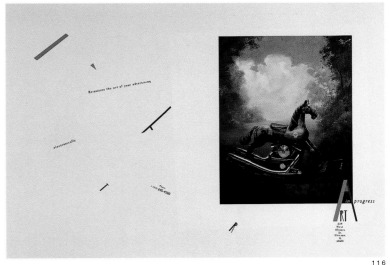

116

■ **110-113** ART DIRECTOR: JERRY KETEL COPYWRITER: CARL LOEB AGENCY: BANG BANG BANG CLIENT: HIPBONE STUDIO COUNTRY: USA ■ **110-113** THESE ADVERTISEMENTS FOR A LIVE-MODEL DRAWING STUDIO HAD TO SHOW THE FIGURE AND YET HAVE A HUMOROUS TOUCH. ● **110-113** «WIR HABEN MEHR UNMÖGLICHE POSITIONEN ZU BIETEN ALS DAN QUAYLE.» «SCHAUEN SIE SICH DEN NABEL VON JEMANDEM ANDEREN AN.» «SCHLÄGT STILLEBEN BEI WEITEM.» «INZWISCHEN SITZEN DIE MEISTEN IHRER FREUNDE ZUHAUSE VOR DEM FERNSEHER (UND SEHEN SICH DIE GLÜCKSKETTE AN).» ▲ **110-113** «NOUS AVONS PLUS DE POSES IMPOSSIBLES À OFFRIR QUE DAN QUAYLE»; «REGARDEZ LE NOMBRIL DE QUELQU'UN D'AUTRE»; «BAT DE LOIN TOUTES LES NATURES MORTES»; «PENDANT CE TEMPS-LÀ, LA PLUPART DE VOS AMIS SONT ASSIS DE-VANT LEUR TÉLÉ EN TRAIN DE REGARDER LA ROUE DE LA FORTUNE». D'UNE CAMPAGNE PUBLICITAIRE POUR UN ATELIER DE DESSINS DE NUS.

■ **114-116** ART DIRECTOR/DESIGNER: DON MORAVICK PHOTOGRAPHERS: LAURIE RUBIN (114), PAM HALLER (115, 116) ELECTRONIC IMAGING: ART IN PROGRESS AGENCY: ART IN PROGRESS CLIENT: WACE USA/ART IN PROGRESS COUNTRY: USA ■ **114-116** ADS SHOWCASING EXAMPLES OF WORK THAT WAS DONE USING THE ELECTRONIC IMAGING CAPABILITIES OF A STUDIO. ● **114-116** HIER WERDEN BEISPIELE ELEKTRONISCHER BILDVER-ARBEITUNG EINES STUDIOS GEZEIGT. ▲ **114-116** EXEMPLES D'IMAGES RETRAVAILLÉES SUR ORDINATEUR CRÉÉES PAR UN STUDIO DE DESIGN.

# We're not the only convention city known for sidewalk art.

The art you'll find on the streets of Portland, Oregon, requires more than a can of spray paint and an attitude.

Of course, we do have some defaced buildings. It's just that we commission them: everything from sweeping floralscapes to thought-provoking sculptures.

And there is plenty of action on Portland's streets. Visitors are likely to be greeted by a Rose Parade or an Artquake (not as earth shattering as some quakes but a dazzling display in its own right), or Saturday Market, our nine-month waterfront salute to mankind's craftiness.

And we admit that our sidewalks are littered. With roving musicians, horse-drawn carriages and sidewalk cafes.

Such tranquility is seldom interrupted. Even the light-rail trains are peaceful as they quietly whisk thousands back and forth between downtown Portland and the Oregon Convention Center.

Now, would you prefer a convention site filled with eyesores, or one that soothes the eye?

## Portland, Oregon
Things look different here.

*The 500,000 sq. ft. Oregon Convention Center is Portland's largest work of art.*

117

# We're Rather Reluctant To Admit What Our Waitress In Seattle Gave A Guest For Lunch.

Her name is Trenna Adams and she had help from three others who work the afternoon shift in our Coffee Garden. What they did for a frequent guest during the recent holidays is actually sort of heartwarming.

But we'd rather not go into details here. Because, the truth is, they couldn't do this sort of thing all the time. Still, their generosity is definitely worth mentioning because it's so typical of the attitude our people have. They jump through hoops every day. In fact, the culture here has produced a level of service that is so exceptional we believe it extends beyond what you'll find at any comparable hotel.

And from the looks of the mail we've been getting, our guests seem to agree. But that's just an ad talking. If your travel plans include the eleven western states, we'd sure like to prove it to you in real life.

Now if you're still curious what happened with the bird, call 1-800-RED LION and Trenna will tell you in her own words.

Or call the same number for reservations. Who knows? You might experience something so special, we'll have to make yet another one of these ads.

## RED LION HOTELS & INNS

118

119

120

121

122

Apparently, Breakfast Cereal Isn't The Only Thing
That Can Be Fortified With Iron.

Sage Cowles
Age 67

Recent studies show that people 50+ are just as receptive to exercise as younger people. For information on classes and our free booklet—Getting Started On Your Own—call 780-1447. Take Care Now. United Hospital

123

What Kind Of Shape Is The Future Of Our Country In?

Unfortunately kids today aren't in very good shape. You can help strengthen our future by calling for a free booklet—The President's Fitness Challenge—on child fitness. To get yours call 780-1447. Take care now. United Hospital

124

If You Think Predicting The Stock Market Is Stressful,
Try Predicting The Weather.

Worrying too much about things you can't do anything about can create stress that is unhealthy. Our free booklet will help you learn how to cope with stress. Call 780-1447 for your copy. Take care now. United Hospital

125

■ 123-125 ART DIRECTOR: RANDY HUGHES PHOTOGRAPHERS: SHAWN MICHIENZI (123, 124), STOCK (125) COPYWRITER: JERRY FURY AGENCY: CLARITY COVERDALE RUEFF CLIENT: THE UNITED HOSPITAL COUNTRY: USA ■ 123-125 HEALTH AND FITNESS BOOKLETS OF UNITED HOSPITAL. ● 123-125 GESUNDHEITS- UND FITNESSBROSCHÜREN EINER KRANKENVERSICHERUNG. ▲ 123-125 BROCHURES D'UNE ASSURANCE MALADIE.

■ 126-128 ART DIRECTORS: CHRIS PAYNE (126, 127), ROHAN CAESAR DESIGNER: CONDON PAYNE TERRY COPYWRITER: JOE DI STEFANO AGENCY: SSB CLIENT: COLONIAL MUTUAL LIFE COUNTRY: AUSTRALIA ■ 126-128 INSURANCE PROGRAMS. ● 126-128 VERSICHERUNG. ▲ 126-128 ASSURANCE.

■ 129 ART DIRECTOR/DESIGNER: KENT SUTER PHOTOGRAPHER: MICHAEL JONES COPYWRITER: DAVE NEWMAN AGENCY: BORDERS, PERRIN & NORRANDER CLIENT: U.S. BANK COUNTRY: USA ■ 129 NEWSPAPER ADVERTISEMENT. ● 129 AUFRUF AN ORGANSPENDER. ▲ 129 APPEL AUX DONNEURS D'ORGANES.

# WHAT WOULD YOU DO IF YOU HAD TO RETIRE TOMORROW?

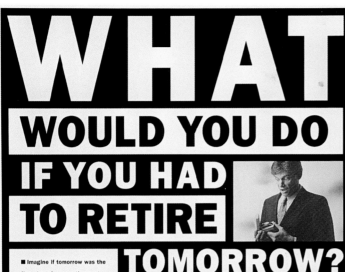

■ Imagine if tomorrow was the first day of your retirement. Imagine if, after working hard to establish a comfortable lifestyle, you were left with not much more than a handshake and the traditional gold watch. ■ Fortunately, you still have a number of years to plan for retirement. To plan for the future you want to have, rather than one you "have to have". Because it's important to realise that the compulsory superannuation provision from employers is unlikely to be enough to maintain your lifestyle. ■ Personal superannuation is not something you can afford to turn your back on. ■ That's why Colonial mutual has developed a personal superannuation plan called Superwise. It can be designed to match your needs and is flexible enough to change as your circumstances do. Contributions can also be adjusted annually to offset the effects of inflation. ■ Superwise is an effective method of ensuring that the sum you receive on retirement amounts to what you need, rather than something much less. That's why you need to start your Superwise plan as soon as possible, to give yourself enough time to comfortably build this sum over a number of years. ■ And, because Superwise is a plan for your future, it's reassuring to know it's from Colonial mutual, one of Australia's most experienced Life Offices. ■ For information, contact your adviser or Colonial mutual office. After all, if you're like most people, you'll want to retire to a future that you've planned.

**Colonial mutual**
Principal Office: 330 Collins St, Melbourne, Vic. 3000
Phone: (03) 607 6111. Offices around Australia.
The Colonial Mutual Life Assurance Society Limited.
A.C.N. 004 021 809          SSB CML522/NAT

126

# IN TEN YEARS TIME I WANT TO:

Everyone reading this sentence would have a very different way of completing it. ■ However, right at the moment, all the statements would have one thing in common. They are merely dreams. And for many of us they would remain so, simply because turning them into reality requires one key element. ■ Money. ■ As we all know, it's easier to spend than to save. Yet, if you were to calculate how much you've earned over the years, it might astonish you to realise how little you have to show for it. ■ To help you overcome this hurdle, Colonial mutual recommends that you pay yourself first, by way of an effective personal savings plan. ■ So the first person to benefit from your pay packet will be you. ■ Colonial mutual Lifewise is a disciplined and flexible savings plan with contributions that can be indexed to counter inflation and paid automatically through your Bank, Credit Union or Building Society. ■ Under current legislation, you receive the proceeds fully "tax-paid" after 10 years. (A fully taxed investment would have to earn considerably more to give you the same after-tax return.) And there are also tax concessions that apply on withdrawal of the proceeds before 10 years. ■ Equally important is that Lifewise comes from Colonial mutual, one of Australia's most experienced Life Offices. ■ For all information, contact your adviser or Colonial mutual office. The sooner you do, the sooner you can start paying yourself first and filling the blanks in your future.

**Colonial mutual**
Principal Office: 330 Collins St, Melbourne, Vic. 3000
Phone: (03) 607 6111. Offices around Australia.
The Colonial Mutual Life Assurance Society Limited.
A.C.N. 004 021 809          SSB CML523/NAT

127

# IMAGINE LOSING YOUR JOB BY ACCIDENT

It's the most unexpected way of finding yourself out on the street. It has nothing to do with layoffs, budget cutbacks, or the recession. ■ It has to do with having an unexpected accident or illness. One which could keep you off work for months, even years. ■ These days, very few employers can afford to hold your position indefinitely. ■ What's more, your bills and other such commitments like the mortgage, the car and school fees certainly will not wait until you're back on your feet again. ■ Often, the financial consequences can be more debilitating than the accident itself. ■ That's why Colonial mutual has developed IncomeGuard, one of the most flexible and appropriate income protection plans available. Up to six benefit and qualifying periods can be mixed and matched in one policy. So variables such as your income, lifestyle, occupation, employment benefits and more can be catered for in one customised plan. ■ Importantly, cover is linked to your occupation and income, with no reduction in benefits if either should change. And IncomeGuard comes from Colonial mutual, one of Australia's most experienced Life Offices. ■ If you need more information, you should contact your financial adviser or local Colonial mutual office today. That way, if you lose your job through an accident or illness, you can spend your time getting better rather than feeling worse.

**Colonial mutual**
Principal Office: 330 Collins St, Melbourne, Vic. 3000
Phone: (03) 607 6111. Offices around Australia.
The Colonial Mutual Life Assurance Society Limited.
A.C.N. 004 021 809          SSB CML524/NAT

128

# HAPPINESS IS BEING AN ORGAN DONOR.

**OREGON DONOR PROGRAM**

*Feel good knowing you can help someone long after you're gone. Carry an organ donor card.*

129

# THINGS ARE NEVER QUITE THE SAME AFTER A TRIP TO THE MODERN

SAN FRANCISCO MUSEUM OF MODERN ART · 401 VAN NESS AVENUE · 415/252-4000

130

# EDVARD MUNCH.

# FORSVINNER?

23. januar 1944 fikk verden vite at en av århundrets aller største billedkunstnere hadde testamentert 1.112 malerier, 17.689 grafiske trykk, ca. 5000 akvareller og tegninger og seks skulpturer til Oslo by.

45 år senere forvaltes Edvard Munchs kunst bak sponplater og falmede gardiner, på vegger som repareres med tape for å skjule sprekker i panelet hvor vannet tidvis har fått fritt løp. I kjellerens magasiner er luftfuktighet og temperatur så høy at konserveringsforholdene er meget dårlige. Redusert bemanning har ført til at alle tilbud til barn og ungdom er avlyst. Og de som kommer for å oppleve skattene, mange av dem har reist halve jorden rundt bare for det, blir møtt av tistler langs veggene, flekkede gulvtepper, avskallet maling og nedslitte møbler.

Det mangler 20 millioner for at Munch-Museet skal kunne fremstå som et representativt senter for Edvard Munch og hans kunst. Og et verdig monument over kulturnasjonens ansvar for en av verdens mest generøse kunstdonasjoner.

Som i dag står i fare for å bli solgt for alle vinder, bare for at litt skal bli igjen.

Politikerne toer sine hender. De finner ikke budsjettmessig dekning for det som trengs. Men å krangle om ansvar og skyld, gavner bare tiden. Og her er det den som er truselen. En tier fra hver av oss til Munch-Museets Stiftelse, gir 40 millioner kroner. Mer skal det ikke til.

Men det haster. Før det bare er politikernes beklagelser igjen av Munchs storslåtte donasjon.

Støtt Munch-Museet og gi ditt bidrag til Munch-Museets Stiftelse; bankgiro 7068.05.13315 eller postgiro 0823.0.93.73.20. Beløpet går uavkortet til å ruste opp Munch-Museet.

FOLKETIEREN TIL MUNCH-MUSEET

131

# TRØST.

# TIL LITEN NYTTE.

23. januar 1944 fikk verden vite at en av århundrets aller største billedkunstnere hadde testamentert 1.112 malerier, 17.689 grafiske trykk, ca. 5000 akvareller og tegninger og seks skulpturer til Oslo by.

45 år senere forvaltes Edvard Munchs kunst bak sponplater og falmede gardiner, på vegger som repareres med tape for å skjule sprekker i panelet hvor vannet tidvis har fått fritt løp. I kjellerens magasiner er luftfuktighet og temperatur så høy at konserveringsforholdene er meget dårlige. Redusert bemanning har ført til at alle tilbud til barn og ungdom er avlyst. Og de som kommer for å oppleve skattene, mange av dem har reist halve jorden rundt bare for det, blir møtt av tistler langs veggene, flekkede gulvtepper, avskallet maling og nedslitte møbler.

Det mangler 20 millioner for at Munch-Museet skal kunne fremstå som et representativt senter for Edvard Munch og hans kunst. Og et verdig monument over kulturnasjonens ansvar for en av verdens mest generøse kunstdonasjoner.

Som i dag står i fare for å bli solgt for alle vinder, bare for at litt skal bli igjen.

Politikerne toer sine hender. De finner ikke budsjettmessig dekning for det som trengs. Men å krangle om ansvar og skyld, gavner bare tiden. Og her er det den som er truselen. En tier fra hver av oss til Munch-Museets Stiftelse, gir 40 millioner kroner. Mer skal det ikke til.

Men det haster. Før det bare er politikernes beklagelser igjen av Munchs storslåtte donasjon.

Støtt Munch-Museet og gi ditt bidrag til Munch-Museets Stiftelse; bankgiro 7068.05.13315 eller postgiro 0823.0.93.73.20. Beløpet går uavkortet til å ruste opp Munch-Museet.

FOLKETIEREN TIL MUNCH-MUSEET

132

# DET SYKE BARN.

# FORSØMMES.

23. januar 1944 fikk verden vite at en av århundrets aller største billedkunstnere hadde testamentert 1.112 malerier, 17.689 grafiske trykk, ca. 5000 akvareller og tegninger og seks skulpturer til Oslo by.

45 år senere forvaltes Edvard Munchs kunst bak sponplater og falmede gardiner, på vegger som repareres med tape for å skjule sprekker i panelet hvor vannet tidvis har fått fritt løp. I kjellerens magasiner er luftfuktighet og temperatur så høy at konserveringsforholdene er meget dårlige. Redusert bemanning har ført til at alle tilbud til barn og ungdom er avlyst. Og de som kommer for å oppleve skattene, mange av dem har reist halve jorden rundt bare for det, blir møtt av tistler langs veggene, flekkede gulvtepper, avskallet maling og nedslitte møbler.

Det mangler 20 millioner for at Munch-Museet skal kunne fremstå som et representativt senter for Edvard Munch og hans kunst. Og et verdig monument over kulturnasjonens ansvar for en av verdens mest generøse kunstdonasjoner.

Som i dag står i fare for å bli solgt for alle vinder, bare for at litt skal bli igjen.

Politikerne toer sine hender. De finner ikke budsjettmessig dekning for det som trengs. Men å krangle om ansvar og skyld, gavner bare tiden. Og her er det den som er truselen. En tier fra hver av oss til Munch-Museets Stiftelse, gir 40 millioner kroner. Mer skal det ikke til.

Men det haster. Før det bare er politikernes beklagelser igjen av Munchs storslåtte donasjon.

Støtt Munch-Museet og gi ditt bidrag til Munch-Museets Stiftelse; bankgiro 7068.05.13315 eller postgiro 0823.0.93.73.20. Beløpet går uavkortet til å ruste opp Munch-Museet.

FOLKETIEREN TIL MUNCH-MUSEET

133

Handel
MESSIAH

WE LEAVE NO STONE
UNTURNED IN REVEALING
HANDEL'S ETERNAL
MASTERPIECE AS IT WAS
FIRST PERFORMED ON
APRIL 13.1742.

Messiah;
Like

MINNEAPOLIS CHAMBER SYMPHONY          612.989.5151

*polished* TO
PERFECTION, WE'LL
PRESENT THE COMPLETE
PERFORMANCE ON
APRIL 13.1992. 250 YEARS
LATER TO BE EXACT.

Before

MONDAY APRIL 13.1992

7:00 P.M.

WORLD THEATER

ST. PAUL

PATRICIA KENT, SOPRANO; SUSAN SACQUITNE DRUCK, ALTO;
ROBERT JOHNSON, TENOR; HUGH GIVENS BASS-BARITONE
THE SEBASTIAN SINGERS
CHAMBER CHORUS OF THE BACH SOCIETY OF MINNESOTA
PAUL OAKLEY MUSIC DIRECTOR

TICKETS ARE $12.50 AND $10.50. SENIOR CITIZENS, STUDENTS, AND CHILDREN ARE HALF PRICE.

134

612.989.5151

Beethoven
Smiles

A SET JAW.
A BULLDOG BROW.
A MAN INTENSELY
DEDICATED TO HIS
ART. YET DESPITE
THESE IMAGES,
BEETHOVEN
*could smile.*

SATURDAY MARCH 7.1992

8:00 P.M.

WORLD THEATER

ST. PAUL

MINNEAPOLIS CHAMBER SYMPHONY

EDMUND BATTERSBY, PIANO

Swafford
WORLD PREMIERE

Beethoven
PIANO CONCERTO #4
SYMPHONY #4

135

MINNEAPOLIS CHAMBER SYMPHONY

612.989.5151   New
Old
Friends

YOU'RE *old friends*
WITH BACH AND MOZART.
NOW MEET THREE
VIRTUALLY UNKNOWN
COMPOSERS WHOSE
WORKS GREATLY ENRICHED
THE 18TH CENTURY.
YOU'LL MAKE THREE
*new friends.*

J. S. Bach     Boyce     Gluck
SUITE #2 IN B MINOR     SYMPHONY #1     SUITE FROM DON JUAN
J. C. Bach               Mozart
SYMPHONY IN B FLAT, OPUS 21, #1     SYMPHONY #29 IN A MAJOR

SATURDAY FEBRUARY 1.1992

8:00 P.M.

WORLD THEATER

ST. PAUL

136

■ **130** ART DIRECTOR: JEREMY POSTAER PHOTOGRAPHER: BOB MIZONO COPYWRITER: BOB KERSTETTER AGENCY: GOODBY BERLIN SILVERSTEIN CLIENT: THE SAN FRANCISCO MUSEUM OF MODERN ART COUNTRY: USA ■ 130 BUS SHELTER PROMOTION. ● 130 «ALLES IST NICHT MEHR GANZ SO WIE VORHER NACH EINER REISE INS MODERN (SAN FRANCISCO MUSEUM OF MODERN ART).» ▲ 130 «RIEN N'EST PLUS COMME AVANT UNE FOIS QUE VOUS AVEZ FAIT UN TOUR DU CÔTÉ DES MODERNES.» (SOUS-ENTENDU L'UNE DES SALLES DU MUSEUM OF MODERN ART À SAN FRANCISCO).

■ **131-133** ART DIRECTOR: STEIN ERIK SELFORS COPYWRITER: ANNE NILSENG AGENCY: SCANECO/YOUNG & RUBICAM CLIENT: EDVARD MUNCH MUSEUM COUNTRY: NORWAY ■ 131-133 THE ACTUAL TITLES OF MUNCH'S PAINTINGS "EDVARD MUNCH", "COMFORT", AND "THE SICK CHILD" READ HERE "EDVARD MUNCH DISAPPEARS?," "COMFORT TO NO AVAIL," AND "THE SICK CHILD SUFFERS;" THE CAMPAIGN WAS TO ALERT THE PUBLIC TO THE BAD STATE OF THE MUNCH MUSEUM IN OSLO. ● 131-133 DIE TITEL DER MUNCH-BILDER «EDVARD MUNCH», «TROST» UND «DAS KRANKE KIND» LAUTEN HIER: «EDVARD MUNCH. VERSCHWINDET?»; «TROST. VERGEBLICH.»; «DAS KRANKE KIND. LEIDET.» DIE KAMPAGNE MACHT AUF DEN SCHLECHTEN ZUSTAND DES MUNCH-MUSEUMS IN OSLO AUFMERKSAM. ▲ 131-133 CES PEINTURES DE MUNCH QUI S'INTITULENT: «EDVARD MUNCH», «CONSOLATION» ET «L'ENFANT MALADE» ONT ÉTÉ COMPLÉTÉS: «EDVARD MUNCH. DISPARU?», «CONSOLATION. EN VAIN», «L'ENFANT MALADE. SOUFFRE». LA CAMPAGNE ATTIRE L'ATTENTION SUR LE MAUVAIS ÉTAT DANS LEQUEL SE TROUVENT LES BÂTIMENTS DU MUSÉE MUNCH.

■ **134-136** ART DIRECTOR: BILL THORBURN DESIGNERS: MATT ELLER, BILL THORBURN COPYWRITER: JERE LANTZ AGENCY: DAYTON'S, HUDSON'S, MARSHALL FIELD'S CLIENT: MINNEAPOLIS CHAMBER SYMPHONY COUNTRY: USA ■ 134-136 THE CAMPAIGN ATTEMPTS TO MAKE KNOWN AND LESS-ER-KNOWN ASPECTS OF MUSIC MORE ACCESSIBLE TO THE PUBLIC. ● 134-136 «DER MESSIAS; WIE ZUVOR.»; «BEETHOVEN LÄCHELT»; «NEUE ALTE FREUNDE». DIESE DOPPELSEITIGEN ANZEIGEN AUS EINER ZEITSCHRIFTENKAMPAGNE BEZWECKEN, DEM PUBLIKUM BEKANNTES UND UNBEKANNTES IN DER MUSIK ZUGÄNGLICHER MACHEN. ▲ 134-136 «LE MESSIE, COMME AUPARAVANT»; «BEETHOVEN SOURIT»; «DE NOUVEAUX VIEUX AMIS». CETTE CAMPAGNE AVAIT POUR BUT DE FAMILIARISER LE PUBLIC AUSSI BIEN AVEC DES CHOSES FAMILIÈRES QU'INCONNUES.

# Just because you're sixteen doesn't mean you can't be up to your eyeballs in debt.

You may be a minor, but your gambling debts may not be. It's not hard for a teenager to run up hundreds of dollars in debts. The time to quit is before you get in too deep. For help, call the Minnesota Compulsive Gambling Hotline. Break the habit before the habit breaks you. **Minnesota Compulsive Gambling Hotline 1-800-437-3641**

137

# MANY POLITICIANS FEEL GUN CONTROL ISSUES COULD END THEIR CAREER.

THEY'RE RIGHT.

**HANDGUN CONTROL®**
CALL 1-900-226-4455.
A LETTER WILL BE SENT IN YOUR NAME TO YOUR CONGRESS
OFFICIAL URGING SUPPORT OF STRONGER GUN LAWS.

138

# Are you losing your husband to some skinny bitch?

For some people, compulsive gambling can become an obsession. It takes over lives, changes personalities, and ruins marriages. If someone you love needs help quitting, contact the Compulsive Gambling Hotline. **Minnesota Compulsive Gambling Hotline 1-800-437-3641**

139

# UNFORTUNATELY, ONE OF THE FEW PUBLIC OFFICIALS TO TAKE A STAND ON GUN CONTROL IS FORCED TO DO IT FROM A CHAIR.

**HANDGUN CONTROL®**
CALL 1-900-226-4455.
A LETTER WILL BE SENT IN YOUR NAME TO YOUR CONGRESS
OFFICIAL URGING SUPPORT OF STRONGER GUN LAWS.

140

# Is your MP helping his friends make a killing?

Last Friday, Parliament debated, but failed to pass, the Wild Mammals (Protection) Bill.

To stop this happening again, the new Parliament must have a majority of MPs who support a ban on blood sports.

So ask your MP if he or she is friends with the hunters. Ask what their party has to say about it. Then, in the general election, you'll know what to do with your vote.

For an action pack, telephone IFAW on 0272 244742.

**If you're against hunting, vote against hunting.** IFAW

141

# Imagine a vet taking ten minutes to stab your dog to death. This is how a whale is killed "humanely."

[body text partially illegible]

IFAW

142

# If this appals you, hound your MP.

A survey showed *80% of the British population to be against fox and stag hunting.

Those who enjoy this barbaric rural pastime have very few supporters amongst the electorate.

But sadly, many in Parliament. Find out if your MP is one of them. Find out where his or her party stands on blood sports.

For an action pack, call IFAW on 0272 244742.

**If you're against hunting, vote against hunting.** IFAW

143

# This Thursday, you can vote to unseat him.

[body text partially illegible]

**If you're against hunting, vote against hunting.** IFAW

144

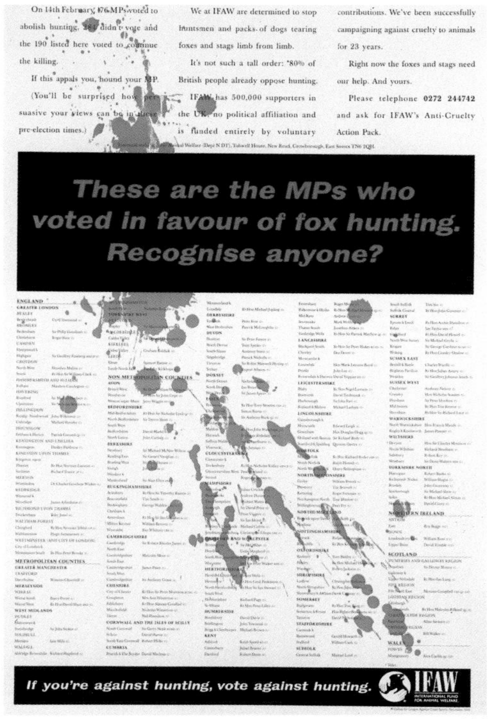

On 14th February 476 MPs voted to abolish hunting. They didn't vote and the 190 listed here voted to continue the killing.

If this appals you, hound your MP.

(You'll be surprised how persuasive your views can be in pre-election times.)

We at IFAW are determined to stop huntsmen and packs of dogs tearing foxes and stags limb from limb.

It's not such a tall order: 80% of British people already oppose hunting.

IFAW has 500,000 supporters in the UK, no political affiliation and is funded entirely by voluntary

contributions. We've been successfully campaigning against cruelty to animals for 23 years.

Right now the foxes and stags need our help. And yours.

Please telephone 0272 244742 and ask for IFAW's Anti-Cruelty Action Pack.

## These are the MPs who voted in favour of fox hunting. Recognise anyone?

[list of MPs — illegible]

**If you're against hunting, vote against hunting.** IFAW

145

■ **137, 138** ART DIRECTOR: JAC COVERDALE PHOTOGRAPHER: STEVE UMLAND COPYWRITER: BILL JOHNSON AGENCY: CLARITY COVERDALE RUEFF CLIENT: MINNESOTA INSTITUTE OF HEALTH COUNTRY: USA ■ **137, 138** A TOLL-FREE HOTLINE NUMBER FOR GAMBLERS AND THEIR FAMILIES. ● **137, 138** BERATUNG FÜR SPIELER BZW. IHRE FAMILIEN. ▲ **137, 138** SERVICE DE CONSEILS QUI S'ADRESSE AUX JOUEURS OU À LEURS FAMILLES.

■ **139, 140** ART DIRECTOR/DESIGNER/COPYWRITER: KEVIN AMTER AGENCY: AGENCY X CLIENT: HANDGUN CONTROL INC. COUNTRY: USA ■ **139, 140** A PUBLIC AWARENESS CAMPAIGN TO FURTHER SUPPORT THE LOBBY FOR STRICTER GUN LAWS. ● **139, 140** ANZEIGEN FÜR EIN STRIKTERES GESETZ IN BEZUG AUF DEN VERKAUF VON WAFFEN AN PRIVATE. ▲ **139, 140** ANNONCES POUR UN CONTRÔLE PLUS STRICT DES VENTES D'ARMES AU PUBLIC.

■ **141-145** ART DIRECTORS: ROSIE ARNOLD (141, 143) MIKE WELLS (142), GARY DENHAM (144, 145) PHOTOGRAPHER: MATT STUCKEY (142) ILLUSTRATOR: OLIVIA BEASLEY (143) COPYWRITER: CHARLES HENDLEY (141, 143), TOM HUDSON (142), BARBARA NOKES (144, 145) AGENCY: BARTLE BOGLE HEGARTY CLIENT: INTERNATIONAL FUND FOR ANIMAL WELFARE COUNTRY: GREAT BRITAIN ■ **141-145** ADS FROM CAMPAIGNS FOR A HUNTING LAW AND AGAINST THE BRUTAL KILLING OF WHALES. ● **141-145** ANZEIGEN AUS EINER KAMPAGNE FÜR EIN JAGDGESETZ UND GEGEN DIE BRUTALE ABSCHLACHTUNG VON WALEN. ▲ **141-145** CAMPAGNES POUR UNE LOI SUR LA CHASSE ET CONTRE LE MASSACRE DES BALEINES.

# TOO BAD FAMILIES TORN APART BY SUBSTANCE ABUSE AREN'T THIS EASY TO PUT BACK TOGETHER.

If you or someone you know is affected by alcohol or drug problems, call for help. 1-800-622-7422. 24 hours. Rhode Island Council On Alcoholism and Other Drug Dependence

147

How would you like to meet this in a dark alley?

It's pro-choice or no choice. Vote for pro-choice candidates. Speak out. Volunteer. Citizens for the Right to Choose. 223-0251

148

■ **147** ART DIRECTOR: GREG BOKOR COPYWRITER: KARA GOODRICH AGENCY: LEONARD MONAHAN LUBARS & KELLY CLIENT: RHODE ISLAND COUNCIL ON ALCOHOLISM & OTHER DRUG DEPENDENCE COUNTRY: USA ■ **147** THIS PUBLIC SERVICE POSTER WAS ACTUALLY TORN AND PUT BACK TOGETHER WITH TAPE. ● **147** «SCHADE. DURCH RAUSCHMITTEL ZERRISSENE FAMILIEN LASSEN SICH NICHT SO LEICHT WIEDER ZUSAMMENSETZEN.» ▲ **147** «DOMMAGE. LES FAMILLES DÉCHIRÉES À CAUSE DE LA CONSOMMATION DE DROGUE NE SE RECONSTITUENT PAS SI FACILEMENT QUE CELA.»

■ **148** ART DIRECTOR: JERRY KETEL COPYWRITER: ALLYSON WRIGHT AGENCY: BANG, BANG, BANG CLIENT: CITIZENS FOR THE RIGHT TO CHOOSE COUNTRY: USA ■ **148** THE MEDIUM BECOMES THE MESSAGE. THE HANGER REFLECTS THE DANGER OF HAVING NO LEGAL RIGHT TO CHOOSE AN ABORTION. ● **148** DAS MEDIUM WIRD DIE BOTSCHAFT. DER KLEIDERBÜGEL BEZIEHT SICH AUF DIE GEFAHR, KEINE MÖGLICHKEIT ZUR LEGALEN ABTREIBUNG ZU HABEN. ▲ **148** LE SUPPORT EST LE MESSAGE. LE PORTE-MANTEAU FAIT ALLUSION AU DANGER QUE REPRÉSENTE LA PÉNALISATION DE L'AVORTEMENT.

BROCHURES

BROCHÜREN

BROCHURES

149

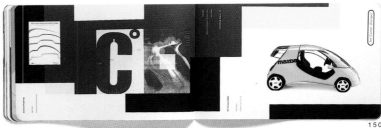

150

151

152

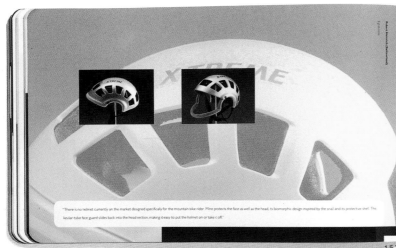

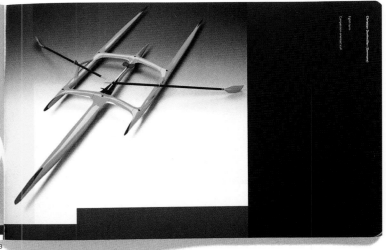

153

154

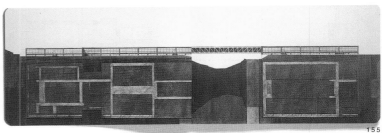

155

156

157

■ 149-157 Art Director: REBECA MENDEZ Designers: REBECA MENDEZ, DARIN BEAMAN, DARREN NAMAYE Photographer: STEVEN A. HELLER Copywriters: STUART I. FROLICK, DAVID R. BROWN, KAREN JACOBSON Agency: ART CENTER DESIGN OFFICE Client: ART CENTER COLLEGE OF DESIGN Country: USA ■ 149-157 THE FORMAL STRUCTURE OF THE CATALOG 1993-94 OF THE ART CENTER COLLEGE OF DESIGN IN PASADENA KEYS ON THE SCHOOL'S DISTINCTIVE ARCHITECTURE. THE ROUNDED CORNERS, A SUBTLE REFERENCE TO THE U.S. PASSPORT, CONVEY OFFI-CIALITY, CONTRASTING WITH AND FURTHER SOFTENING THE HIGHLY STRUCTURED DESIGN. ● 149-157 DIE FORMALE STRUKTUR DES KATALOGS 1993-94 DES ART CENTER COLLEGE OF DESIGN IN PASADENA BEZIEHT SICH AUF DIE BESONDERE ARCHITEKTUR DER SCHULE. DIE ABGERUNDE-TEN ECKEN, EINE ANSPIELUNG AUF DEN AMERIKANISCHEN PASS, GEBEN DEM KATALOG ETWAS OFFIZIELLES UND DIENEN ALS GEGENGEWICHT ZUM DURCHSTRUKTURIERTEN DESIGN. ▲ 149-157 L'ORGANISATION FORMELLE DU CATALOGUE 1993-94 DU ART CENTER COLLEGE OF DESIGN S'APPUIE SUR L'ARCHITECTURE DU BÂTIMENT DE CETTE ÉCOLE. LES ANGLES ARRONDIS, UNE ALLUSION AU PASSEPORT AMÉRICAIN, LUI DON-NENT UN CARACTÈRE OFFICIEL ET OFFRENT UN CONTRASTE INTÉRESSANT AVEC LE DESIGN RIGOUREUSEMENT STRUCTURÉ DE L'ENSEMBLE.

158

159

■ 158, 159 Art Directors: JOHN PYLYPCZAKY/DITI KATONA Designer: DITI KATONA Photographer: KAREN LEVY Agency: CONCRETE DESIGN COMMUNICATIONS INC. Client: LIDA BADAY Country: CANADA ■ 158, 159 BROCHURE INTRODUCING THE NEW SPRING LINE OF A FASHION DESIGNER. THE WIRE BINDING IS COVERED BY TAPE WITH A LINEN CHARACTER. ● 158, 159 BROSCHÜRE FÜR DIE FRÜHJAHRSMODE EINER MODE-SCHÖPFERIN. DIE KLAMMERHEFTUNG WIRD DURCH DEN KLEBSTREIFEN MIT LEINENCHARAKTER VERDECKT. ▲ 158, 159 BROCHURE POUR LA COL-LECTION PRINTEMPS-ÉTÉ D'UNE CRÉATRICE DE MODES. L'AGRAFAGE DE LA RELIURE EST CAMOUFLÉE SOUS UN RUBAN ADHÉSIF IMITATION LIN.

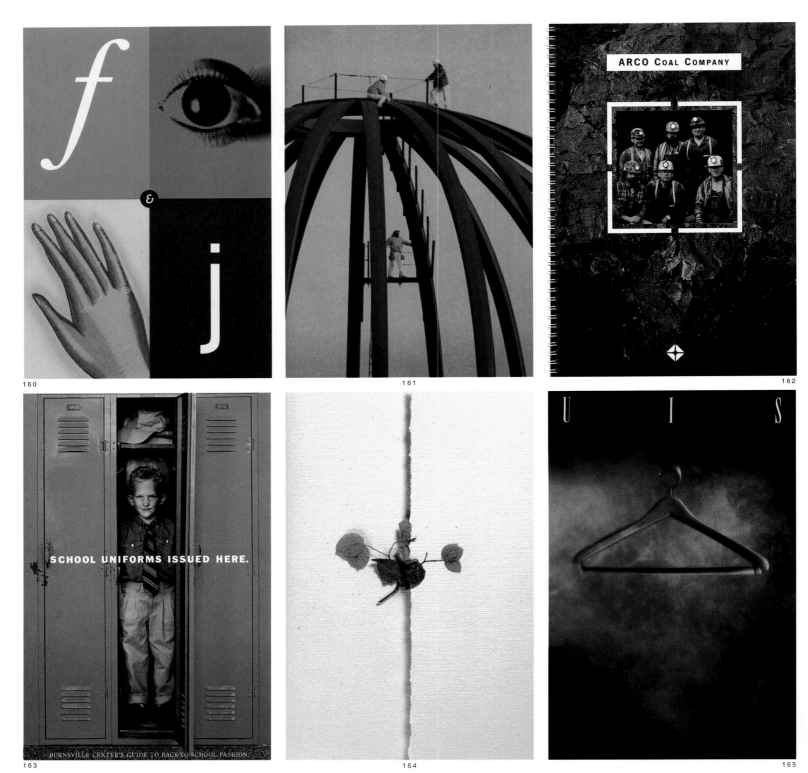

■ **160** ART DIRECTOR: DOUGLAS MAY, LYNN BERNICK DESIGNER: CANDACE·BUCHANAN AGENCY: MAY & CO. CLIENT: FRIEND & JOHNSON COUNTRY: USA ■ **161** ART DIRECTOR/DESIGNER: DOUG WOLFE AGENCY: HAWTHORNE/WOLFE CLIENT: MCCARTHY CONSTRUCTION COUNTRY: USA ■ **162** ART DIRECTOR: DAVID BILOTTI DESIGNER: DAVID MELLEN AGENCY: DAVID MELLEN DESIGN CLIENT: ARCO COAL COMPANY COUNTRY: USA ■ **163** ART DIRECTOR: JAC COVERDALE PHOTOGRAPHER: SHAWN MICHIENZI/BUZZSAW AGENCY: CLARITY COVERDALE RUEFF CLIENT: BURNSVILLE CENTER COUNTRY: USA ■ **164** ART DIRECTOR/DESIGNER: MICHAEL BROCK AGENCY: MICHAEL BROCK DESIGN CLIENT: FRED SANDS ESTATES COUNTRY: USA ■ **165** ART DIRECTORS: KEVIN B. KUESTER, BRENT MARMO DESIGNER: TIM SAUER PHOTOGRAPHER: JOE PACZKOWSKI AGENCY: THE KUESTER GROUP CLIENT: UIS, INC. COUNTRY: USA ■

166

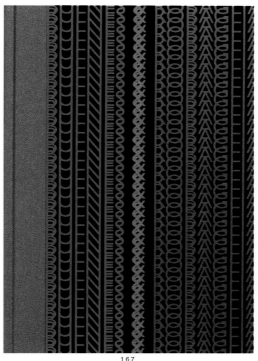

167

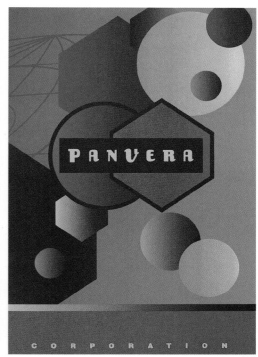

168

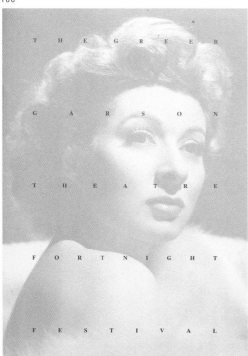

169

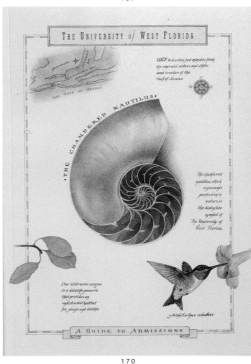

170

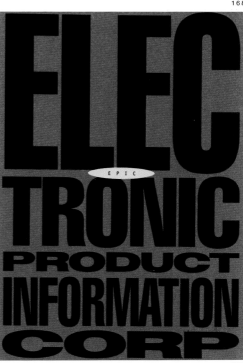

171

166 Art Director: DOUG AKAGI Designers: DOUG AKAGI, SHARRIE BROOKS, LENORE BARTZ Photographer: PAUL MARGOLIES Client: US WINDPOWER Country: USA ■ 167 Art Directors: JOSÉ BULNES, ANTOINE ROBAGLIA Client: BULNES & ROBAGLIA Country: FRANCE ■ 168 Art Directors: KEVIN WADE, DANA LYTLE Designer: KEVIN WADE Agency: PLANET DESIGN COMPANY Client: PANVERA CORP. Country: USA ■ 169 Art Director/Designer: THOMAS VASQUEZ Client: MEADOWS SCHOOL OF THE ARTS Country: USA ■ 170 Art Director: ANTHONY RUTKA Designers: ANTHONY RUTKA, MATT DAVIS Illustrator: ANATOLY DVERIN Agency: RUTKA WEADOCK DESIGN Client: UNIVERSITY OF WEST FLORIDA Country: USA ■ 171 Art Directors/Designers: LAURIE ELLIS, JAN ELLIS Agency: ELLIS DESIGN Client: ELECTRONIC PRODUCT INFORMATION CORP. Country: USA

172

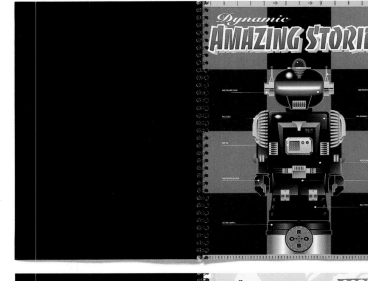

173

176

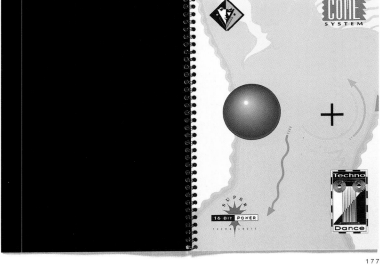

177

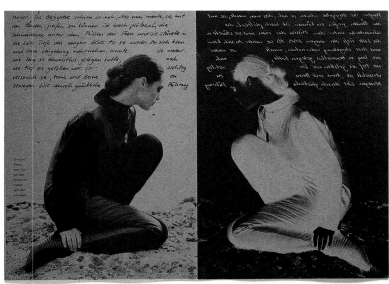

180

181

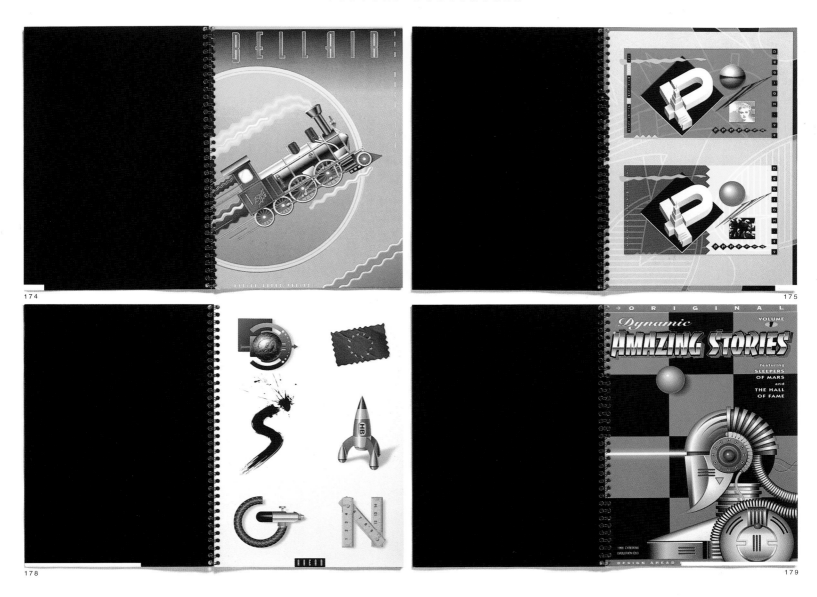

174

175

178

179

■ **172-179** DESIGNER: RALF STUMPF AGENCY: DESIGN AHEAD CLIENT: DESIGN AHEAD COUNTRY: GERMANY ■ **172-179** THIS SELF-PROMOTIONAL BROCHURE OF A DESIGN STUDIO WAS PRODUCED COMPLETELY ON A MAC, INCLUDING PRINT FILMS. ● **172-179** DIESE EIGENWERBUNGSBROSCHÜRE WURDE VOLLSTÄNDIG AUF EINEM MAC ERSTELLT, EINSCHLIESSLICH DER DRUCKFILME. ▲ **172-179** CETTE BROCHURE AUTOPROMOTIONNELLE D'UN STUDIO DE DESIGN A ÉTÉ ENTIÈREMENT RÉALISÉE SUR UN POSTE DE CAO MACINTOSH, Y COMPRIS LES FILMS POUR L'IMPRESSION.

■ **180, 181** ART DIRECTOR: URSULA GEBENDINGER PHOTOGRAPHER: STEFAN INDLEKOFER STYLIST: JEANNETTE GLOOR COPYWRITER: BRUNO TOBLER AGENCY: ATELIER DIENER AG CLIENT: JEANNETTE GLOOR COUNTRY: SWITZERLAND ■ **180, 181** "CONTRASTS", THE 1992/93 FALL/WINTER COLLECTION BY FASHION DESIGNER JEANNETTE GLOOR. IT WAS PRINTED AS DUPLEX ON PACKAGING CELLULOSE. THE COPY ON THE COVER CONSISTS OF NUMEROUS DEFINITIONS OF BLACK AND WHITE. ● **180, 181** DIE KOLLEKTION FÜR HERBST/WINTER 92/93 VON JEANNETTE GLOOR. DER KATALOG IST ALS DUPLEX AUF PACK-ZELLULOSE GEDRUCKT. DER TEXT AUF DEM UMSCHLAG BESTEHT AUS ZAHLREICHEN DEFINITIONEN VON SCHWARZ UND WEISS. ▲ **180, 181** LA COLLECTION AUTOMNE-HIVER 92/93 DE JEANNETTE GLOOR. LE CATALOGUE EST IMPRIMÉ DOUBLE-TON SUR UNE PÂTE POUR PAPIER D'EMBALLAGE. LE TEXTE DE LA COUVERTURE EST COMPOSÉ D'UNE ÉNUMÉRATION DE QUALIFICATIFS DU NOIR ET DU BLANC.

182

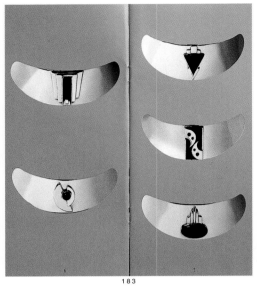

183

184

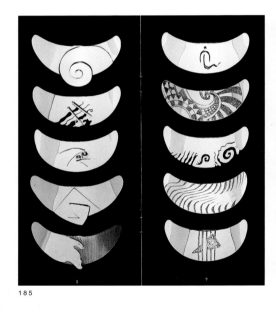

185

186

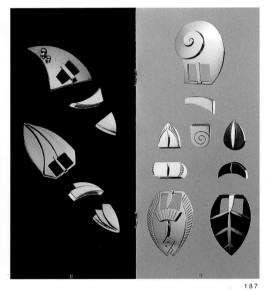

187

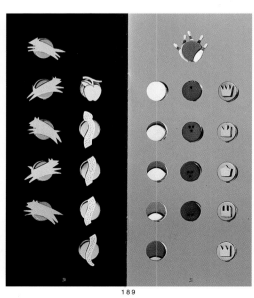

188

189

190

■ **182-190** ART DIRECTOR/DESIGNER: LUIS ACEVEDO PHOTOGRAPHER: RICHARD REENS AGENCY: RBMM CLIENT: MANO A MANO INC. COUNTRY: USA ■ **182-190** ACCENT CLIPS DESIGNED BY LUIS ACEVEDO AND CRAFTED IN STERLING SILVER ARE PRESENTED IN THIS SMALL BROCHURE. IT SHOWS DETAILS OF THE CLIPS AND THEIR EFFECT AS ACCESSORIES ON GARMENTS. ● **182-190** CLIPS UND SCHNALLEN, VON LUIS ACEVEDO ENTWORFEN UND IN STERLING-SILBER HERGESTELLT, SIND GEGENSTAND DIESER BROSCHÜRE. ▲ **182-190** CETTE BROCHURE PRÉSENTE DES CRÉATIONS DE LUIS ACEVEDO, DES BOUCLES DE CEINTURES ET DES CLIPS FABRIQUÉS EN ARGENT STERLING. ILS SONT ÉGALEMENT MONTRÉS SUR DES VÊTEMENTS.

■ **191** DESIGNER: JEFFREY MORRIS AGENCY: STUDIO MORRIS CLIENT: ICF COUNTRY: USA ■ **191** PRODUCT BROCHURE OF AN OFFICE FURNITURE COMPANY. ● **191** PRODUKTBROSCHÜRE EINES BÜROMÖBELFABRIKANTEN. ▲ **191** BROCHURE D'UN FABRICANT DE MEUBLES DE BUREAU.

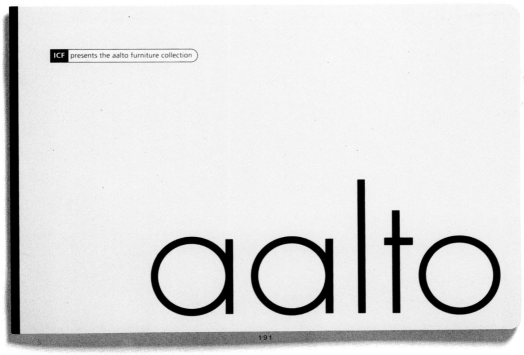

191

192

■ **192** ART DIRECTOR/DESIGNER: MICHAEL BAVIERA PHOTOGRAPHER: ARTEMIDE AGENCY: BBV CLIENT: WOHNFLEX COUNTRY: SWITZERLAND ■ **192** INVITATION TO AN EXHIBITION OF THE MILANO-VENEZIA COLLECTION OF ARTEMIDE. TO PROVIDE AN ILLUSION OF THE TRANSPARENCY OF THE MURANO GLASS FROM WHICH THESE LAMPS WERE MADE, PARCHMENT PAPER WAS USED FOR THE CARDS. ● **192** EINLADUNG ZU EINER AUSSTELLUNG DER MILANO VENEZIA-KOLLEKTION VON ARTEMIDE. UM DIE TRANSPARENZ DER LEUCHTEN AUS MURANO-GLAS WIEDERZUGEBEN, WURDE DIE KARTE AUF TRANSPARENTPAPIER GEDRUCKT. ▲ **192** INVITATION À UNE EXPOSITION DE LA COLLECTION MILANO-VENEZIA DE ARTEMIDE. AFIN DE RENDRE L'EFFET DE TRANSPARENCE DU VERRE DE MURANO, LA CARTE A ÉTÉ IMPRIMÉE SUR PAPIER TRANSPARENT.

■ **193-195** ART DIRECTOR: JENNIFER MORLA DESIGNERS: JENNIFER MORLA, SHARRIE BROOKS COPYWRITER: DAVID LEVI STRAUSS AGENCY: MORLA DESIGN CLIENT: CAPP STREET PROJECT COUNTRY: USA ■ **193-195** THE DIE-CUT ELIPSES ON THIS FOLDER ARE A MEANS OF ISOLATING THE TITLE FROM THE REMAINING TEXT DESCRIBING THE CAPP STREET PROJECT, AN EXPERIMENTAL ART PROJECT. ● **193-195** DIE OVALEN AUSSTANZUNGEN DIESES UMSCHLAGS DIENEN DAZU, DEN TITEL DER BROSCHÜRE VOM ÜBRIGEN TEXT ZU ISOLIEREN, DER DAS CAPP STREET PROJECT, EIN EXPERIMENTELLES KUNSTPROJEKT, BESCHREIBT. ▲ **193-195** LES DÉCOUPES À L'EMPORTE-PIÈCE DE CETTE COUVERTURE PERMETTENT D'ISOLER LE TITRE DU RESTE DU CONTENU. LE TEXTE DÉCRIT LE CAPP STREET PROJECT, UN PROJET ARTISTIQUE EXPÉRIMENTAL.

■ **196, 197** ART DIRECTOR/ILLUSTRATOR/COPYWRITER: MICHAEL CRONAN DESIGNERS: MICHAEL CRONAN, DIANA HOWARD PHOTOGRAPHER: TERRY LORANT AGENCY: CRONAN DESIGN CLIENT: CRONAN ARTEFACT COUNTRY: USA ■ **196, 197** WALKING MAN IS A LINE OF CLOTHING DESIGNED BY MICHAEL CRONAN FOR HARD-WORKING PEOPLE LOOKING FOR PRACTICAL, NO-NONSENSE CLOTHES. ● **196, 197** WALKING MAN IST EINE BEKLEIDUNGSLINIE FÜR HART ARBEITENDE LEUTE, DIE PRAKTISCHE, UNKOMPLIZIERTE KLEIDUNG BRAUCHEN. ▲ **196, 197** WALKING MAN EST UNE LIGNE DE VÊTEMENTS CRÉÉE PAR MICHAEL CRONAN POUR TOUS LES TYPES DE TRAVAIL MANUEL: L'ACCENT EST MIS SUR L'ASPECT PRATIQUE.

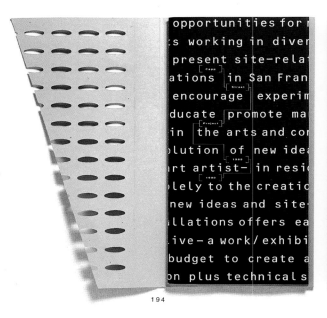

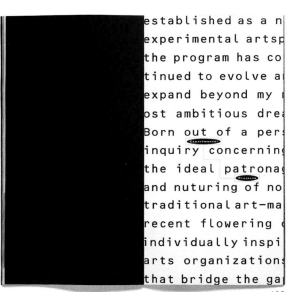

193

194

195

■ **198, 199** ART DIRECTOR: DIETER SIEGER PHOTOGRAPHER: MICHAEL SIEGER AGENCY: SIEGER DESIGN CLIENT: MARSBERGER GLASWERKE RITZENHOFF GMBH COUNTRY: GERMANY ■ **198, 199** COVER AND SPREAD FROM A BROCHURE INTRODUCING THE GIFT PRODUCTS OF RITZENHOFF. ● **198, 199** UMSCHLAG UND DOPPELSEITE AUS EINER BROSCHÜRE, IN DER DIE GESCHENKARTIKEL VON RITZENHOFF VORGESTELLT WERDEN. ▲ **198, 199** COUVERTURE ET DOUBLE PAGE D'UNE BROCHURE DANS LAQUELLE LES ARTICLES CADEAUX DE LA FIRME RITZENHOFF SONT PRÉSENTÉS.

■ **200, 201** ART DIRECTOR/DESIGNER: HIROYUKI HAYASHI ILLUSTRATOR: TAKANORI AIBA AGENCY: GRAPHICS & DESIGNING INC. CLIENT: SHINHYORON COUNTRY: JAPAN ■ **200, 201** COVER AND SPREAD OF A CATALOG PRESENTING THE LABYRINTHINE DRAWINGS OF A JAPANESE ARTIST. ● **200, 201** UMSCHLAG UND DOPPELSEITE AUS EINEM KATALOG, IN DEM LABYRINTH-ZEICHNUNGEN EINES JAPANISCHEN KÜNSTLERS VORGESTELLT WERDEN. ▲ **200, 201** COUVERTURE ET DOUBLE PAGE D'UN CATALOGUE QUI RASSEMBLE DES LABYRINTHES DESSINÉS PAR UN ARTISTE JAPONAIS.

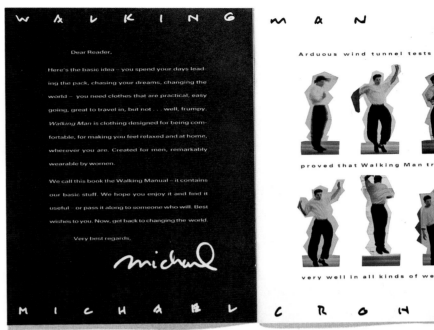

196

197

198

199

200

201

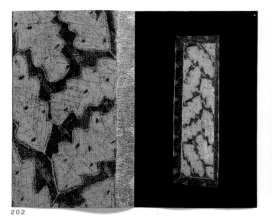

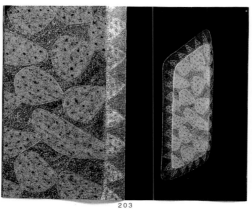

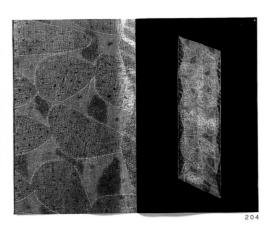

202                 203                 204

205                 206

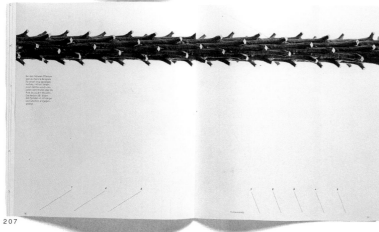

207                 208

*At the end of a long day when our pencils
are dull and our minds are not far
behind, this is what we find ourselves
thinking about: Rain (whether it will
stop). Inspiration (whether it will come
back). Rent (whether it will get paid).
Art (whether the dead guys who made it
will be mad at us for ripping off their
ideas). Architecture (whether it can*

overcome the influence of cartoons and
strip malls). Relationships (whether it's
possible to make the good ones last and
the bad ones go away). Clients (see
"Relationships"). Design Annuals
(whether they're worth the paper they're
printed on). Self-promotion pieces (see
"Design Annuals"). Heaven (whether
there is one, and if so, what typeface

209                 210                 211

■ **202-204** Art Director/Designer: HIROYUKI HAYASHI Photographer: MASAYA NAKAMURA Agency: GRAPHICS & DESIGNING INC. Client: MASAHIRO MAEDA Country: JAPAN ■ **202-204** CATALOG FOR AN EXHIBITION BY JAPANESE CERAMIST MASAHIRO MAEDA. ● **202-204** KATALOG FÜR DIE AUSSTELLLUNG DES JAPANISCHEN TÖPFERS MASAHIRO MAEDA. ▲ **202-204** LE CATALOGUE D'EXPOSITION D'UN POTIER JAPONAIS.

■ **205-208** Art Director/Designer/Illustrator/Client: JOHANNES PFEIFER Country: GERMANY ■ **205-208** THIS CATALOG ENTITLED "SPIRALS, SCREWS AND GROWING RINGS" IS THE THESIS WORK OF A DESIGN STUDENT. ● **205-208** DIESER KATALOG MIT DEM TITEL «SPIRALEN, SCHRAUBEN, WACHSENDE RINGE» IST DIE DIPLOMARBEIT EINES DESIGN-STUDENTEN. ER BEFASST SICH MIT DEN URFORMEN, SO WIE SIE IN DER NATUR AUF-TAUCHEN. ▲ **205-208** CE CATALOGUE INTITULÉ «SPIRALES, VIS ET ANNEAUX» EST LE TRAVAIL DE DIPLÔME D'UN ÉTUDIANT EN DESIGN.

212

■ **209-211** Art Directors: KURT HOLLOMON, STEVE SANDSTROM Designer: KURT HOLLOMON Photographer: MARK HOOPER Illustrator: WARD SCHUMAKER Copywriter: PETER WEGNER Agency/Client: SANDSTROM DESIGN Country: USA ■ **209-211** THIS PROMOTIONAL PORTFOLIO IS HAND-PRODUCED. THE PROJECTS ARE REPRESENTED ON ADHESIVE PRINTS WHICH CAN EASILY BE EXCHANGED. ● **209-211** DIESE EIGENWER-BUNGSMAPPE IST VON HAND PRODUZIERT. DIE PROJEKTE SIND AUF EINGEKLEBTEN DRUCKEN DARGESTELLT. ▲ **209-211** CE DOSSIER AUTO-PROMOTIONNEL A ÉTÉ RÉALISÉ À LA MAIN. LES PROJETS SONT PRÉSENTÉS SOUS FORME DE PHOTOS IMPRIMÉES COLLÉES SUR LA PAGE.

■ **212** Designer: GREY DESIGN Photographer: TODD HAIMAN Client: TODD HAIMAN PHOTOGRAPHY Country: USA ■ **212** SELF-PROMOTIONAL BROCHURE OF A PHOTOGRAPHER. ● **212** BROSCHÜRE EINES PHOTOGRAPHEN. ▲ **212** BROCHURE AUTOPROMOTIONNELLE D'UN PHOTOGRAPHE.

213

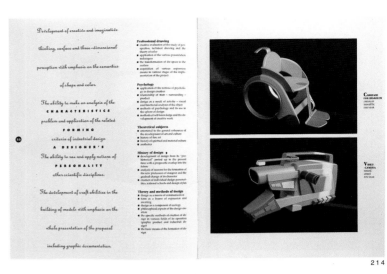

214

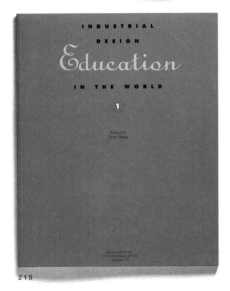

215

216

217

■ **213-217** ART DIRECTOR/DESIGNER: EDI BERK PHOTOGRAPHER: DRAGAN ARRIGLER AGENCY: KROG CLIENT: SECRETARIAT OF THE 17TH WORLDESIGN ICSID CONGRESS COUNTRY: SLOVENIA ■ **213-217** COVER AND SPREADS FROM A CATALOG PRESENTING THE WORK OF STUDENTS FROM INDUSTRIAL DESIGN SCHOOLS IN VARIOUS COUNTRIES. ● **213-217** UMSCHLAG UND DOPPELSEITEN EINES KATALOGES, IN DEM ANLÄSSLICH EINES KONGRESSES DIE STUDENTENARBEITEN VON INDUSTRIE-DESIGNSCHULEN AUS VERSCHIEDENEN LÄNDERN VORGESTELLT WERDEN. ▲ **213-217** D'UN CATALOGUE PUBLIÉ À L'OCCASION D'UNE EXPOSITION PRÉSENTANT LES TRAVAUX D'ÉTUDIANTS EN DESIGN INDUSTRIEL DE DIVERS PAYS.

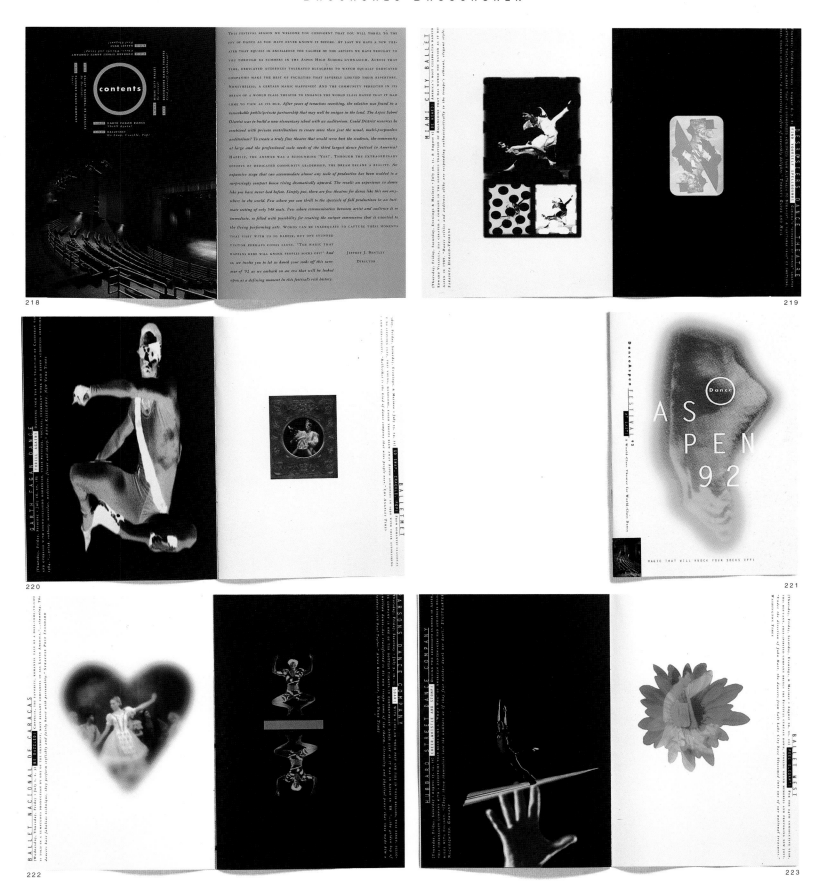

■ **218-223** ART DIRECTOR: JAMIE KOVAL DESIGNERS: JAMIE KOVAL, CURTIS SCHREIBER PHOTOGRAPHERS: VARIOUS COPYWRITER: JEFFREY BENTLEY AGENCY: VSA PARTNERS INC. CLIENT: DANCE ASPEN COUNTRY: USA ■ **218-223** THIS BROCHURE FOR A NEWLY COMPLETED THEATER IN ASPEN HAD TO FUNCTION AS AN IMAGE PIECE, NEWSPAPER INSERT AND DIRECT MAIL PIECE. ● **218-223** DIESE BROSCHÜRE FÜR EIN NEUES THEATER IN ASPEN MUSSTE ALS IMAGE-BROSCHÜRE, ZEITUNGSBEILAGE UND DIRECT MAIL GEEIGNET SEIN. ▲ **218-223** CETTE BROCHURE POUR UN NOUVEAU THÉÂTRE DEVAIT ÊTRE UTILISÉ À LA FOIS COMME BROCHURE DE PRESTIGE, SUPPLÉMENT DE JOURNAUX ET DOCUMENT DE MARKETING DIRECT.

224

225

226

227

228

■ **224-228** DESIGNER: IVAN FERNANDEZ PHOTOGRAPHER: DAVID VANCE COUNTRY: USA ■ **224-228** SELF-PROMOTIONAL BOOKLET OF PHOTOGRAPHER DAVID VANCE. THE PHOTOS ARE GLUED-ON. ● **224-228** EIGENWERBUNGSBROSCHÜRE DES PHOTOGRAPHEN DAVID VANCE. DIE BILDER SIND EINGEKLEBT. ▲ **224-228** BROCHURE AUTOPROMOTIONNELLE DU PHOTOGRAPHE DAVID VANCE. LES PHOTOS SONT COLLÉES COMME DANS UN ALBUM.

■ **229-237** ART DIRECTOR: CHERYL HELLER DESIGNER: ANNE ROUQUETTE PHOTOGRAPHERS: ALBERT WATSON (230, 231, 233, 235-238), NADAV KANDER (234) COPYWRITER: GEOFF CURRIER AGENCY: WELLS RICH GREENE BDDP CLIENT: S.D. WARREN COMPANY COUNTRY: USA ■ **229-237** THIS BROCHURE FOR A WARREN PAPER QUALITY SHOWS ARTIFACTS USED BY GREAT EXPLORERS. THE IMPROVISED SNOW GOGGLES, USED ON THE 1845 FRANKLIN EXPEDITION TO THE NORTH POLE, WERE MADE OF LEATHER AND WIRE MESH. ● **229-237** DIESE BROSCHÜRE FÜR EINE PAPIERSORTE ZEIGT GEGENSTÄNDE VON EXPEDITIONEN GROSSER FORSCHER. DIE SCHNEEBRILLE AUS DER FRANKLIN-EXPEDITION ZUM NORDPOL IM JAHRE 1845 BESTAND AUS LEDER UND MASCHENDRAHT. ▲ **229-237** CETTE BROCHURE PRÉSENTANT UNE QUALITÉ DE PAPIER BRILLANT MONTRE DES OBJETS UTILISÉS PAR QUELQUES GRANDS EXPLORATEURS. LES LUNETTES DE SOLEIL IMPROVISÉES QUI FIGURENT SUR LA COUVERTURE ONT SERVI LORS DE L'EXPÉDITION FRANKLIN AU POLE NÔRD EN 1845; ELLES ONT ÉTÉ FABRIQUÉES À L'AIDE DE CUIR ET DE TOILE MÉTALLIQUE.

229

230

231

232

233

234

235

236

237

238
239
240
241
242
243

■ **238-243** ART DIRECTOR: MICHAEL BIERUT DESIGNERS: MICHAEL BIERUT, LISA CERVENY AGENCY: PENTAGRAM DESIGN CLIENT: MOHAWK PAPER MILLS COUNTRY: USA ■ **238-243** THIS MOHAWK PAPER-QUALITY BROCHURE IS DEDICATED TO THE SUBJECT OF DESIGN AND IS MEANT TO BE KEPT BY THE RECIPIENT. THE IDEA, ASIDE FROM PRESENTING PAPER QUALITIES, IS TO PRESENT MOHAWK AS A THOUGHTFUL CITIZEN IN THE DESIGN COMMUNITY. ● **238-243** DIESE BROSCHÜRE, MIT DER PAPIERQUALITÄTEN VORGESTELLT WERDEN, IST DEM THEMA DESIGN GEWIDMET, MIT DEM ZIEL, DASS SIE VOM EMPFÄNGER AUFGEHOBEN WIRD. ▲ **238-243** CETTE BROCHURE, DANS LAQUELLE SONT MISES EN ÉVIDENCE LES QUALITÉS DES PAPIERS DE CE FABRICANT, EST CONSACRÉE AU DESIGN. IL S'AGISSAIT ICI DE SOULIGNER LE RÔLE QUE JOUE MOHAWK DANS CETTE BRANCHE.

■ **244-249** ART DIRECTOR: KIT HINRICHS DESIGNER: AMY CHAN PHOTOGRAPHER: BOB ESPARZA, TERRY HEFFERNAN COPYWRITER: DELPHINE HIRASUNA AGENCY: PENTAGRAM DESIGN, SAN FRANCISCO CLIENT: SIMPSON PAPER COUNTRY: USA ■ **244-249** THE WINNERS OF THE SIMPSON PRINTED PAPER COMPETITION ARE PRESENTED IN THIS ANNUAL BROCHURE. ● **244-249** DIE GEWINNER DES ALLJÄHRLICH DURCHGEFÜHRTEN DRUCKMEDIEN-WETTBEWERBS DES PAPIERHERSTELLERS SIMPSON WERDEN IN DIESER BROSCHÜRE VORGESTELLT. ▲ **244-249** LES GAGNANTS DU CONCOURS ANNUEL DE MÉDIAS IMPRIMÉS, ORGANISÉ PAR LE FABRICANT DE PAPIER SIMPSON, SONT PRÉSENTÉS DANS CETTE BROCHURE.

THE PATH FROM CONCEPTUAL IDEA TO PRINTED PIECE IS FRAUGHT WITH COUNTLESS CHALLENGES. SO WHEN A JOB IS BEAUTIFULLY EXECUTED FROM START TO FINISH, CONGRATULATIONS ARE WELL DESERVED. THE ANNUAL SIMPSON PRINTED PAPER COMPETITION WAS ESTABLISHED TO RECOGNIZE OUTSTANDING WORKS PRINTED ON SIMPSON PAPERS OVER THE PREVIOUS 12 MONTHS. THIS YEAR'S PANEL OF DISTINGUISHED JUDGES INCLUDED KIT HINRICHS, LESLEE AVCHEN, LOUISE FILI AND TAMOTSU YAGI. FROM A FIELD OF OVER A THOUSAND ENTRIES, THEY SELECTED 22 EXCEPTIONAL PIECES EXHIBITING EXCELLENCE IN CREATIVITY, DESIGN AND PRINT PRODUCTION. THREE PARTICULARLY IMPRESSIVE WORKS WERE HONORED WITH SPECIAL JUDGES' AWARDS. ALL OF THE WINNING ENTRIES ARE ON DISPLAY IN A NATIONAL TRAVELING EXHIBITION.

244

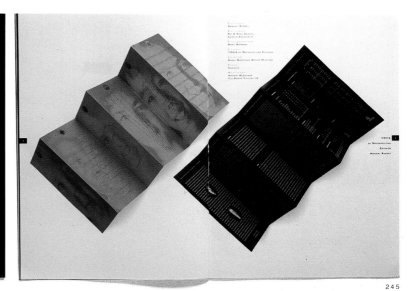

245

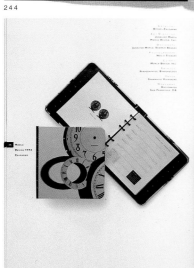

246

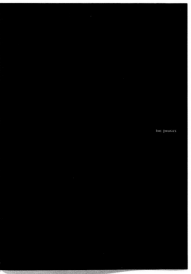

247

248

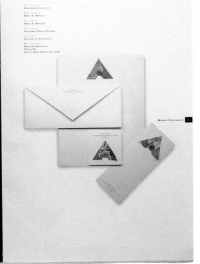

249

250

From Empress Josephine to John Steinbeck, people have pursued their passion for nature by collecting natural things for pleasure and practical purpose. Like a close-up camera lens, collections enhance our appreciation for the world around us by focusing attention on details sometimes missed in nature's profusion. In so doing, they can heighten scientific awareness, inspire creativity, and reveal the fascinating variety within nature, as well as the beauty and uniqueness of each species. Wonderful facets of nature are evident in the new multi-colored flecked look and textured Cord™ finish in Simpson's expanded collection of EverGreen Text and Cover papers, made from 50% recycled fiber including 10% postconsumer waste. These unique additions, each available in three colors, bring even greater dimension to EverGreen's original palette of 13 soft, earthy hues and are a natural evolution of our popular EverGreen line.

251

252

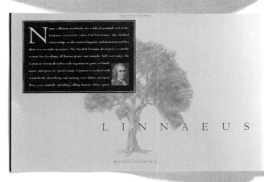

253

254

UPON MOVING TO NEW MEXICO, AMERICAN ARTIST GEORGIA O'KEEFFE (1887-1986) BECAME FASCINATED BY THE SUN-BLEACHED ANIMAL SKELETONS SCATTERED OVER THE DESERT AND BEGAN COLLECTING THEM FOR THE STARK SIMPLICITY OF THEIR FORM. ■ SO ENAMOURED WAS O'KEEFFE WITH THE BONES THAT SHE EVEN PACKED THEM IN A BARREL AND SHIPPED THEM TO NEW YORK SO SHE COULD CONTINUE PAINTING THEM WHILE THERE, MUCH TO THE INITIAL DISPLEASURE OF HER HUSBAND, PHOTOGRAPHER ALFRED STIEGLITZ. ■ "THE BONES SEEM TO CUT SHARPLY TO THE CENTER OF SOMETHING THAT IS KEENLY ALIVE ON THE DESERT EVEN THO' IT IS VAST AND EMPTY AND UNTOUCHABLE — AND KNOWS NO KINDNESS WITH ALL ITS BEAUTY," SHE WROTE. ■ SEEING DRIED BONES AS THE ESSENCE OF THE SOUTHWEST, O'KEEFFE MADE ANIMAL SKULLS AS WELL AS OTHER DESERT FINDS A FREQUENT THEME IN HER PAINTINGS OF NEW MEXICO.

255

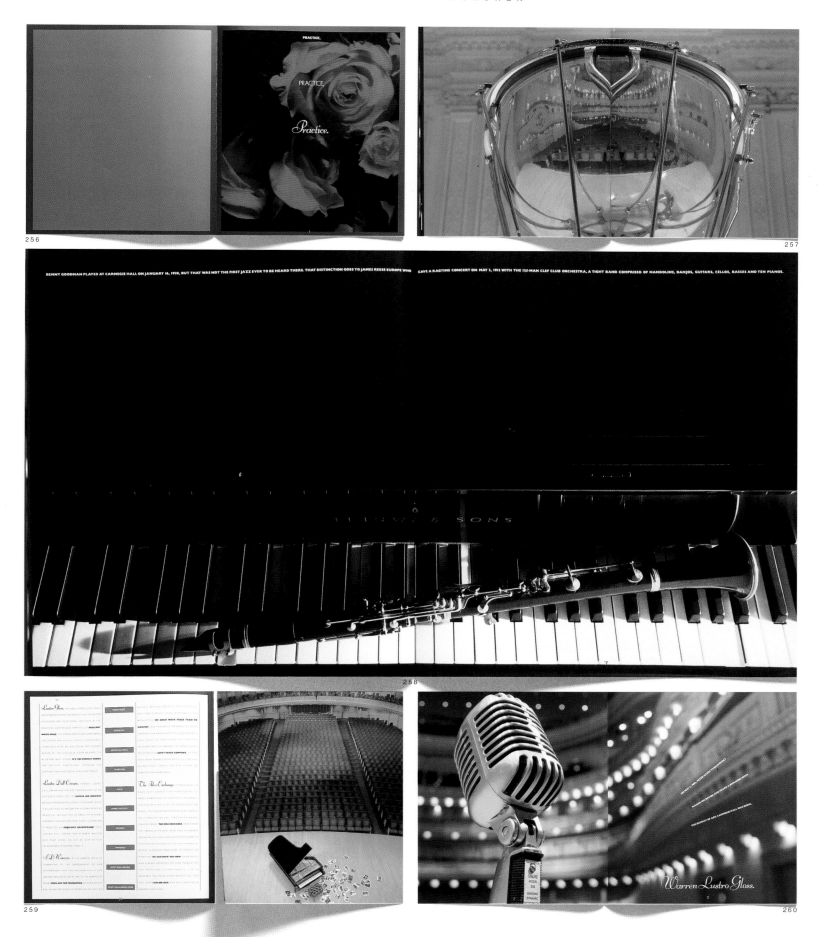

256

257

258

259

260

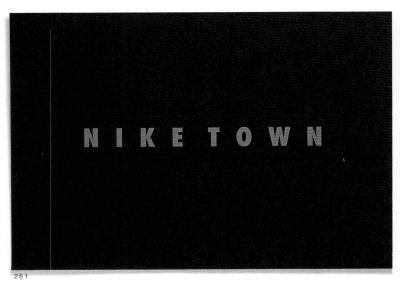

261

262

263

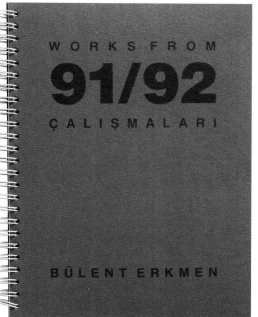

264

265

266

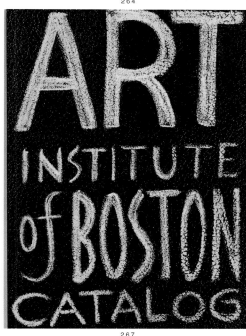

267

268

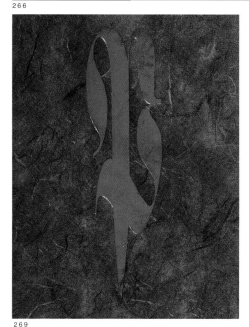

269

270

271

Unless otherwise noted
dimensions are in inches and
in order of height, width and
depth

272

273

274

275

276

277

278

279

280

281

282

283

■ **272-277** Art Director: MICHAEL BIERUT Designers: MICHAEL BIERUT, DORIT LEV Photographer: MICHAEL GALATIS Agency: PENTAGRAM DESIGN Client: PETER JOSEPH GALLERY Country: USA ■ **272-277** BAROQUE MODERNISM. THE LAYOUT OF THIS EXHIBITION CATALOG IS MEANT TO REFLECT THE ROBUST QUALITY OF THE WROUGHT-IRON FURNITURE DESIGNED BY ALBERT PALEY. ● **272-277** BAROCKER MODERNISMUS – DAS LAYOUT DIESES KATALOGES SOLLTE DIE ROBUSTHEIT DER EISENMÖBEL VON ALBERT PALEY WIEDERGEBEN. ▲ **272-277** LE BAROQUE MODERNE – LA MISE EN PAGES DE CE CATALOGUE D'EXPOSITION DEVAIT SUGGÉRER LA ROBUSTESSE DES MEUBLES EN MÉTAL D'ALBERT PALEY.

■ **278-283** Art Director/Photographer/Client: FRANK M. OREL Country: GERMANY ■ **278-283** "HANDLE WITH CARE"—SELF-PROMOTION OF A PHOTOGRAPHER. ● **278-283** «HANDLE WITH CARE» – EIGENWERBUNG EINES PHOTOGRAPHEN. ▲ **278-283** AUTOPROMOTION D'UN PHOTOGRAPHE.

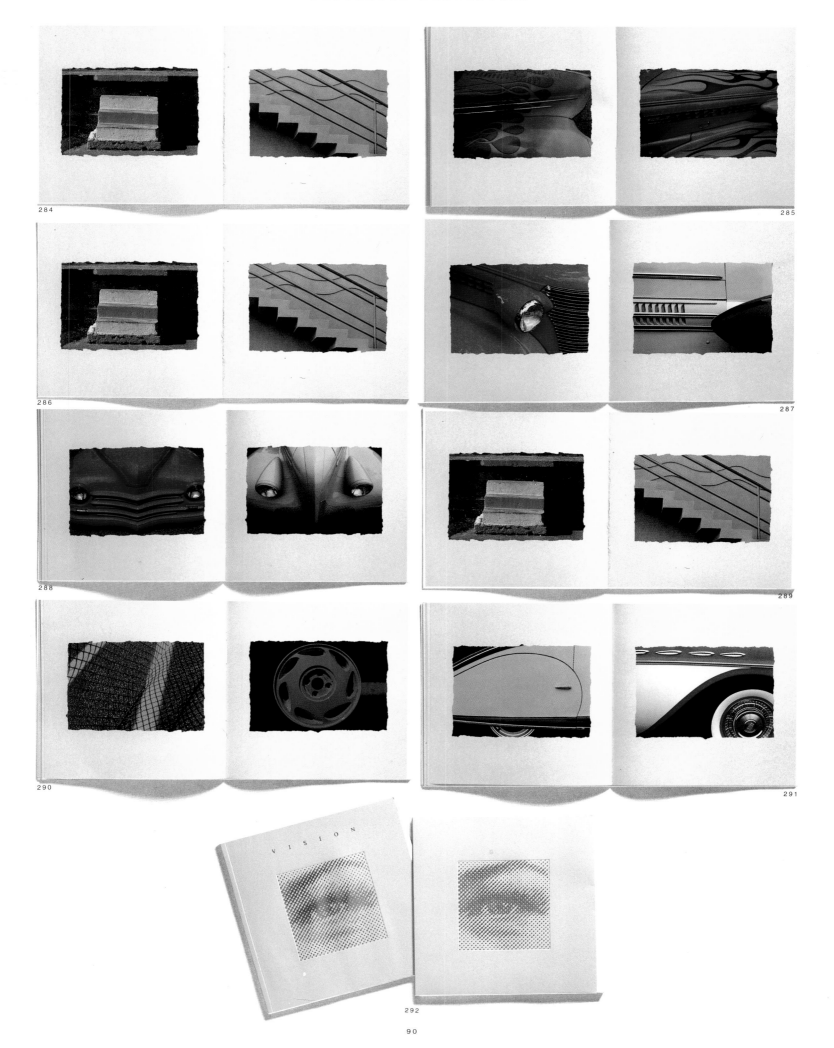

284

285

286

287

288

289

290

291

292

293

294

295

296

297

298

■ 284-292 ART DIRECTOR/DESIGNER/PHOTOGRAPHER: JULIUS FRIEDMAN AGENCY: IMAGES CLIENT: HENNEGAN COMPANY COUNTRY: USA ■ 284-292 THE COLOR QUALITY OFFERED BY A PRINTING FIRM IS DEMONSTRATED IN THIS BOOKLET. ● 284-292 DIE QUALITÄT DES FARBDRUCKS WIRD IN DIESER BROSCHÜRE DEMONSTRIERT. ▲ 284-292 CETTE BROCHURE MET EN VALEUR LA QUALITÉ D'IMPRESSION EN COULEURS D'UNE IMPRIMERIE.

■ 293-298 ART DIRECTOR/DESIGNER: BRYAN L. PETERSON PHOTOGRAPHER: ROBB DEBENPORT AGENCY: PETERSON & COMPANY CLIENT: MOHAWK PAPER COUNTRY: USA ■ 293-298 EACH OF THE SPREADS IN THIS BROCHURE FEATURES A QUOTE RELATING TO THE THEME OF THE PHOTO. ● 293-298 JEDE DOPPELSEITE DIESER BROSCHÜRE ENTHÄLT EIN ZITAT, DAS SICH AUF DAS THEMA DER PHOTOGRAPHIE BEZIEHT. ▲ 293-298 CHAQUE DOUBLE PAGE DE CETTE BROCHURE D'UN FABRICANT DE PAPIER PROPOSE UNE CITATION QUI SE RAPPORTE AU THÈME DE LA PHOTO.

■ **299** ART DIRECTOR: MICHAEL DENNY DESIGNERS: JOHN BATESON, RACHAEL DINNIS PHOTOGRAPHER: CHRISTOPHER RIDLEY IMAGE MANIPULATION: IQ VIDEOGRAPHICS AGENCY: ROUNDEL DESIGN GROUP CLIENT: RAILFREIGHT DISTRIBUTION, BRITISH RAILWAYS BOARD COUNTRY: GREAT BRITAIN ■ **299** CORPORATE BROCHURE FOR BRITISH RAIL'S INTERMODAL FREIGHT OPERATION DEMONSTRATING THEIR COMMITMENT TO PROVIDING A SERVICE THAT MAKES THE MOST OF NEW TECHNOLOGY. ● **299** BROSCHÜRE FÜR DIE FRACHTABTEILUNG DER BRITISCHEN EISENBAHNEN, DIE FÜR IHREN KUNDENSERVICE DIE MÖGLICHKEITEN NEUER TECHNOLOGIEN AUSSCHÖPFT. ▲ **299** BROCHURE CRÉÉE POUR LE SERVICE DE FRET DES CHEMINS DE FER BRITANNIQUES QUI UTILISENT TOUTES LES RESSOURCES DES NOUVELLES TECHNOLOGIES POUR SATISFAIRE LEURS CLIENTS.

■ **300** ART DIRECTORS: STEVE GIBBS, WILLIE BARONET DESIGNER: STEVE GIBBS PHOTOGRAPHER: JOE CARLSON AGENCY: GIBBS BARONET CLIENT: ALLSTEEL COUNTRY: USA ■ **300** INTRODUCTION OF A NEW SERIES OF OFFICE SEATING. THE PRESENTATION HIGHLIGHTS THE LINES OF THE CHAIRS. ● **300** EINE NEUE SERIE VON BÜROSTÜHLEN WIRD VORGESTELLT. ▲ **300** PRÉSENTATION D'UNE NOUVELLE LIGNE DE SIÈGES DE BUREAU.

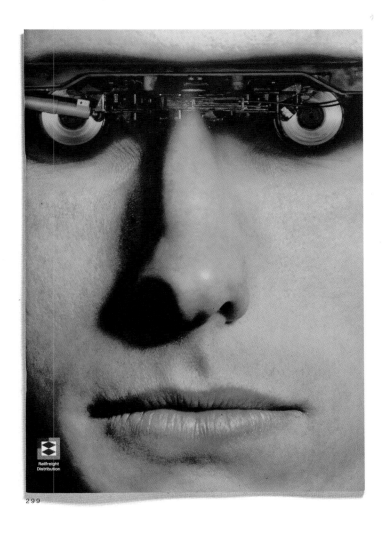

299

300

■ **301** ART DIRECTOR/DESIGNER/PHOTOGRAPH: OSWALD LUKOSSEK CLIENT: SOMMER EINRICHTUNGSHAUS COUNTRY: GERMANY ■ **301** CONCEPTS, PLANNING AND CONSULTATION ARE OFFERED ALONG WITH THE FURNITURE OF THIS COMPANY. ● **301** KONZEPTE, PLANUNG UND BERATUNG SOWIE MÖBEL WERDEN HIER ANGEBOTEN. DAS MOTTO DES KATALOGS: WIR HABEN EINE GANZE REIHE VON KÖPFEN, DIE IHNEN HELFEN, IHRE PROBLEME ZU LÖSEN. ▲ **301** CE FABRICANT DE MEUBLES PROPOSE ICI, OUTRE SON PRODUIT, DES CONCEPTS, UNE PLANIFICATION ET UN SERVICE DE CONSEILS.

■ **302** ART DIRECTOR/DESIGNER: DAVID LLOYD BECK AGENCY: SIBLEY/PETEET DESIGN CLIENT: NOVIKOFF, INC. COUNTRY: USA ■ **302** THIS BROCHURE INTRODUCES METAPLAN, A NEW MODULAR FURNITURE SYSTEM. ● **302** MIT DIESER BROSCHÜRE WIRD EINE NEUE LINIE VON MÖBELSYSTEMEN UNTER DEM NAMEN METAPLAN VORGESTELLT. ▲ **302** DE NOUVEAUX SYSTÈMES DE MOBILIER MODULAIRE METAPLAN SONT PRÉSENTÉS ICI.

■ (FOLLOWING SPREAD) **303-315** ART DIRECTOR/DESIGNER: MICHAEL VANDERBYL PHOTOGRAPHER: PATERSON PHOTOGRAPHIC COPYWRITER: MICHAEL KEILHAUER AGENCY: VANDERBYL DESIGN CLIENT: KEILHAUER INDUSTRIES COUNTRY: USA ■ **303-315** PRODUCT BROCHURES FOR A PRODUCER OF HIGH-END FURNITURE, INTENDED TO PROJECT A NEW IMAGE OF THE FIRM AND THE MODERNITY OF THEIR PRODUCTS. ● (NÄCHSTE DOPPEL-SEITE) **303-315** BROSCHÜREN FÜR EINEN HERSTELLER HOCHWERTIGER MÖBEL. ES GALT, EIN NEUES IMAGE DES HERSTELLERS UND DIE MODER-NITÄT DER MÖBEL HERAUSZUSTELLEN. ▲ (DOUBLE PAGE SUIVANTE) **303-315** BROCHURES PRODUITS POUR UN FABRICANT DE MEUBLES HAUT DE GAMME. IL S'AGISSAIT DE METTRE L'ACCENT SUR LA NOUVELLE IMAGE DE LA FIRME AINSI QUE SUR LA MODERNITÉ DE SES MEUBLES.

301

302

■ (FOLLOWING SPREAD) **316-322** ART DIRECTOR: MICHAEL VANDERBYL DESIGNERS: MICHAEL VANDERBYL, PATRICIA GLOVER PHOTOGRAPHER: CHARLY FRANKLIN COPYWRITER: PENNY BENDA AGENCY: VANDERBYL DESIGN CLIENT: RUCKER FULLER COUNTRY: USA ■ **316-322** THE DESIGN, COPY AND PHOTOGRAPHY OF THIS CORPORATE BROCHURE ARE MEANT TO CONVEY THE MESSAGE THAT THE COMPANY RUCKER FULLER IS AN INNOVATIVE, MULTIFACETED, SERVICE-ORIENTED PRODUCER OF OFFICE FURNITURE, WHICH HAS BEEN IN BUSINESS FOR OVER EIGHTY YEARS. ● (NÄCHSTE DOPPELSEITE) **316-322** DESIGN, TEXT UND PHOTOS DIESER BROSCHÜRE SOLLEN EINE INNOVATIVE, VIELSEITIGE, SERVICEORIENTIERTE FIRMA PRÄSENTIEREN, DIE BÜROMÖBEL HERSTELLT. ▲ (DOUBLE PAGE SUIVANTE) **316-322** LE DESIGN, LE TEXTE ET LES PHOTOS DE CETTE BROCHURE DEVAIENT SUGGÉRER L'ESPRIT D'INNOVATION, LA DIVERSIFICATION ET LA QUALITÉ DES SERVICES QU'OFFRE CE FABRICANT DE MEUBLES.

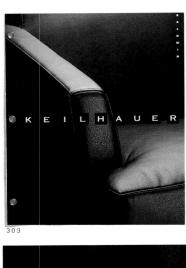

303

304

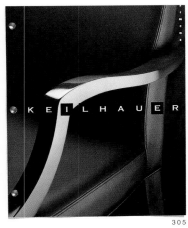

305

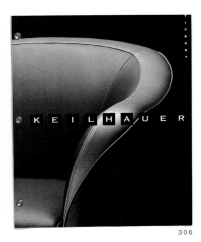

306

307

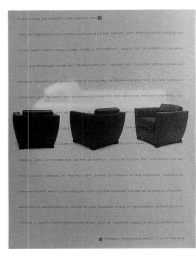

308

309

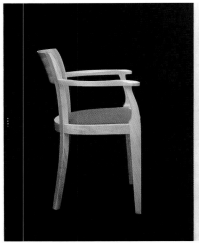

310

311

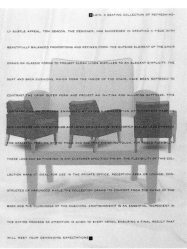

312

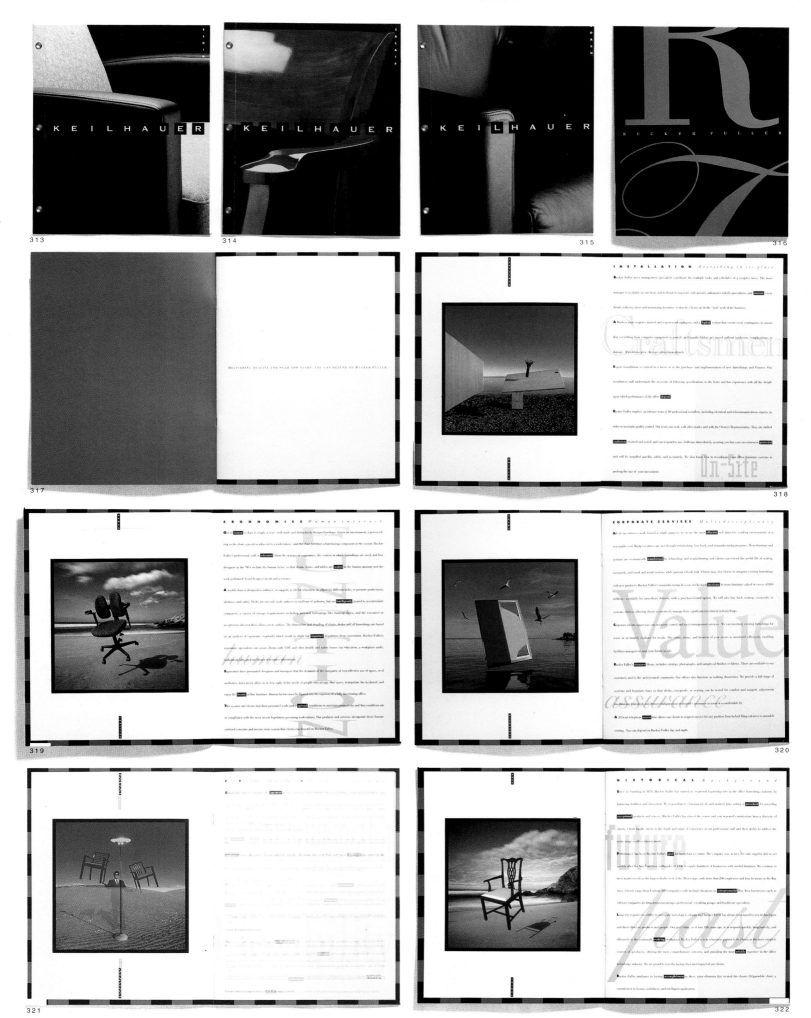

313

314

315

316

317

318

319

320

321

322

■ **323-328** ART DIRECTOR: REBECA MENDEZ DESIGNERS: DARREN NAMAYE, REBECA MENDEZ PHOTOGRAPHER: STEVEN A. HELLER COPYWRITER: KAREN JACOBSON AGENCY: ART CENTER COLLEGE OF DESIGN OFFICE CLIENT: ART CENTER COLLEGE OF DESIGN COUNTRY: USA ■ **323-328** THE ART CENTER'S "VIEWBOOK" WAS DESIGNED AS AN OVERVIEW FOR CANDIDATES. IT PROVIDES A BRIEF INTRODUCTION TO THE COLLEGE AND ITS PROGRAMS, AS WELL AS EXAMPLES OF COMPLETED STUDENT WORK IN MAJOR FIELDS OF STUDY. ● **323-328** DAS «VIEWBOOK» DES ART CENTER COLLEGE OF DESIGN IST ALS ERSTE INFORMATION FÜR INTERESSIERTE STUDENTEN GEDACHT. ES ENTHÄLT EINE KURZE EINFÜHRUNG ÜBER DAS COLLEGE, DAS STUDIENPROGRAMM UND BEISPIELE VON STUDENTENARBEITEN AUS DEN WICHTIGSTEN BEREICHEN. ▲ **323-328** LE «VIEWBOOK» DU ART CENTER COLLEGE OF DESIGN A ÉTÉ CONÇU EN TOUT PREMIER LIEU POUR INFORMER LES INTÉRESSÉS: IL CONTIENT UNE BRÈVE INFORMATION SUR L'ÉCOLE, LE PROGRAMME DES COURS ET DES EXEMPLES DE TRAVAUX D'ÉTUDIANTS DES BRANCHES PRINCIPALES.

■ **329-331** ART DIRECTOR/DESIGNER: REBECA MENDEZ PHOTOGRAPHERS: STEVEN A. HELLER, EIKA AOSHIMA COPYWRITERS: KAREN JACOBSON, ANNA GANAHL AGENCY: ART CENTER DESIGN OFFICE CLIENT: ART CENTER COLLEGE OF DESIGN COUNTRY: USA ■ **329-331** THIS ENVELOPE CONTAINS ART CENTER POSTCARDS THAT, IN A MINIMUM OF SPACE, DEPICT MANY ASPECTS OF CAMPUS LIFE, COLLEGE FACILITIES AND EXAMPLES OF STUDENT WORK. ● **329-331** DIESER UMSCHLAG (GEÖFFNET UND GESCHLOSSEN GEZEIGT) ENTHÄLT POSTKARTEN DES ART CENTER COLLEGE OF DESIGN, DIE AUF KLEINEM RAUM VIELE ASPEKTE DES CAMPUS-LEBENS, EINRICHTUNGEN UND EINE AUSWAHL VON STUDENTENARBEITEN ZEIGEN. ▲ **329-331** CETTE POCHETTE RENFERME DES CARTES POSTALES DU ART CENTER COLLEGE OF DESIGN. ON A AINSI PU PRÉSENTER SUR UN MINIMUM D'ESPACE LE CAMPUS, LES INSTALLATIONS À LA DISPOSITION DES ÉTUDIANTS ET QUELQUES EXEMPLES DE LEURS TRAVAUX.

■ **332** Art Directors: KLAS BJRKMAN, FLISA HEDMAN Designers: KLAS BJRKMAN, FLISA HEDMAN Photographer: MATS LILJEDAHL Copywriter: BO ANNELL Agency: BJRKMAN & MITCHELL Client: ANNELL LJUS + FORM Country: SWEDEN ■ 332 THIS FOLDER PRESENTS A NEW LIGHT FIXTURE DESIGN BY ARCHITECT CLAES KOCK. ● 332 IN DIESER BROSCHÜRE WIRD EINE NEUE AUFHÄNGUNG FÜR LEUCHTEN VORGESTELLT. DESIGNER IST DER ARCHITEKT CLAES KOCK. ▲ 332 CETTE BROCHURE PRÉSENTE UN NOUVEAU LUMINAIRE DESSINÉ PAR L'ARCHITECTE CLAES KOCK.

■ **333** Art Director: SHINNOSUKE SUGISAKI Designer: SHINNOSUKE SUGISAKI Agency: ZOO INC. Client: NANBA CITY Country: JAPAN ■ 333 FRONT PAGE OF A LARGE-FORMAT FOLDER SERVING AS A CATALOG FOR AN EXHIBITION OF INDUSTRIAL DESIGNER TOSHIYUKI KITA. ● 333 VORDERSEITE EINES GROSSFORMATIGEN FALTKATALOGS FÜR EINE AUSSTELLUNG DES JAPANISCHEN INDUSTRIEDESIGNERS TOSHIYUKI KITA. ▲ 333 PREMIÈRE PAGE D'UN CATALOGUE DÉPLIANT DE GRAND FORMAT POUR UNE EXPOSITION DU DESIGNER INDUSTRIEL TOSHIYUKI KITA.

   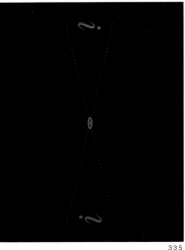

332        333        334        335

■ **334** Art Director: SIMONE IMMEL Copywriter: RITA GISSEL Agency: WUNDERMAN CATO JOHNSON Client: IPTA GMBH Country: GERMANY ■ 334 COVER MADE OF CORRUGATED CARTON WITH A CUT-OUT FIELD FOR THE TITLE "A CASE FOR IPTA—WAREHOUSING WITH A METHOD." ● 334 DER UMSCHLAG DIESER BROSCHÜRE IST AUS WELLKARTON MIT AUSGESTANZTEM FELD FÜR DEN TITEL. ▲ 334 COUVERTURE DE CARTON ONDULÉ AVEC DÉCOUPE À L'EMPORTE-PIÈCE LAISSANT VOIR LE TITRE, POUR UNE BROCHURE PRÉSENTANT UN SYSTÈME D'ENTREPOSAGE.

■ **335-340** Art Director/Designer: LUIS ACEVEDO Photographer: RICHARD REENS Copywriter: SCOTT SIMMONS Agency: RBMM/THE RICHARDS GROUP Client: RICHARD REENS Country: USA ■ 335-340 COVER AND SPREADS FROM A SMALL PROMOTIONAL BROCHURE FOR A PHOTOGRAPHER. ● 335-340 KLEINE WERBEBROSCHÜRE FÜR EINEN PHOTOGRAPHEN. ▲ 335-340 COUVERTURE ET PETITE BROCHURE POUR UN PHOTOGRAPHE.

336

337

338

339

340

■ 341, 342 ART DIRECTOR: CHERYL HELLER DESIGNERS: CHERYL HELLER, ANNE ROUQUETTE PHOTOGRAPHER: CLINT CLEMENS COPYWRITER: GEOFF CURRIER CLIENT: S.D. WARREN COMPANY COUNTRY: USA ■ 341, 342 THE ELEPHANT ON THE COVER ON THIS PROMOTIONAL BROCHURE IS PART OF A HERD OF EIGHT AFRICAN ELEPHANTS, THE CENTERPIECE OF THE AKELEY MEMORIAL HALL OF AFRICAN MAMMALS. THE SIX SCARLET TANAGERS ARE ALSO PART OF THE MUSEUM'S COLLECTION. ● 341, 342 DER ELEFANT AUF DEM UMSCHLAG DIESER BROSCHÜRE FÜR EINE PAPIERQUALITÄT GEHÖRT ZU EINER HERDE VON ACHT AFRIKANISCHEN ELEPHANTEN IN EINEM AMERIKANISCHEN MUSEUM. DIE VÖGEL GEHÖREN AUCH ZUR MUSEUMSSAMMLUNG. ▲ 341, 342 L'ÉLÉPHANT SUR LA COUVERTURE DE CETTE BROCHURE FAIT PARTIE D'UN TROUPEAU DE HUIT ÉLÉPHANTS QUI SONT EXPOSÉS DANS LA SALLE DES MAMMIFÈRES D'AFRIQUE. LES OISEAUX FONT ÉGALEMENT PARTIE DES COLLECTIONS DU MUSÉE.

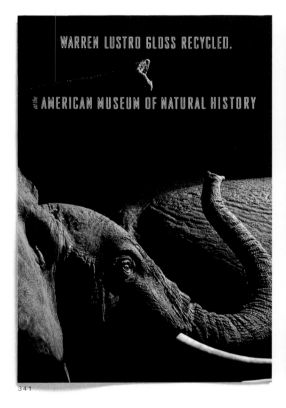

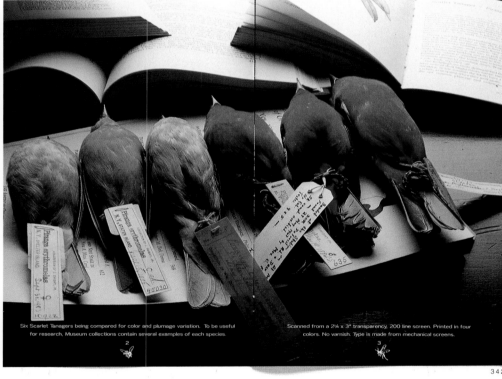

Six Scarlet Tanagers being compared for color and plumage variation. To be useful for research, Museum collections contain several examples of each species.

Scanned from a 2¼ x 3" transparency, 200 line screen. Printed in four colors. No varnish. Type is made from mechanical screens.

341

342

■ 343-348 ART DIRECTOR: STEVE TOLLESON DESIGNERS: STEVE TOLLESON, DONNA ANDERSON, BOB AUFULDISH, DAVID ANTHONY PHOTOGRAPHER: BRIAN FESSENDEN COPYWRITER: LINDSAY BEAMAN CLIENT: TOLLESON DESIGN COUNTRY: USA ■ 343-348 THESE SELF-PROMOTIONAL BROCHURES FOR A DESIGN STUDIO ILLUSTRATE THREE AREAS OF THEIR ACTIVITY: IDENTITY, MISCELLANEOUS, ANNUAL REPORTS. ● 343-348 DIESE PROMOTIONSBROSCHÜREN EINES DESIGNSTUDIOS BETREFFEN DREI BEREICHE IHRER TÄTIGKEIT: ERSCHEINUNGSBILDER, VERSCHIEDENES, JAHRESBERICHTE. ▲ 343-348 CES BROCHURES AUTOPROMOTIONNELLES D'UN STUDIO DE DESIGN ILLUSTRENT QUELQUES-UNS DE SES SECTEURS D'ACTIVITÉ.

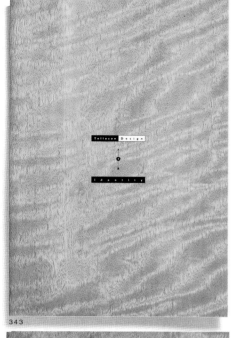

343

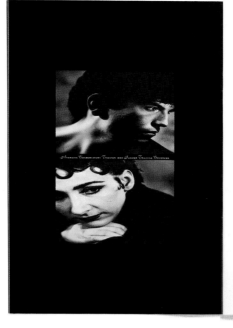

344

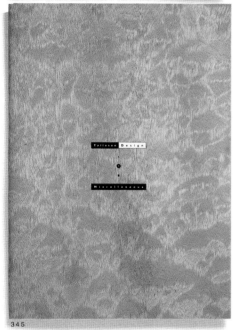

345

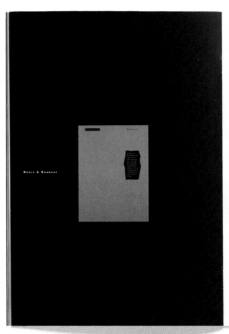

346

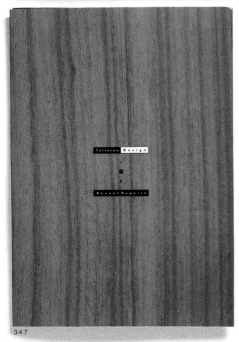

347

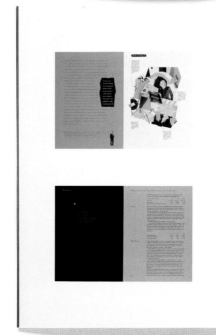

348

349

350

351

352

353

354

355

356

357

■ **349** ART DIRECTOR/DESIGNER: HANS KENTIE CLIENT: LUXAFORM INTERNATIONAL COUNTRY: GERMANY ■ **349** BOX CONTAINING VARIOUS FURNITURE BROCHURES. ● **349** SCHACHTEL FÜR VERSCHIEDENE MÖBELPROSPEKTE. ▲ **349** BOITE CONTENANT DIVERS PROSPECTUS DE MEUBLES.

■ **350** ART DIRECTOR/DESIGNER: BÜLENT ERKMEN CLIENT: A.T. CROSS COMPANY COUNTRY: TURKEY ■ **350** COVER OF A CATALOG FOR AN ART EXHIBITION. ● **350** UMSCHLAG EINES KATALOGS FÜR EINE KUNSTAUSSTELLUNG. ▲ **350** COUVERTURE DU CATALOGUE D'UNE EXPOSITION.

■ **351, 358-361** ART DIRECTOR: ANTONIO PEREZ ESCOLANO AGENCY: DISENO Y COMUNICACION S.A. CLIENT: DISENO Y COMUNICACION S.A. COUNTRY: SPAIN ■ **351, 358-361** COVER AND SPREADS OF A SELF-PROMOTIONAL BROCHURE FOR A DESIGN STUDIO. ● **351, 358-361** UMSCHLAG UND DOPPELSEITEN EINER EIGENWERBUNGSBROSCHÜRE EINES DESIGNSTUDIOS. ▲ **351, 358-361** AUTOPROMOTION D'UN STUDIO DE DESIGN.

■ **352** Art Director/Designer: KLAUS BIETZ Agency: HWL & PARTNER DESIGN Client: GALERIE VON OERTZEN Country: GERMANY ■ **352** INVITATION TO A FRANKFURT EXHIBITION OF THE WORKS OF THREE AUSTRALIAN DESIGNERS. ● **352** EINLADUNG ZU EINER AUSSTELLUNG VON DREI AUSTRALISCHEN DESIGNERN IN FRANKFURT. ▲ **352** INVITATION À UNE EXPOSITION DE TROIS DESIGNERS AUSTRALIENS À FRANCFORT.

■ **353** Art Director/Designer: ERICH FALKNER Agency: GGK WIEN Client: PORSCHE AUSTRIA GESMBH & CO. Country: AUSTRIA ■ **353** BOX CONTAINING A PROMOTIONAL GIFT AND BROCHURE ON THE VOLKSWAGEN PASSAT. ● **353** DIESE BOX FÜR DEN VW PASSAT ENTHÄLT EIN WERBEGESCHENK UND EINE BROSCHÜRE. ▲ **353** CETTE BOÎTE RENFERME UN CADEAU PROMOTIONNEL ET UNE BROCHURE SUR LA VOLKSWAGEN PASSAT.

■ **354** Art Directors: JOYCE NESNADNY, MARK SCHWARTZ Designer: JOYCE NESNADNY Agency: NESNADNY & SCHWARTZ Client: CLEVELAND INSTITUTE OF ART Country: USA ■ **354** THIS BROCHURE PROVIDES INTERESTED CANDIDATES WITH INFORMATION ON THE LACOSTE SCHOOL OF THE ARTS IN PROVENCE, FRANCE. ● **354** DIESE BROSCHÜRE INFORMIERT ÜBER DAS PROGRAMM DER LACOSTE SCHOOL OF ARTS KUNSTSCHULE IN DER PROVENCE. ▲ **354** CETTE BROCHURE CONTIENT DES INFORMATIONS SUR LE PROGRAMME D'UNE ÉCOLE D'ART SITUÉE EN PROVENCE.

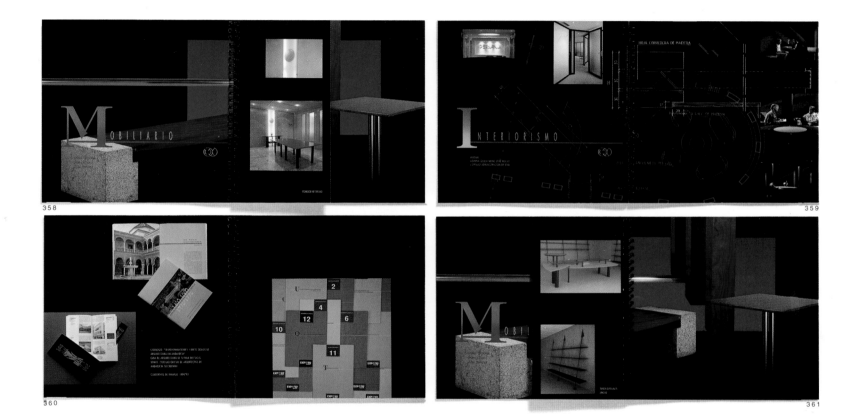

358

359

360

361

■ **355** Art Director: SAUL TORRES Designer: SAUL TORRES Photographer: GILLES LARRAIN Agency: EISENBERG ASSOCIATES Client: THE MEADOWS MUSEUM Country: USA ■ **355** EXHIBITION CATALOG FOR NEW YORK BASED PHOTOGRAPHER GILLES LARRAIN. ● **355** AUSSTELLUNGSKATALOG FÜR DEN IN NEW YORK LEBENDEN PHOTOGRAPHEN GILLES LARRAIN. ▲ **355** CATALOGUE D'EXPOSITION DU PHOTOGRAPHE GILLES LARRAIN.

■ **356** Creative Director: LESLIE LEVENTMAN Art Director: SCOTT WADLER Designer: GAIL RIGELHAUPT Agency: MTV NETWORKS CREATIVE SERVICES/RIGELHAUPT DESIGN Client: COMEDY CENTRAL Country: USA ■ **356** BLIND-EMBOSSED COVER OF A BROCHURE PRESENTING THE PROGRAM OF COMEDY CENTRAL TV. ● **356** BLINDGEPRÄGTER UMSCHLAG FÜR DAS PROGRAMM EINES UNTERHALTUNGSSENDERS DES FERNSEHENS. ▲ **356** COUVERTURE GAUFRÉE À SEC ORNANT LE PROGRAMME D'UN ÉMETTEUR D'ÉMISSIONS DE VARIÉTÉS DE LA TÉLÉVISION AMÉRICAINE.

■ **357** Art Director: JACK ANDERSON Designers: JACK ANDERSON, PAULA COX, DAVID BATES, LIAN NG, LEO RAYMUNDO Agency/Client: HORNALL ANDERSON DESIGN WORKS Country: USA ■ **357** COVER (CORRUGATED CARDBOARD) OF HORNALL ANDERSON'S "A DECADE OF DESIGN." ● **357** VORDERSEITE EINES LEPORELLOPROSPEKTES ZUM 10JÄHRIGEN BESTEHEN VON HORNALL ANDERSON DESIGN WORKS. ▲ **357** PREMIÈRE PAGE (CARTON ONDULÉ) D'UN DÉPLIANT EN ACCORDÉON RÉALISÉ À L'OCCASION DU 10E ANNIVERSAIRE DE HORNALL ANDERSON DESIGN WORKS.

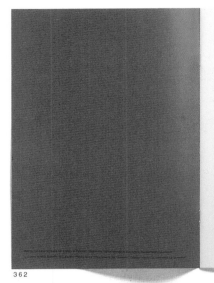

## BEAUTIFUL HEAT

Heat and comfort are for us humans inseparably linked: heat is visible and tangible well-being. We see heat in a rich scale of colours, ranging from blazing signal red to the more subdued warm tones of the colours of the earth. • All day and every day man's attention is centred on the sources from which he draws heat. In the beginning it was the open fire and the smouldering incandescent glow in the centre of the room. Later the fire was shifted from the floor to the hearth and the stove. Chimneys and stoves became formative elements in the culture of living. This we can see in the artistically decorated and magnificently painted glazed ovens which adorned patrician residences in the past. • About 150 years ago the first central heating systems were built and installed. For a long time the heating elements presented a rather ugly picture, exclusively dedicated to the performance of their technical function. They were therefore mainly hidden behind covering structures of varying visual appeal. But the next development in radiator design demonstrated that sources of heat could also be aesthetic: creativity and manual skill combined with the passage of years to make elegant radiators which not only fulfilled their technical functions but also – by their design alone – communicated a feeling of cosiness and comfortable living. • Heat – even when performing its technical function – had again become a source of beauty. Heating radiators fulfil in their colour and shape a whole range of demands in the internal architecture of the home. In one case this can mean their separate arrangement in the configuration of the room; in other circumstances – for example in bathrooms – they gladly step forward to emphasize the architectural design. Sometimes they are well rounded – soft shapes are suitable – while in other cases flat structures impart the desired harmony of the room. • The Zehnder Group with their generous range of products meet all technical and architectural demands. Let us inspire you with our flow of ideas on radiators. You can satisfy your longing for comfort and the beauty of heat as you run through the models shown in the following pages.

362

GRILLE RADIATORS    CONVECTORS    OVERHEAD RADIANT PANEL STRIPS

363

TUBULAR RADIATORS

364

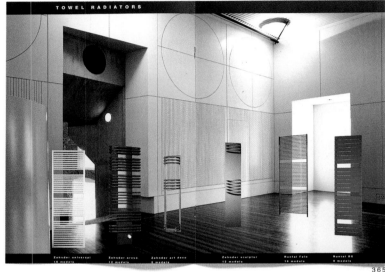

TOWEL RADIATORS

365

366

■ 362-366 ART DIRECTOR: GIANNI BERTOSSA PHOTOGRAPHER: RUEDI FISCHLI COPYWRITER: ERNST BOHREN AGENCY: RENZEN & PARTNER CLIENT: ZEHNDER HOLDING COUNTRY: SWITZERLAND ■ 362-366 THE CLIENT IS A LEADING MANUFACTURER OF RADIATORS. THE BACKGROUND PHOTOGRAPHS WERE TAKEN IN A SWISS CASTLE. THE SYNTHESIS OF TRADITION AND MODERN ARCHITECTURE SEEMED TO BE THE PERFECT SETTING FOR THE PRODUCTS. ● 362-366 DER AUFTRAGGEBER GEHÖRT ZU DEN BEDEUTENDSTEN HERSTELLERN VON HEIZKÖRPERN. DIE HINTERGRUNDAUFNAHMEN WURDEN IM CASTEL GRANDE IN BELLINZONA GEMACHT. DIE SYNTHESE VON TRADITION UND MODERNER ARCHITEKTUR SCHIEN EIN PERFEKTER RAHMEN FÜR DIE PRODUKTPALETTE. ▲ 362-366 LE CLIENT EST L'UN DES PLUS GRANDS FABRICANTS DE RADIATEURS. LES DÉCORS DE L'ARRIÈRE-PLAN ONT ÉTÉ PHOTOGRAPHIÉS DANS LE CASTEL GRANDE, UN CHÂTEAU FORT DE BELLINZONE, EN SUISSE. OFFRANT UNE SYNTHÈSE DE LA TRADITION ET DE L'ARCHITECTURE MODERNE, IL FOURNISSAIT LE DÉCOR IDÉAL POUR CES PRODUITS.

Viele Möbeldesigner
entwerfen **Möbel**
und es kommt
**Schrott** dabei
heraus. Ich
mache es
einfach umgekehrt,
und deshalb bin ich
auch kein
Möbeldesigner.

367

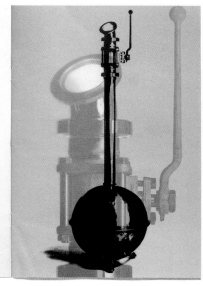

368

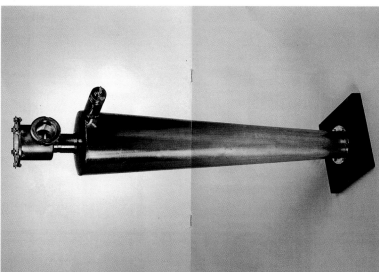

369

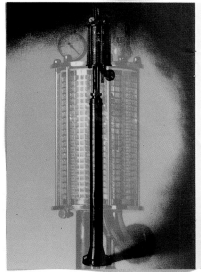

1957 N e u   g e b o r e n
1976-81 Architektur Studium mit
Abschluss Dipl. Ing.
D ü s s e l d o r f
1982-84 Gasthörerschaft HDK,
B e r l i n
1985-86 Assistenz bei Stahl-
bildhauer Jeff Lowe,
L o n d o n
A u s s t e l l u n g e n
1985 Gallerie Voll-Art, Berlin
1986 Gallerie Bel-Etage, Düsseldorf
1987 Möbelle, Düsseldorf
1988 Leo Kirch Gruppe, München
1989 Havelock Walk Studios, London
1989 Kunstpalast, Düsseldorf
1989 Möbelmesse, Köln
1990 Robin des Bois, Paris
Piet Neiser lebt und arbeitet als
Architekt und Künstler in Düsseldorf.
Kontakt :Stratenweg 45 4000 Düsseldorf 12
Tel.(0211) 660 300 / (0211) 29 75 13

370

schrottlampen
piet neiser

371

■ **367-371** ART DIRECTOR/DESIGNER: MICHAELA NEISER PHOTOGRAPHERS: HUMA ROSENTALSKI, BERND AHRENDS COPYWRITER: PIET NEISER CLIENT: PIET NEISER COUNTRY: GERMANY ■ **367-371** "IN CREATING FURNITURE, MANY FURNITURE DESIGNERS CREATE TRASH; I DO IT THE OTHER WAY AROUND." THIS CATALOG PRESENTS THE TRASH LAMPS OF ARCHITECT PIET NEISER. ● **367-371** DIE SCHROTTLAMPEN VON PIET NEISER, VORGESTELLT IN EINEM KATALOG. ▲ **367-371** LES «LAMPES DE RÉCUPÉRATION» DE PIET NEISER SONT PRÉSENTÉES DANS CE CATALOGUE.

372

373

374

375

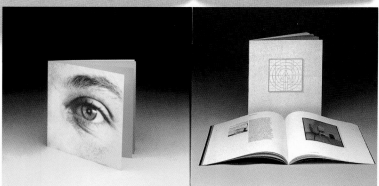

376

377

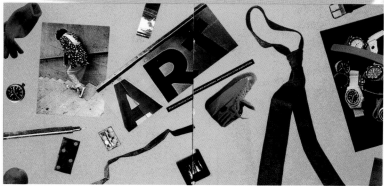

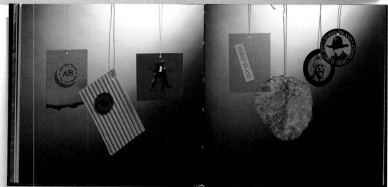

378

379

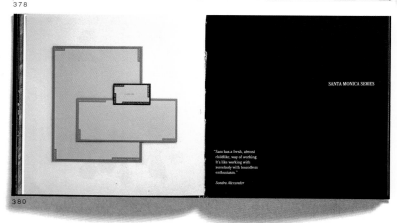

380

381

382

383

■ **372-382** ART DIRECTOR/DESIGNER: SAM SMIDT PHOTOGRAPHERS: VARIOUS AGENCY/CLIENT: SAM SMIDT INC. COUNTRY: USA ■ **372-382** A COMPACT MINI PORTFOLIO OF RECENT PROJECTS DONE BY SAM SMIDT STUDIO. ● **372-382** EIN KOMPAKTES MINI-PORTFOLIO, DAS DIE NEUSTEN ARBEITEN DES SAM SMIDT STUDIOS PRÄSENTIERT. ▲ **372-382** UN MINI PORTFOLIO RENFERMANT LES TRAVAUX LES PLUS RÉCENTS DU STUDIO SAM SMIDT.

■ **383** ART DIRECTORS: JOEL FULLER, CLAUDIA DECASTRO DESIGNER: CLAUDIA DECASTRO PHOTOGRAPHER: GALLEN MEI AGENCY: PINKHAUS DESIGN CORP. CLIENT: GILBERT PAPER COUNTRY: USA ■ **383** THE THEME OF THIS PROMOTIONAL BROCHURE FOR THE PAPER QUALITY GILBERT OXFORD IS THE CONSTANCY OF IMPORTANT THINGS. ● **383** THEMA DIESER BROSCHÜRE FÜR DIE PAPIERQUALITÄT GILBERT OXFORD IST DIE BESTÄNDIGKEIT WICHTIGER DINGE. ▲ **383** LE SUJET DE CETTE BROCHURE POUR LES PAPIERS GILBERT OXFORD EST LA PERMANENCE DES CHOSES IMPORTANTES.

■ **384** ART DIRECTOR/DESIGNER/ILLUSTRATOR: PAUL BLACK AGENCY: THE DESIGN GROUP – JRSK CLIENT: SPECIALIZED BIKE COUNTRY: USA ■ **384** THIS CARTON FOLDER WITH GLUED-ON LABEL CONTAINS INFORMATION AND ORDER FORMS FOR SPECIALIZED BIKE DEALERS. ● **384** DIESE KARTON-MAPPE MIT AUFGEKLEBTEM ETIKETT ENTHÄLT INFORMATIONEN ÜBER EINE FAHRRADMARKE UND BESTELLFORMULARE FÜR HÄNDLER. ▲ **384** CE DOSSIER EN CARTON RENFERME DES INFORMATIONS SUR UNE MARQUE DE VÉLO ET DES BONS DE COMMANDE DESTINÉS AUX DÉTAILLANTS.

■ **385, 386** ART DIRECTORS: ERWIN SCHMÖLZER, KRISTIN KONIAREK DESIGNER: KRISTIN KONIAREK PHOTOGRAPHER: RUDI KREMAIER COPYWRITER: ISOLDE OZLBERGER AGENCY: ATELIER FÜR KUNST UND DESIGN ERWIN SCHMÖLZER CLIENT: ALFRED SCHROT KG COUNTRY: AUSTRIA ■ **385, 386** DIRECT MAIL PIECES FOR A GOURMET RESTAURANT. ONE SERVES AS AN ANNOUNCEMENT OF THEIR VENISON WEEKS AND THE OTHER EMPHA-SIZES THAT THE RESTAURANT IS OPEN ON SUNDAYS. ● **385, 386** DIRECT MAIL FÜR EIN RESTAURANT. ▲ **385, 386** DOCUMENTS DE MAILING DI-RECT POUR UN RESTAURANT: IL Y EST QUESTION DE «SEMAINES DE LA CHASSE» ET DU SERVICE «SPÉCIAL DIMANCHE» DE CET ÉTABLISSEMENT.

385

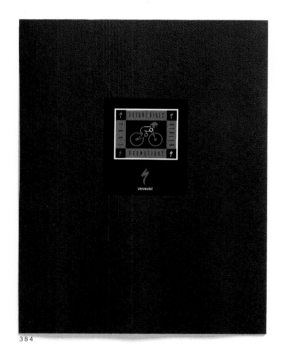

386

384

387

■ **387** ART DIRECTOR: MICHAEL BROCK DESIGNERS: MICHAEL BROCK, ROBERT PEAK PHOTOGRAPHER: ROBERT PEAK AGENCY: MICHAEL BROCK DESIGN CLIENT: WARNER HOME VIDEO COUNTRY: USA ■ **387** CATALOG COVER INCORPORATING THE WARNER BROTHERS LOGO. ● **387** DAS WARNER BROTHERS LOGO IST AUF DIESEM KATALOGUMSCHLAG ABGEBILDET. ▲ **387** LE LOGO DE WARNER BROTHERS EN COUVERTURE D'UN CATALOGUE.

■ **388-396** ART DIRECTOR/DESIGNER: KERRY GRADY PHOTOGRAPHER: GEOF KERN ILLUSTRATORS: KERRY GRADY V. OTTO, ANN FIELD COPYWRITER: RALPH CAPLAN AGENCY: KERRY GRADY DESIGN CLIENT: NEENAH PAPER COUNTRY: USA ■ **388-396** THIS BOOK ACTS AS A SALES TOOL FOR PRINTING PAPERS, PROVIDING IMPORTANT INFORMATION WHILE ENTERTAINING THE CUSTOMER. ● **388-396** DIESE BROSCHÜRE FÜR DRUCKPAPIERE ENT-HÄLT WICHTIGE INFORMATIONEN UND UNTERHÄLT GLEICHZEITIG DEN KUNDEN. ▲ **388-396** CETTE BROCHURE PRÉSENTANT DES PAPIERS POUR IMPRESSION SERT DE MATÉRIEL DE VENTE. ELLE RENFERME DES INFORMATIONS IMPORTANTES TOUT EN ÉTANT DISTRAYANTE POUR LE CLIENT.

397

398

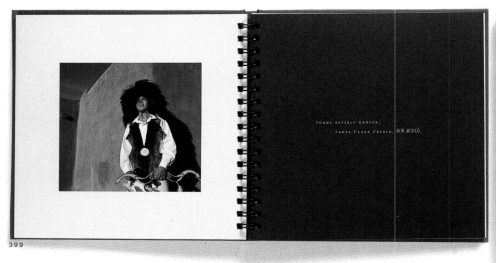

399

400

401

402

■ **397, 398** Art Director/Designer: JEAN McCARTNEY Photographer: PATRICIA HEAL Stylist: KEITH JOHNSTON Agency: IN-HOUSE, WEST POINT PEPPERELL Client: MARTEX, WEST POINT PEPPERELL, INC. Country: USA ■ **397, 398** THE FALL 1992 LINE OF MARTEX BED LINENS. THE SETTINGS REFLECT THE STYLE OF THE DESIGNS. SHOWN IS THE "MALAKAR" DESIGN. ● **397, 398** DIE MARTEX-BETTWÄSCHE-KOLLEKTION HERBST 92. GEZEIGT IST DAS DESIGN «MALAKAR». ▲ **397, 398** LA COLLECTION AUTOMNE/HIVER DES LINGES DE MAISON MARTEX: ICI, LA LIGNE «MALAKAR».

■ **399, 400** Art Director: RODNEY RASCONA Designer: THE KOTTLER CALDERA GROUP Photographer/Client: RODNEY RASCONA Country: USA ■ **399, 400** "LOCATION"—A SELF-PROMOTIONAL BOOK FOR THE PHOTOGRAPHER. SHOWN IS A YOUNG BUFFALO DANCER IN NEW MEXICO. ● **399, 400** »LOCATION« – EIN EIGENWERBUNGSBÜCHLEIN DES PHOTOGRAPHEN. DAS BILD ZEIGT EINEN JUNGEN BÜFFEL-TÄNZER IN NEUMEXIKO. ▲ **399, 400** «LOCATION» – UN PETIT LIVRE AUTOPROMOTIONNEL DU PHOTOGRAPHE. L'IMAGE MONTRE UN JEUNE DANSEUR-BUFFLE DU NOUVEAU-MEXIQUE.

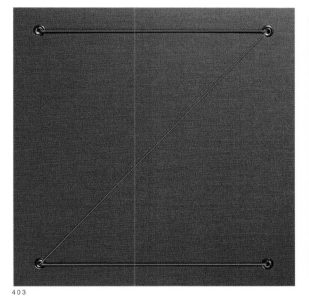

403

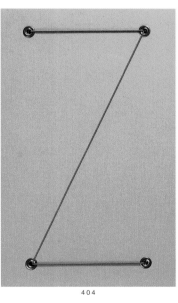

404

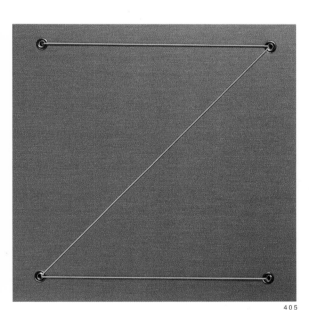

405

■ **401, 402** Art Director/Designer: PATRICIA A. EYNON Photographer: LISA POMEROY Country: USA ■ **401, 402** THIS STUDENT PROJECT WAS INTENDED TO SHOW THE POSSIBILITIES OF COMPUTERIZED MANIPULATION OF A BLACK-AND-WHITE PHOTOGRAPH. ● **401, 402** BEI DIESEM STUDIENPROJEKT GING ES UM DIE VERSCHIEDENEN MÖGLICHKEITEN DER COMPUTERMANIPULATION EINES SCHWARZWEISSPHOTOS. ▲ **401, 402** CE PROJET AVAIT POUR OBJECTIF DE MONTRER LES POSSIBILITÉS DE LA MANIPULATION D'UNE IMAGE EN NOIR ET BLANC SUR ORDINATEUR.

■ **403-405** Art Directors/Designers: MARK SCHWARTZ, JOYCE NESNADNY Agency: NESNADNY & SCHWARTZ Client: Z CONTEMPORARY CUISINE Country: USA ■ **403-405** MENU COVERS THAT ALLOW EASY CHANGES OF INSERTS. THE Z IS FORMED BY A RUBBER BAND. ● **403-405** MENU-UMSCHLÄGE, DIE EINEN LEICHTEN AUSTAUSCH DER EINLAGEBLÄTTER ERMÖGLICHEN. DAS Z BESTEHT AUS EINEM GUMMIBAND. ▲ **403-405** DES COUVERTURES DE MENUS SOLIDES, QUI PERMETTENT DE CHANGER FACILEMENT LES FEUILLETS INTERNES. LE Z EST FAIT D'UNE ÉLASTIQUE.

408

409

410

411

412

413

■ **406, 407** ART DIRECTOR/DESIGNER/ILLUSTRATOR: SHARON WERNER AGENCY: WERNER DESIGN WERKS INC. CLIENT: MICK FREUND COUNTRY: USA ■ **406, 407** "MY EX-WIFE'S RECIPES." THIS COOK-BOOK SERIES IS FOR THE SINGLE OR NEWLY SINGLE MAN—SET UP INTO EVENTS LIKE FIRST DATE, LAST DATE. IT ALSO CONTAINS SUGGESTIONS FOR SETTING THE RIGHT ATMOSPHERE. ● **406, 407** «DIE REZEPTE MEINER EX-FRAU» – DIESE KOCH-BÜCHER SIND FÜR FRISCH GESCHIEDENE MÄNNER ODER SINGLES BESTIMMT; SIE SIND NACH ANLÄSSEN WIE 'ERSTE EINLADUNG' ODER 'LETZTE EINLADUNG' EINGETEILT. ▲ **406, 407** «LES RECETTES DE MON EX-FEMME» – CES LIVRES DE CUISINE SONT DESTINÉS TOUT SPÉCIALEMENT AUX HOMMES DIVORCÉS OU AUX CÉLIBATAIRES; ILS SONT CONÇUS PAR SUJETS, TELS QUE «PREMIÈRE INVITATION» OU «DERNIÈRE INVITATION».

■ **408-413** ART DIRECTOR: MAX RINDLISBACHER PHOTOGRAPHER: MICHAEL WISSING AGENCY: ASGS/BBDO CLIENT: MICHAEL WISSING COUNTRY: GERMANY ■ **408-413** THE SELF-PROMOTIONAL CATALOG OF GERMAN PHOTOGRAPHER MICHAEL WISSING COMES IN A LARGE METAL BOX. ● **408-413** DER EIGENWERBUNGSKATALOG DES DEUTSCHEN PHOTOGRAPHEN MICHAEL WISSING WIRD IN EINER ALUMINIUMSCHACHTEL PRÄSENTIERT. ▲ **408-413** LE CATALOGUE AUTOPROMOTIONNEL DU PHOTOGRAPHE ALLEMAND MICHAEL WISSING EST PRÉSENTÉ DANS UN COFFRET EN MÉTAL.

414

415

416

417

418

419

■ 414-419 ART DIRECTORS: LANA RIGSBY, ANDY DEARWATER ILLUSTRATOR: ANDY DEARWATER CLIENT: ZOOLOGICAL SOCIETY OF HOUSTON COUNTRY: USA ■ 414-419 SPREADS FROM A BROCHURE COMMEMORATING THE 25TH ANNIVERSARY OF THE HOUSTON ZOOLOGICAL SOCIETY. THE THEME OF THE ILLUMINATED CAPS—THE COVER CLOSES WITH A Z—IS CARRIED THROUGH THE WHOLE BOOK. ● 414-419 DOPPELSEITEN AUS EINER BROSCHÜRE DER ZOOLOGISCHEN GESELLSCHAFT VON HOUSTON. DAS THEMA ILLUMINIERTER INITIALEN – DER SCHUTZUMSCHLAG WIRD MIT EINEM Z GESCHLOSSEN – ZIEHT SICH DURCH DIE GANZE BROSCHÜRE. ▲ 414-419 DOUBLES PAGES D'UNE BROCHURE PUBLIÉE À L'OCCASION DES 25 ANS D'EXISTENCE DE LA SOCIÉTÉ ZOOLOGIQUE D'HOUSTON. LE THÈME DE L'INITIALE ENLUMINÉE SE POURSUIT À TRAVERS TOUT L'OUVRAGE.

■ 420 DESIGN DIRECTOR: TOM GEISMAR DESIGNER: CATHY SCHAEFER PHOTOGRAPHER: KAREN YAMAUCHI AGENCY: CHERMAYEFF & GEISMAR INC. CLIENT: THE KNOLL GROUP COUNTRY: USA ■ 420 THESE BROCHURES BELONG TO A SERIES SPECIFYING STANDARDS FOR THE GRAPHIC SYSTEMS DEVELOPED FOR KNOLL. THE COVER IMAGERY ABSTRACTLY REFLECTS THE BROCHURES' CONTENTS BY OVERLAPPING COLORS TO CREATE THE GRID USED IN THE DESIGN OF STATIONERY AND FORMS. ● 420 DIESE BROSCHÜREN ENTHALTEN FÜR KNOLL ENTWICKELTE GRAPHISCHE GESTAL-TUNGSVORSCHRIFTEN. DIE ÜBERLAGERTEN FARBFELDER SIND EINE ABSTRAKTION DER ETABLIERTEN RASTER FÜR DIE BRIEFSCHAFTEN UND FORMULARE. ▲ 420 CES BROCHURES CONTIENNENT DES RÈGLES DE CONCEPTION GRAPHIQUE MISES AU POINT POUR KNOLL. LES SUPERPOSI-TIONS DE COULEURS SYMBOLISENT LES TRAMES POUR PAPIERS À LETTRES ET FORMULAIRES, QUI SONT PRÉSENTÉES DANS CES BROCHURES.

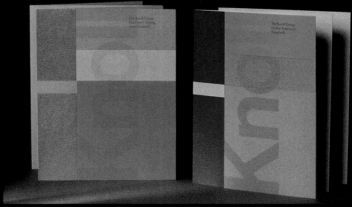

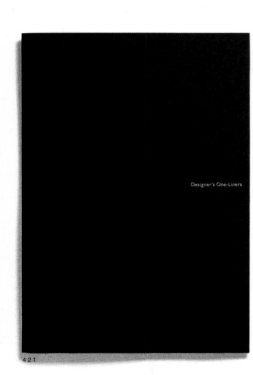

421

422

423

424

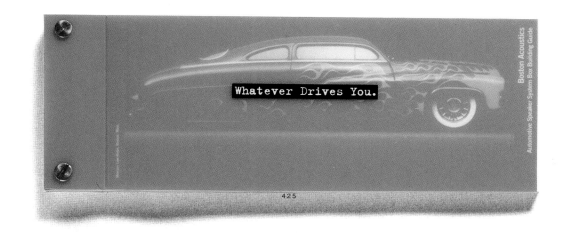

■ **421-424** ART DIRECTOR/DESIGNER: MICHAEL SKJEI AGENCY: M. SKJEI DESIGN CO. CLIENT: SHAY, SHEA, HSIEH & SKJEI COUNTRY: USA ■ **421-424** THROUGHOUT THIS SMALL BOOKLET, ONE-LINE QUOTES OF INTERNATIONALLY KNOWN ARCHITECTS AND DESIGNERS ARE PRESENTED. ● **421-424** IN DIESEM BÜCHLEIN SIND DURCHGEHEND AUF EINER ZEILE ZITATE VON BEKANNTEN ARCHITEKTEN UND DESIGNERN WIEDERGEGEBEN. ▲ **421-424** DANS CE LIVRE, ON A INSCRIT SUR UNE SEULE LIGNE DES CITATIONS DE GRANDS ARCHITECTES ET DESIGNERS DU MONDE ENTIER.

■ **425, 426** ART DIRECTOR: BRUCE CROCKER DESIGNERS: BRUCE CROCKER, MARTIN SORGER AGENCY: CROCKER INC. CLIENT: BOSTON ACOUSTICS COUNTRY: USA ■ **425, 426** THIS BROCHURE PROVIDES THE CONSUMER WITH SPECIFICATIONS ON CAR AUDIO SPEAKERS WHILE AT THE SAME TIME SERVING AS AN INSTALLATION GUIDE. THE SCREW BINDING ALLOWS FOR EASY EXCHANGE OF PAGES; ITS TRANSPARENT PLASTIC COVER PROVIDES STABILITY AND PROTECTION. ● **425, 426** DIESE BROSCHÜRE ENTHÄLT ANGABEN FÜR DIE VERBRAUCHER ÜBER AUTORADIOS; GLEICH-ZEITIG DIENT SIE ALS ANLEITUNG FÜR MONTEURE. DIE SCHRAUBEN-BINDUNG ERLAUBT DAS AUSTAUSCHEN EINZELNER SEITEN. DER UMSCHLAG AUS TRANSPARENTEM PLASTIK VERLEIHT DER BROSCHÜRE ZUSÄTZLICH STABILITÄT. ▲ **425, 426** CETTE BROCHURE RENFERME DES INFORMA-TIONS POUR L'UTILISATEUR D'AUTO-RADIOS; EN MÊME TEMPS, ELLE SERT DE MODE D'EMPLOI POUR LES MONTEURS. LA RELIURE VISSÉE PER-MET D'ÉCHANGER AU BESOIN QUELQUES PAGES. LA COUVERTURE EN PLASTIQUE CONFÈRE À CETTE BROCHURE UNE PLUS GRANDE STABILITÉ.

■ **427** Art Director: TERRANCE ZACHARKO Designers: TERRANCE ZACKARKO, SANDI DUYVEWAARDT Photographer: ROBIN BARTHOLICK Agency: ZACHARKO DESIGN PARTNERSHIP Client: ISLAND PAPER MILLS COMPANY Country: CANADA ■ **427** BROCHURE FOR A NEW LINE OF RECYCLED PAPERS. ● **427** BROSCHÜRE FÜR UMWELT-PAPIER. ▲ **427** COUVERTURE D'UNE BROCHURE POUR UNE NOUVELLE SORTE DE PAPIER RECYCLÉ.

■ **428** Art Director: ROLAND MATTICZK Designer: MONIKA VAN HELDEN Photographer: THOMAS RÄSE Agency: SEHSTERN Client: DJH-LANDESVERBAND Country: GERMANY ■ **428** TRAVEL CATALOG AND OFFICIAL INDEX OF THE YOUTH HOSTELS OF BERLIN-BRANDENBURG. THE CUT-OUTS IN THE BRANDENBURGER GATE OFFER A VIEW OF A LANDSCAPE TYPICAL FOR THE REGION. ● **428** REISEKATALOG UND VERZEICHNIS DER JUGENDHERBERGEN DES LANDESVERBANDES BERLIN-BRANDENBURG. DIE AUSSCHNITTE IM BRANDENBURGER TOR LASSEN EINE FÜR DIE GEGEND TYPISCHE LANDSCHAFT ERKENNEN. ▲ **428** CATALOGUE DE VOYAGES ET INDEX OFFICIEL DES AUBERGES DE JEUNESSE DE L'AGGLOMÉRATION BERLIN-BRANDEBOURG. LES DÉCOUPES DANS LA PORTE DE BRANDEBOURG LAISSENT ENTREVOIR UN PAYSAGE TYPIQUE DE LA RÉGION.

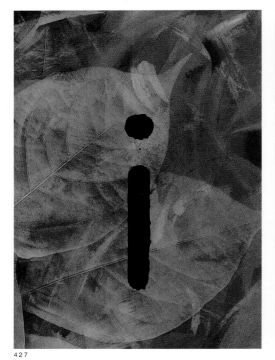

427                               428                               429

■ **429** Art Director: TIM LARSEN Designers: MARK KUNDMANN, MONA MARQUARDT Agency: LARSEN DESIGN OFFICE Client: CORE OF UNDERSTANDING CONFERENCE COMMITTEE Country: USA ■ **429** THIS TWO-COLOR BOOKLET WAS DESIGNED ON THE COMPUTER. OVERLAYS AND MERGING OF IMAGES HEIGHTEN ITS IMPACT. TARGETED AT DESIGN EDUCATORS AND STUDENTS, IT BRINGS TO LIGHT ISSUES EXAMINED AT THE CORE OF UNDERSTANDING CONFERENCE. ● **429** DIESE BROSCHÜRE WURDE MIT DEM COMPUTER HERGESTELLT, WOBEI ÜBERLAGERUNGEN UND VERSCHMELZUNGEN VON BILDERN FÜR SPANNUNG SORGEN. SIE INFORMIERT DESIGN-PROFESSOREN UND STUDENTEN ÜBER EINE KONFERENZ ÜBER DIE ROLLE DES DESIGNS. ▲ **429** CETTE BROCHURE A ÉTÉ RÉALISÉE SUR ORDINATEUR; LES SUPERPOSITIONS ET LES FONDUS D'IMAGES RENFORCENT SON IMPACT. ELLE INFORME LES PROFESSEURS ET LES ÉTUDIANTS DE DESIGN SUR DES CONFÉRENCES CONSACRÉ AU RÔLE DU DESIGN.

■ **430-435** Art Director/Illustrator: ANDY DEARWATER Copywriter: JO ANN STONE Agency: DEARWATER DESIGN Client: ANGLO SHOPPING & TRADING INC. Country: USA ■ **430-435** METAPHORICAL NAUTICAL IMAGES WERE USED IN THIS BROCHURE OF A SHIP BROKER IN ORDER TO ILLUSTRATE HOW VISION AND INDEPENDENCE CAN MEAN GREATER BENEFITS TO CLIENTS. ● **430-435** DIE METAPHORISCHEN BILDER IN DIESER BROSCHÜRE SOLLEN ZEIGEN, DASS VISION UND UNABHÄNGIGKEIT DEN KUNDEN GRÖSSERE VORTEILE BRINGEN. ▲ **430-435** LES IMAGES MÉTAPHORIQUES DE CETTE BROCHURE DOIVENT DÉMONTRER QUE LA VISION ET L'INDÉPENDANCE PEUVENT APPORTER AUX CLIENTS DES AVANTAGES APPRÉCIABLES.

430

Anglo Shipping & Trading is a charter brokerage firm. Based in Houston, our sphere of operations is worldwide. We help producers and traders ship bulk liquid products and gases around the globe; consult on shipping needs; and buy and sell vessels. Clients demand one thing of us: the best deals that can be fixed. Our reputation in the marketplace stems from our track record of making such deals on a consistent basis. We can do this because of our vision, independence, and sensitivity to clients' profit margins.

431

Our business at Anglo Shipping & Trading is about searching for and finding optimum short-term and long-term transportation opportunities, whatever and wherever they may be, and we are aggressive in this pursuit. Our staff is trained to see the complete picture. We know, or we will

VISION

find out, which products are moving, which aren't, and where; where vessels are; who's reliable; who's fair. The value we bring to clients is our ability to look at data freshly and combine it so that these clients achieve their shipping and trading objectives with predictability.

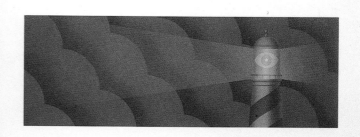

432

As an independent company, Anglo Shipping & Trading has an advantage: We maneuver easily in this business. The benefit to clients is simply this: they come first. The entire international shipping market is at their disposal through us. And we know the market as well as anyone

INDEPENDENCE

in the business. Furthermore, by dealing direct with clients, ship owners, charterers, and brokers, we have everyone's attention. This gives our clients negotiating leverage. Our flexibility also means that we can respond to the unexpected quickly and with much greater control.

433

Trade is about profit. Profit is about margins. And margins can be narrow in shipping and trading markets. So we direct transportation strategies to effect the highest savings and protect client profit margins. Whatever the need — from handling a charter for spot voyages,

PROFIT

day-to-day single shipments, or affreightment contracts, to determining the form of transportation with the least liability, to negotiating vessel purchases and sales — Anglo Shipping & Trading is an extension of our clients, with mutual economic interests and goals.

434

If you aren't already familiar with Anglo Shipping & Trading or would like additional information on our services and experience in this business, we invite your inquiry, 24-hours a day, everyday. We will be more than happy to make a case for how the vision and independence we bring to your projects can positively affect your profitability in the shipping and trading marketplace. You can reach us by phone at

713/623-8544; telex 376-5205; and fax 713/623-8728. Our address is 4600 Post Oak Place, Suite 153, Houston, Texas 77027, U.S.A.

435

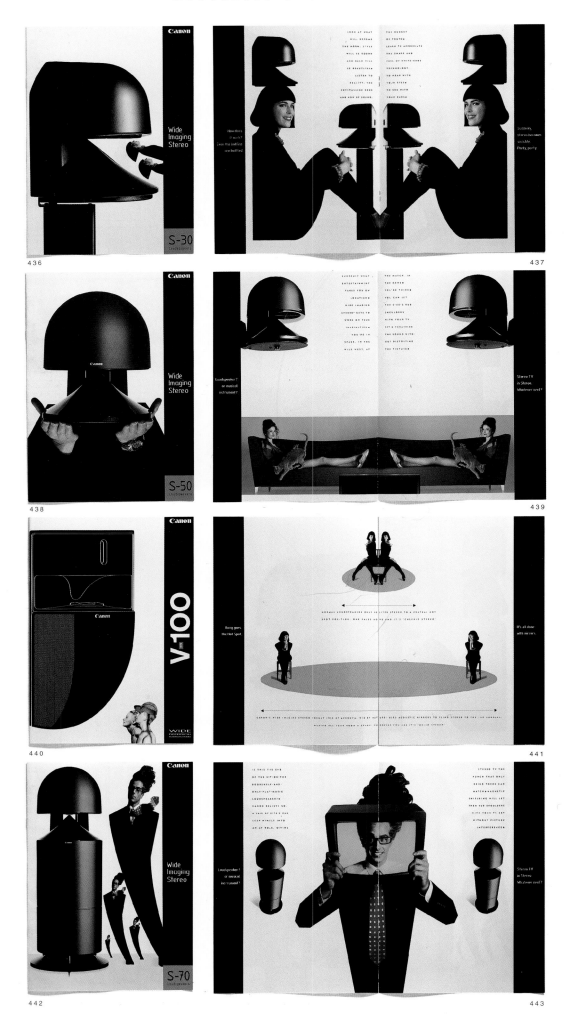

436

437

438

439

440

441

442

443

444

■ 436-443 ART DIRECTOR/DESIGNER: BILL PROCTER PHOTOGRAPHER: JOHN WALLACE ILLUSTRATORS: ANDREJ KLIMOWSKI, DAVID PENNEY AGENCY: BILL PROCTER LTD. CLIENT: CANON AUDIO U.K. COUNTRY: GREAT BRITAIN ■ 436-443 CANON PRODUCT BROCHURES. ● 436-443 UMSCHLÄGE UND DOPPELSEITEN VON CANON-PRODUKTBROSCHÜREN. ▲ 436-443 COUVERTURES ET DOUBLES PAGES DE BROCHURES POUR LES PRODUITS CANON.

■ 444 ART DIRECTOR/DESIGNER: JOHN SAYLES COPYWRITER: DOROTHY ANDERSON STUDIO: SAYLES DESIGN CLIENT: THE ANDERSON FAMILY ■ 444 THIS CUSTOM-MADE BOX AND THE BROCHURE INSIDE WERE DEVELOPED TO COMMEMORATE A FAMILY REUNION. THE BROCHURE COVER IS FROM LEATHER SCRAPS. ● 444 DIESE SCHACHTEL, VON HAND GEMACHT, UND DIE BROSCHÜRE SIND ERINNERUNGEN AN EIN FAMILIENTREFFEN. ▲ 444 CES BOITES FAITES MAIN ET LES BROCHURES QU'ELLES RENFERMENT ONT ÉTÉ CONÇUES EN SOUVENIR D'UNE RÉUNION DE FAMILLE.

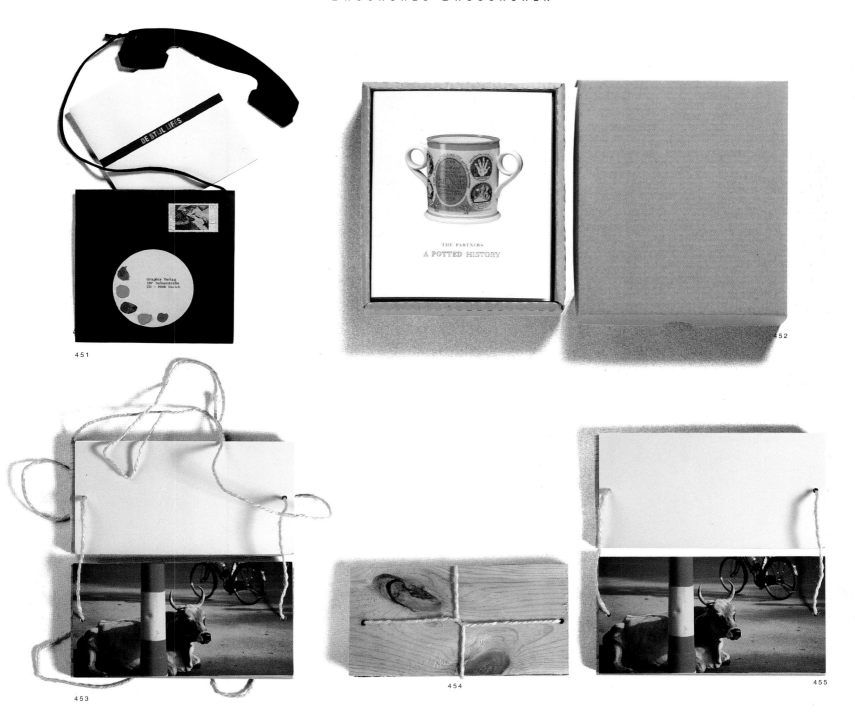

451

452

453

454

455

■ **445-450** ART DIRECTOR: RAPHAEL SENZAMICI PHOTOGRAPHER: RAPHAEL SENZAMICI AGENCY: MANDRILL DESIGNS CLIENT: PIERRE GAGNAIRE COUNTRY: FRANCE ■ **445-450** COVERS FOR THE MENU AND WINE LIST OF A RESTAURANT IN FRANCE. ● **445-450** UMSCHLÄGE FÜR SPEISE- UND WEINKARTEN EINES RESTAURANTS IN FRANKREICH. ▲ **445-450** COUVERTURES DES MENUS ET DE LA CARTE DES VINS D'UN GRAND RESTAURANT.

■ **451** ART DIRECTORS: ROLAND SCHNEIDER, MICHAELA BAUER CLIENT: BAUER'S BÜRO COUNTRY: GERMANY ■ **451** ANNOUNCEMENT OF A CHANGE IN TELEPHONE NUMBER. THE COLORED DOTS ON THE DIAL WERE HAND-PAINTED. ● **451** ANKÜNDIGUNG EINER NEUEN TELEPHONNUMMER. DIE FARBIGEN PUNKTE AUF DER WÄHLSCHEIBE WURDEN VON HAND AUFGEMALT. ▲ **451** ANNONCE D'UN CHANGEMENT DE NUMÉRO DE TÉLÉPHONE.

■ **452** ART DIRECTOR: DAVID STUART DESIGNERS: PETER CARROW, GLEN STONE PHOTOGRAPHER: PETER MARSHALL AGENCY/CLIENT: THE PARTNERS COUNTRY: GREAT BRITAIN ■ **452** YEAR ONE IS PAPER, TWO IS COTTON, NINE IS POTTERY—FOLLOWING THIS OLD CUSTOM, POTTERY WAS THE SUBJECT OF THIS DESIGN STUDIO'S BROCHURE COMMEMORATING NINE YEARS OF BUSINESS. ● **452** EIN JAHR IST PAPIER, ZWEI SIND BAUMWOLLE, NEUN KERAMIK – ENTSPRECHEND DIESEM ALTEN BRAUCH WAR KERAMIK DAS THEMA EINER BROSCHÜRE ZUM NEUNJÄHRIGEN BESTEHEN EINES DESIGNSTUDIOS. ▲ **452** UNE ANNÉE EST SYMBOLISÉE PAR LE PAPIER, DEUX PAR LE COTON, NEUF PAR LA CÉRAMIQUE – CONFORMÉMENT À CETTE TRADITION, LA CÉRAMIQUE ÉTAIT LE SUJET DE CETTE BROCHURE PUBLIÉE À L'OCCASION DU 9E ANNIVERSAIRE D'UN STUDIO DE DESIGN.

■ **453-455** ART DIRECTOR/DESIGNER/PHOTOGRAPHER/CLIENT: JUAN JOSE DIAZ INFANTE COUNTRY: MEXICO ■ **453-455** THIS PORTRAIT OF INDIA SERVED AS SELF-PROMOTION FOR THE DESIGNER. THE BOOK IS BOUND IN WOOD, LIKE THE ORIGINAL SCRIPTURES. ● **453-455** DIESES PORTRÄT INDIENS DIENTE ALS EIGENWERBUNG. DAS BUCH IST WIE DIE ALTEN HEILIGEN BÜCHER IN HOLZ GEBUNDEN. ▲ **453-455** CE PORTRAIT DE L'INDE A ÉTÉ UTILISÉ COMME AUTOPROMOTION D'UN DESIGNER. LE LIVRE EST RELIÉ AVEC DES AIS DE BOIS, COMME LES ANCIENS MANUSCRITS.

# WAAAAAAAAAA!

In case you haven't heard,

Jon & Kathy had a baby.

Hannah Elizabeth Flaming

January 29, 1991

8 lbs. 2 oz.

■ **456** ART DIRECTOR/DESIGNER: JON FLAMING AGENCY: SULLIVAN PERKINS CLIENT: JON & KATHY FLAMING COUNTRY: USA ■ **456** BIRTH ANNOUNCE-
MENT FOR HANNAH FLAMING. ● **456** GEBURTSANZEIGE FÜR HANNAH FLAMING. ▲ **456** ANNONCE DE L'ANNIVERSAIRE DE HANNAH FLAMING.

■ **457** ART DIRECTOR/DESIGNER/ILLUSTRATOR: CRAIG STEWART JACKSON CLIENTS: KATHY HOPPS, TOM GRACE COUNTRY: USA ■ **457** SINCE THE
BABY'S FATHER IS INVOLVED WITH ARCHITECTURE, THE BIRTH ANNOUNCEMENT WAS FASHIONED LIKE A BLUE-PRINT, WITH PHYSICAL ATTRIBUT-
ES WRITTEN AS ARCHITECT'S NOTES. "SITE INSPECTIONS WELCOME." ● **457** DIE GEBURTSANZEIGE WURDE WIE EINE BLAUPAUSE HERGESTELLT,
WEIL DER VATER DES BABYS MIT ARCHITEKTUR ZU TUN HAT. ALLE ANGABEN ÜBER DAS BABY SIND ENTSPRECHEND FORMULIERT UND DARGE-
STELLT. «BESICHTIGUNG WILLKOMMEN». ▲ **457** CE FAIRE-PART DE NAISSANCE A ÉTÉ CONÇU COMME UN BLEU, LE PÈRE DE L'ENFANT TRA-
VAILLANT DANS LE SECTEUR DE L'ARCHITECTURE; LA DESCRIPTION DU BÉBÉ Y A ÉTÉ INSCRITE À LA MANIÈRE DES NOTES D'UN ARCHITECTE.

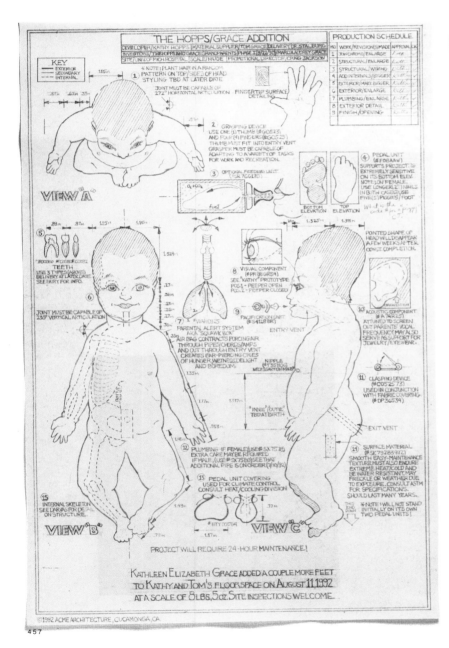

457

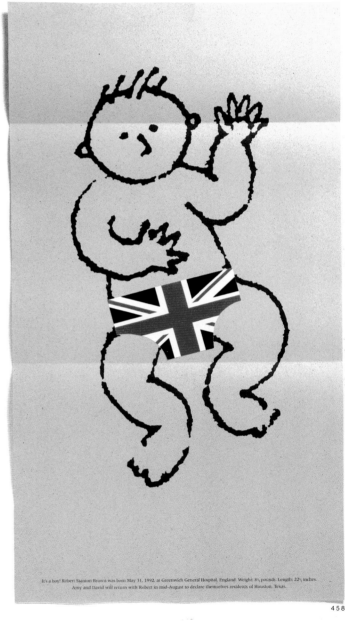

458

■ **458** ART DIRECTOR/DESIGNER/ILLUSTRATOR: ROB WILSON AGENCY: SULLIVAN PERKINS CLIENT: AMY & DAVID DAVIS COUNTRY: USA ■ **458** THIS BIRTH
ANNOUNCEMENT SERVES SIMULTANEOUSLY AS A CHANGE-OF-ADDRESS ANNOUNCEMENT FOR THE PARENTS WHO WERE RETURNING TO
HOUSTON FROM GREAT BRITAIN. COLOR COPIES WERE APPLIED TO THE ONE-COLOR PRINT. ● **458** DIESE GEBURTSANZEIGE KÜNDIGT GLEICH-
ZEITIG DIE RÜCKKEHR DER ELTERN VON ENGLAND NACH USA AN. ▲ **458** CE FAIRE-PART DE NAISSANCE ANNONCE EN MÊME TEMPS LE RETOUR
DES PARENTS AUX USA APRÈS UN SÉJOUR EN ANGLETERRE. DES COPIES COULEURS ONT ÉTÉ COLLÉES SUR L'IMPRIMÉ À UNE COULEUR.

■ **459** ART DIRECTOR: MICHAEL GERBINO DESIGNER: THOMAS BUTERA CLIENT: MICHAEL GERBINO DESIGNS COUNTRY: USA ■ **459** THE TRAIN IN THIS ANNOUNCEMENT SYMBOLIZES NOT ONLY THE MOVING TO A NEW ADDRESS, BUT ALSO THE FACT THAT THE NEW ADDRESS IS RIGHT NEAR NEW YORK'S MAJOR TRAIN DEPOT. ● **459** DER ZUG IN DIESER UMZUGSANZEIGE SYMBOLISIERT NICHT NUR DEN UMZUG, SONDERN AUCH DIE NEUE ADRESSE IN DER NÄHE DES ZUGDEPOTS VON NEW YORK. ▲ **459** SUR CETTE ANNONCE DE DÉMÉNAGEMENT, LE TRAIN NE SYMBOLISE PAS SEULEMENT LE DÉPLACEMENT, IL SIGNALE ÉGALEMENT QUE LA NOUVELLE ADRESSE EST SITUÉE À PROXIMITÉ DU DÉPÔT FERROVIAIRE DE NEW YORK.

■ **460, 461** DESIGNER: LAUREN SMITH CLIENT: LAUREN SMITH DESIGN COUNTRY: USA ■ **460, 461** PACKING MATERIAL WAS USED FOR THIS MOVING ANNOUNCEMENT. ● **460, 461** «DIE HOHE MIETE HAT UNS VERANLASST ZU PACKEN.» UMZUGSANZEIGE NUR AUS VERPACKUNGSMATERIAL ▲ **460, 461** «LE LOYER ÉLEVÉ NOUS A OBLIGÉ À FAIRE NOS VALISES.» ANNONCE DE DÉMÉNAGEMENT. ON N'A UTILISÉ QUE DU MATÉRIEL D'EMBALLAGE.

460

461

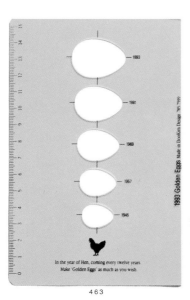

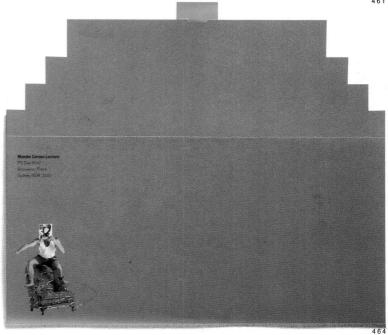

462

463

464

■ **462, 463** ART DIRECTOR: DOO HWANG KIM DESIGNERS: DONGIL LEE, LIWON SHIN CLIENT: DOO KIM DESIGN COUNTRY: SOUTH KOREA ■ **462, 463** A STUDIO'S GREETING CARD FOR 1993, THE YEAR OF THE CHICKEN, WHICH COMES AROUND EVERY TWELVE YEARS. ● **462, 463** DIE NEUJAHRSKARTE EINES DESIGN STUDIOS IM JAHR DES HUHNS (1993), DAS ALLE ZWÖLF JAHRE STATTFINDET. ▲ **462, 463** LA CARTE DE VŒUX D'UN STUDIO DE DESIGN POUR LE NOUVEL AN 1993, QUI SE SITUE SOUS LE SIGNE DU COQ, SELON UN CYCLE QUI SE RENOUVELLE TOUS LES DOUZE ANS.

■ **464** ART DIRECTOR/DESIGNER: ANNE SHACKMAN PHOTOGRAPHER: PAUL HENDERSON-KELLY STUDIO: ANNE SHACKMAN DESIGN CLIENT: MAMBO CARSON LECTURE COUNTRY: AUSTRALIA ■ **464** OUTSIDE OF AN INVITATION TO A LECTURE BY AMERICAN DESIGNER DAVID CARSON. UNFOLDED, THIS ENVELOPE BECOMES A SMALL POSTER. ● **464** AUSSENSEITE EINER EINLADUNG ZU EINEM VORTRAG DES AMERIKANISCHEN DESIGNERS DAVID CARSON. AUSEINANDERGEFALTET WIRD DIESES COUVERT ZU EINEM KLEINEN PLAKAT. ▲ **464** PAGE EXTÉRIEURE D'UNE INVITATION À UNE CONFÉRENCE DU DESIGNER AMÉRICAIN DAVID CARSON. UNE FOIS DÉPLOYÉE, CETTE ENVELOPPE SE TRANSFORME EN PETITE AFFICHE.

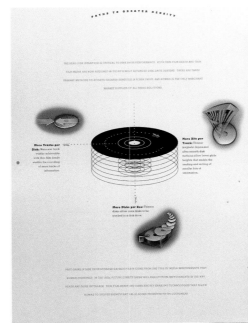

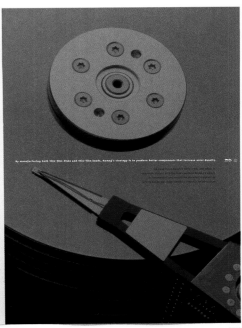

465

466

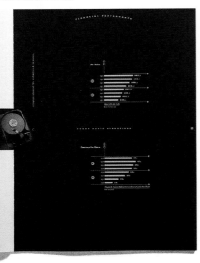

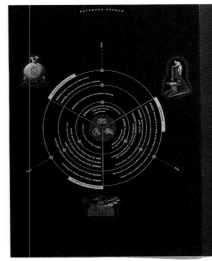

467

468

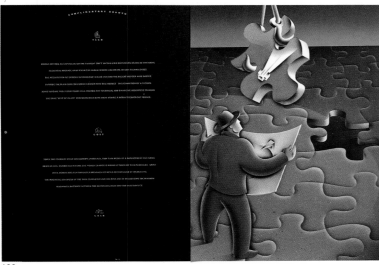

469

470

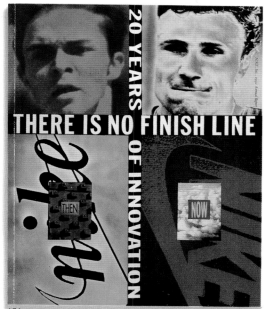

471

472

473

474

■ 465-470 ART DIRECTOR: STEVE TOLLESON DESIGNERS: STEVE TOLLESON, MARK WINN PHOTOGRAPHER: LUIS DELGADO ILLUSTRATOR: JEFF KOEGEL AGENCY: TOLLESON DESIGN CLIENT: KOMAG COUNTRY: USA ■ 465-470 THE 1991 ANNUAL REPORT FOR KOMAG, A MANUFACTURER OF THIN FILM DISKS AND HEADS IN THE FIELD OF MEDIA TECHNOLOGY. ● 465-470 UMSCHLAG UND DOPPELSEITEN AUS DEM JAHRESBERICHT 1991 DER FIRMA KOMAG, HERSTELLER VON DÜNNEN PLATTEN UND TONKÖPFEN IM BEREICH DER MEDIENTECHNOLOGIE. ▲ 465-470 LE RAPPORT ANNUEL 1991 DE LA FIRME KOMAG, FABRICANT DE DISQUES EXTRA-PLATS ET DE TÊTES DE MAGNÉTOPHONES, SPÉCIALISTE DES MÉDIAS DE HAUTE TECHNOLOGIE.

■ 471-474 ART DIRECTOR/DESIGNER: ANN SCHWIEBINGER-MAYER PHOTOGRAPHERS AND PHOTO ILLUSTRATORS: VARIOUS ILLUSTRATOR: JOEL NAKAMURA COPYWRITER: BOB LAMBIE AGENCY: NIKE DESIGN CLIENT: NIKE INC. COUNTRY: USA ■ 471-474 COVERS AND SPREADS FROM THE 1992 NIKE ANNUAL REPORT, CELEBRATING THE FIRM'S 20 YEARS OF EXISTENCE. ● 471-474 DER JAHRESBERICHT 1992 FÜR NIKE ZELEBRIERT DAS ZWANZIG-JÄHRIGE BESTEHEN DES UNTERNEHMENS. ▲ 471-474 LE RAPPORT ANNUEL 1992 DE NIKE CÉLÉBRAIT LE 20E ANNIVERSAIRE DE L'ENTREPRISE.

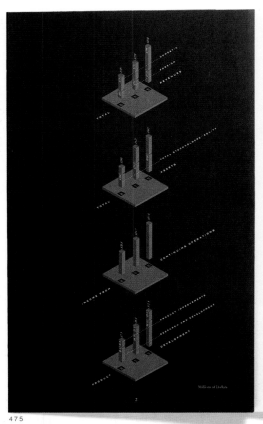

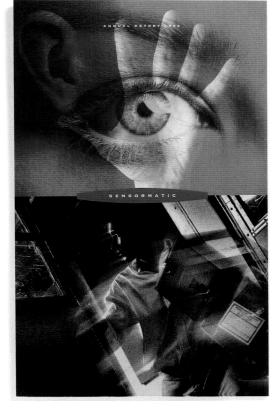

475

476

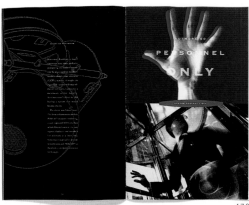

477

478

479

■ **475-479** ART DIRECTOR: NORM LEE DESIGNER: GREG SAMATA PHOTOGRAPHER: MARC NORBERG ILLUSTRATOR: PAUL THOMPSON COPYWRITER: JON LUKOMNIK AGENCY: SAMATA ASSOC. CLIENT: SENSORMATIC ELECTRONICS COUNTRY: USA ■ 475-479 THE 1992 ANNUAL REPORT OF SENSORMATIC, A COMPANY PRODUCING ELECTRONIC SURVEILLANCE SYSTEMS. ● 475-479 DER JAHRESBERICHT 1992 FÜR SENSORMATIC, HERSTELLER VON ELEKTRONISCHEN ÜBERWACHUNGSSYSTEMEN. ▲ 475-479 LE RAPPORT ANNUEL 1992 DE SENSORMATIC, UN FABRICANT DE SYSTÈMES DE SURVEILLANCE.

EDITORIAL

REDAKTIONELL

RÉDACTIONNEL

# COMPUTER KIDS

Sie lernen mit dem Joystick spielen, bevor sie richtig gehen können; sie programmieren, ohne das Buchstabieren schon perfekt zu beherrschen; sie verlieren sich in den bunten Räumen des Bildschirms und wissen noch nicht viel über die Stolpersteine des Lebens. In die Welt der Kinder gehört der Computer wie einst die elektrische Eisenbahn, der Teddybär aus Plüsch und der Legoquader.

Von Hans-Heinrich Pardey
Fotos: Max Aguilera-Hellweg

# COMPUTER KIDS

---

## WER HALT SUCHT, FINDET IHN

## WER DIE MITTE SUCHT, FOLGT DEM GÜRTEL

Von Ingrid Heinrich-Jost   Fotos: Susan Lamér

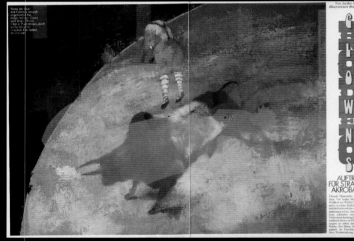

---

### TUCH FÜR SCHWEISS UND TRÄNEN
Von Hans A. Neunzig
Illustrationen: Heinz Edelmann

# GOODWINGS

## AUFTRITT FÜR STRAMME AKROBATEN

Von Jordan Mejias
Illustrationen: Brad Holland

---

# MATTEO THUN

Von Wolfgang Nagel

Fotos: Albrecht Fuchs

# MATTEO THUN

■ **480-487** ART DIRECTOR/DESIGNER: HANS-GEORG POSPISCHIL PHOTOGRAPHERS: MAX AGUILERA-HELLWEG (480, 481), SUSAN LAMÈR (482, 483), ALBRECHT FUCHS (486, 487) ILLUSTRATORS: HEINZ EDELMANN (484), BRAD HOLLAND (485) PUBLISHER: *FRANKFURTER ALLGEMEINE ZEITUNG* COUNTRY: GERMANY ■ **480-487** SPREADS FROM VARIOUS ISSUES OF THE *FRANKFURTER ALLGEMEINE MAGAZIN*. THE SUBJECTS: COMPUTER KIDS, FASHION, HANDKERCHIEFS, RODEO CLOWNS, INDUSTRIAL DESIGNER MATHEO THUN. ● **480-487** DOPPELSEITEN AUS VERSCHIEDENEN AUSGABEN DES *FRANKFURTER ALLGEMEINE MAGAZINS*. DIE THEMEN: COMPUTER KIDS, MODE, TASCHENTÜCHER, RODEO-CLOWNS, DER INDUSTRIE-DESIGN-ER MATHEO THUN. ▲ **480-487** DOUBLES PAGES DE DIVERS NUMÉROS DU *FRANKFURTER ALLGEMEINE MAGAZIN*. LES SUJETS: LES NOUVELLES GÉNÉRATIONS DE L'ÈRE INFORMATIQUE, LA MODE, LES MOUCHOIRS, LES CLOWNS DES RODÉOS, LE DESIGNER INDUSTRIEL MATHEO THUN.

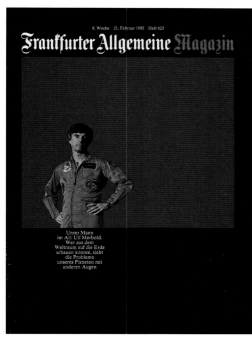

488

489

490

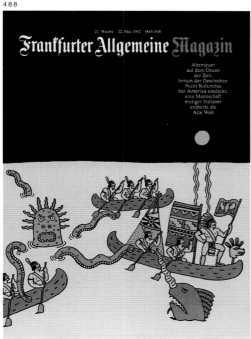

491

492

493

■ **488-493** ART DIRECTOR/DESIGNER: HANS-GEORG POSPISCHIL PHOTOGRAPHERS: WOLFGANG WESENER (488), LILIAN BIRNBAUM (489), SUSAN LAMÈR (492) ILLUSTRATOR: SEYMOUR CHWAST (490, 491, 493), PUBLISHER: *FRANKFURTER ALLGEMEINE MAGAZIN* COUNTRY: GERMANY ■ **488-493** VARIOUS COVERS OF THE *FRANKFURTER ALLGEMEINE MAGAZIN*. ● **488-493** UMSCHLÄGE DES *FAZ* MAGAZINS. ▲ **488-493** COUVERTURES DU *FAZ*-MAGAZIN.

A D

*Jornal de Arte Publicitária,*
*Design & Fotografia A&nD / 19*

As Melhores Fotos do Anos 80' / Fotografia nos Comerciais
/ O Diretor de Arte do Ano / A Publicidade Inglesa/ One Show

494

495

496

■ **494-496** Art Director/Designer: Oswaldo Miranda Photographers: Tyen (494), Kazumi Kurigami (495) Klaus Mitteldorf (496) Agency: Casa de Idéias Client: Inpacel Country: Brazil ■ 494-496 covers of *A&DD*, a journal on advertising and photography. The principal themes of the issues in question: body in motion, cosmetics and perfumes, fashion. ● 494-496 Umschläge von *A&DD*, eine brasilianische Zeitschrift über Werbung und Photographie. Die Hauptthemen der betreffenden Ausgaben: der Körper in Bewegung, Kosmetik und Parfums, Mode. ▲ 494-496 couvertures de *A&DD*, un magazine sur la publicité et la photographie. Les thèmes abordés dans ces numéros étaient les suivants: le corps en mouvement, les cosmétiques et les parfums, la mode.

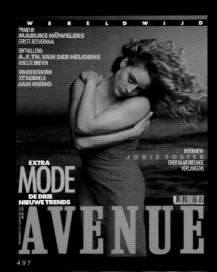

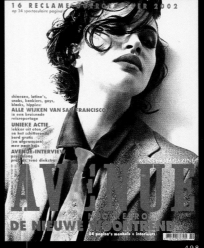

497

498

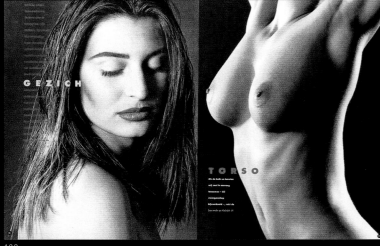

499

500

501

502

## TUSSEN KNOKKE EN DE PANNE VERZUIPT
# BELGIE ZIJN VERDRIET

Met lingerie van Fleur en een jasje van Féraud meedoen aan het paringsritueel bij Charly's. Na de alcoholvrije cocktail bij Majestic lang tafelen bij l'Aquilon of, très entre nous, bij taveerne The Caddie. Ten slotte een beschaafd dansje bij Number 1 of een gokje aan de speeltafel. Portret van de Belgische kust, waar het verval voortschrijdt maar de horeca nog ouderwets van wanten weet. "Glaasje bubbeltjes tussendoor, manneke?"

TEKST IVO WEYEL/FOTOGRAFIE THEO BAART

De Panne: dit is niet wat het schijnt, en zelfs geen rollerskatebaan, maar het winnende ontwerp in een wedstrijd waarbij het erom giag voor de aaneengeschakelde cabines van Rode Kruis- en andere strandhulptroepen een oorspronkelijke vormgeving te bedenken.

503

■ 497-503 ART DIRECTOR/DESIGNER: HANS VAN BLOMMESTEIN PHOTOGRAPHERS: ANNIE LEIBOVITZ (495), BART VAN LEEUWEN (496) ANNA BEEKE (497, 500) BRUNO PEETERS (501) CHARLES VAN HOORICK (502) THEO BAART (503) PUBLISHER: DE GEILLUSTREERDE PERS BV CLIENT: AVENUE COUNTRY: NETHERLANDS ■ 497-503 COVERS AND SPREADS FROM AVENUE: ACTRESS AND FILM DIRECTOR JODIE FOSTER, FASHION INSPIRED BY THE PEOPLE'S REPUBLIC OF CHINA, BEAUTY IN SUMMER, CLAUDIA SCHIFFER IN CHANEL, THE VAMP TYPE OF WOMAN (IN CONNECTION WITH A BEAUTY FEATURE), BELGIUM. ● 497-503 UMSCHLÄGE UND DOPPELSEITEN AUS AVENUE: JODIE FOSTER, SCHAUSPIELERIN UND REGISSEURIN, MODEEINFLÜSSE AUS CHINA, SCHÖNHEIT IM SOMMER, CLAUDIA SCHIFFER IN CHANEL, FRAUENTYP VAMP (EIN SCHÖNHEITSBEITRAG), BELGIEN. ▲ 497-503 COUVERTURES ET DOUBLES PAGES DU MAGAZINE AVENUE: L'ACTRICE ET RÉALISATRICE JODIE FOSTER; LA MODE INSPIRÉE PAR LA CHINE; LA BEAUTÉ EN ÉTÉ; CLAUDIA SCHIFFER EN CHANEL; LE TYPE DE FEMME VAMP (EN RELATION AVEC UN ARTICLE DE BEAUTÉ); LA BELGIQUE.

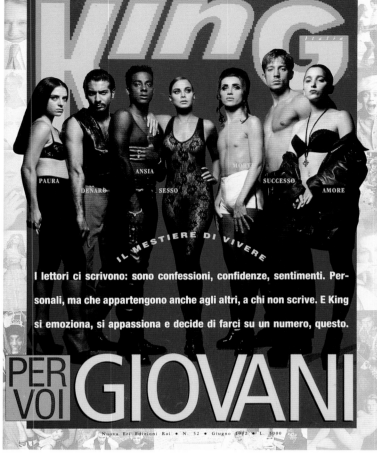

504

505

506

507

508

■ **504-507** Art Director: MARIAPIA COPPIN Photographers: GERRY GAVIGAN (504), MICHEL COMTE (505), GIUSEPPE PINO (506), SHAHRAM SANAI (507) Publisher: NUOVA ERI EDIZIONI RAI Country: ITALY ■ **504-507** COVERS OF ITALIAN MAGAZINE *KING*: ACTOR ANTHONY HOPKINS, READERS OF *KING* MAGAZINE, "IT IS FORBIDDEN FOR MINORS TO BE AS STUPID AS THE GROWN-UPS," "AFTER THE YEARS OF CONFORMISM, HERE COME THE REBELS." ● **504-507** UMSCHLÄGE VON *KING*: DER SCHAUSPIELER ANTHONY HOPKINS; LESER DES MAGAZINS; «ES IST MINDER-JÄHRIGEN VERBOTEN, SO DUMM WIE DIE ERWACHSENEN ZU SEIN»; «NACH JAHREN DES KONFORMISMUS KOMMEN JETZT DIE REBELLEN.» ▲ **504-507** COUVERTURES DU MAGAZINE ITALIEN *KING*: L'ACTEUR ANTHONY HOPKINS, LECTEUR DE CE MAGAZINE; «INTERDIT AUX MINEURS» – IL EST INTERDIT AUX MINEURS D'ÊTRE AUSSI STUPIDES QUE LES ADULTES; «APRÈS DES ANNÉES DE CONFORMISME, PLACE AUX REBELLES».

■ **508** Art Director/Designer: OSWALDO MIRANDA Photographer: JEAN-PAUL GOUDE Agency: CASA DE IDÉIAS Publisher: INPACEL Country: BRAZIL ■ **508** COVER OF *GRAFICA* WITH A PORTRAIT OF GRACE JONES. ● **508** UMSCHLAG VON *GRAFICA* MIT EINEM PORTRÄT DER AMERIKANI-SCHEN SÄNGERIN GRACE JONES. ▲ **508** UN PORTRAIT DE LA CHANTEUSE AMÉRICAINE GRACE JONES EN COUVERTURE DU MAGAZINE *GRAFICA*.

509

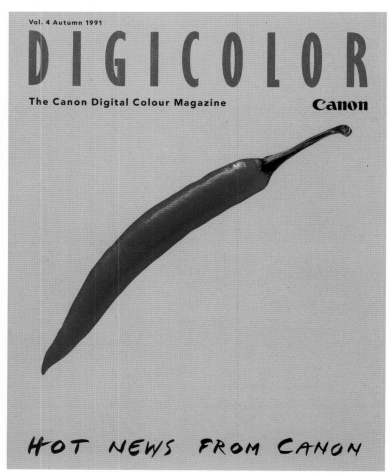

510

■ **509, 510** ART DIRECTOR/DESIGNER: HENNY VAN ECK AGENCY: VAN ECK & VERDIJK PUBLISHER: GRAFISCH VORMGEVERS CLIENT: CANON EUROPE COUNTRY: ■ **509, 510** THE CANON DIGITAL COLOR MAGAZINE IS MEANT FOR PRESENT AND POTENTIAL FUTURE USERS OF CANON COLOR PRODUCTS. ● **509, 510** DAS CANON-MAGAZIN ÜBER DIGITALFARBEN RICHTET SICH AN GEGENWÄRTIGE UND ZUKÜNFTIGE VERWENDER VON CANON-FARBPRODUKTEN. ▲ **509, 510** COUVERTURES DE DEUX NUMÉROS DU MAGAZINE CANON QUI EST CONSACRÉ AUX COULEURS DIGITALISÉS.

■ **511, 512** ART DIRECTOR: HERMAN DYAL DESIGNERS: HERMAN DYAL, SUSAN MCINTYRE AGENCY: FULLER DYAL & STAMPER PUBLISHER: CONTEMPORARY ART MUSEUM COUNTRY: USA ■ **511, 512** COVERS OF *CAM NEWS*, THE NEWSLETTER OF THE CONTEMPORARY ARTS MUSEUM OF HOUSTON. ● **511, 512** UMSCHLÄGE VON *CAM NEWS*, DEM VIERTELJÄHRLICHEN MITTEILUNGSBLATT DES MUSEUMS FÜR ZEITGENÖSSISCHE KUNST IN HOUSTON, TEXAS. ▲ **511, 512** COUVERTURES DE *CAM NEWS*, LE BULLETIN D'INFORMATION DU MUSÉE D'ART MODERNE DE HOUSTON, TEXAS.

fields

O

dreams

Fancy-free. Embroidered (Lesage) gold lamé (Vergé) gown with gold lace (Marescot) lining, Christian Dior.

SHAPE

For Evening, Designers Are Taking Shape Into Bold New Territory.

Opposite page: Black taffeta gown with "dome" skirt,

about $8,460, by Valentino. LaCrasia velvet gloves.

Q

fall's refined appeal

uiet luxury, considered line, beautiful fabrics: These are the qualities that epitomize the new elegance that underlies fall's flashier changes. These are clothes beyond the seasonal vagaries of fashion, yet within their timeless appeal show real, substantive changes that are absolutely of the moment. A sweeping black evening dress that bares only the shoulders in a statement of subtle exposure. A soft gray cashmere worn with matching trousers, in a completely original variation on the suit. "Elegance is understatement," says Calvin Klein. "The woman should stand out, the clothes should not overtake her." There's an integrity of design that allows these pieces to stand on their own. They don't need the glittery camouflage of a wristful of bracelets or strands of necklaces to look finished. "That ethic of jeweled, faxed, scalloped, and tiered is just not in my world anymore," says Isaac Mizrahi. "Now a scent, a defined eyebrow, is all you need." Impeccable in balance, cut, and proportion, these are the clothes that, by virtue of their practicality, their lack of pretension, are the foundation of a great wardrobe. A new grace comes to evening. Opposite page: Black viscose/Lycra turtleneck, drop-waist dress, about $1,375, by Donna Karan.

516                                                                                                                                        517

■ **513–515** CREATIVE DIRECTOR: FABIEN BARON ART DIRECTOR: JOEL BERG DESIGNER: JOHN SVENSSON PHOTOGRAPHERS: FRANCOIS HALARD (513),
MARIO TESTINO (514), PATRICK DEMARCHELIER (515) CLIENT: *HARPER'S BAZAAR* PUBLISHER: CARL PORTALE COUNTRY: USA ■ **513–515** SPREADS
FROM A FASHION FEATURE IN *HARPER'S BAZAAR*. ● **513–515** DOPPELSEITEN AUS EINEM MODEBEITRAG IN DER AMERIKANISCHEN AUSGABE VON
*HARPER'S BAZAAR*. ▲ **513–515** DOUBLES PAGES TIRÉES D'UN ARTICLE DE MODE PARU DANS L'EDITION AMÉRICAINE DE *HARPER'S BAZAAR*.

■ **516, 517** ART DIRECTOR: AGNÈS CRUZ DESIGNERS: AGNÈS CRUZ, VIRGINIO BRUNI TEDESCHI PHOTOGRAPHER: ANNIE LEIBOVITZ (517) PUBLISHER:
L'AUTRE JOURNAL COUNTRY: FRANCE ■ **516, 517** COVERS OF A MONTHLY MAGAZINE. AT LEFT: "WHAT'S NEW?"; AT RIGHT MAGIC JOHNSON. ●
**516, 517** UMSCHLÄGE EINES MONATSMAGAZINS. LINKS: »WAS GIBT'S NEUES?«, RECHTS MAGIC JOHNSON. ▲ **516, 517** DEUX COUVERTURES D'UN
MAGAZINE MENSUEL QUI ABORDE LES QUESTIONS D'ACTUALITÉ OU PRÉSENTE DES PERSONNALITÉS DANS UNE PERSPECTIVE NOUVELLE.

# ICE

THE ROLLING STONE INTERVIEW BY ALAN LIGHT

# T O M
# Cruise

*by* PATRICK GOLDSTEIN

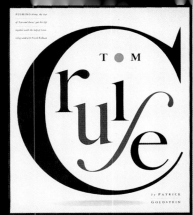

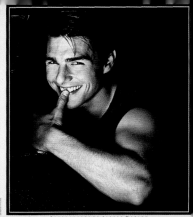

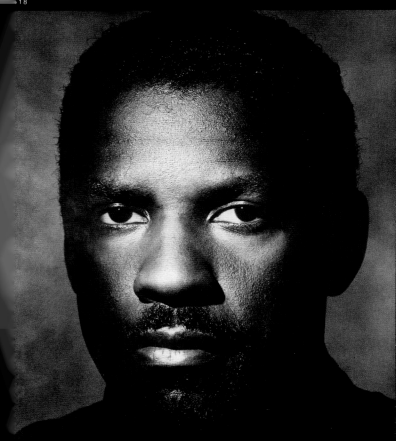

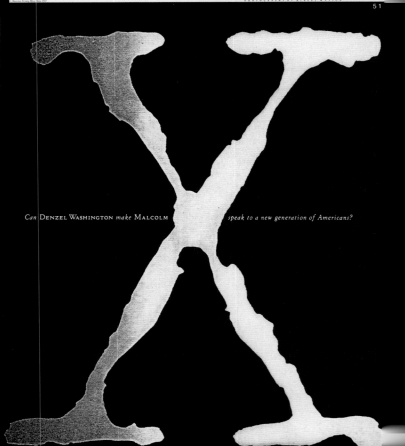

*Can* DENZEL WASHINGTON *make* MALCOLM X *speak to a new generation of Americans?*

# Clint
# EASTWOOD

THE ROLLING STONE
INTERVIEW
BY DAVID BRESKIN

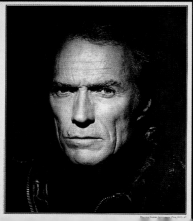

# David
# CRONENBERG

THE · ROLLING · STONE
· I N T E R V I E W ·
BY · DAVID · BRESKIN

**Yo-Yo, Vanessa Williams, Janet Jackson,**

# RollingStone

Cypress Hill's B-Real & Others Speak Out

L.A. BURNING: Ice-T, Jody Watley

**RED HOT CHILI PEPPERS**

The Black Crowes, Lindsey Buckingham

523

**1967 1992**

# RollingStone

AXL ROSE
SPRINGSTEEN
MADONNA
LED ZEPPELIN
CLAPTON
BONNIE RAITT
McCARTNEY
MICHAEL STIPE
ZAGGER
RICHARDS
NEIL YOUNG
DYLAN
RAY CHARLES
LENNON
LITTLE RICHARD
TOWNSHEND
BRIAN WILSON
STING
DON HENLEY
MORRISON
PHIL SPECTOR
BOWIE
JAMES TAYLOR
GARCIA
JONI MITCHELL
BILLY JOEL
ROY ORBISON
ICE-T

## XX

**THE INTERVIEWS**

524

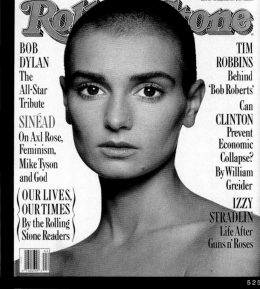

# Rolling Stone

BOB DYLAN
The All-Star Tribute

SINÉAD
On Axl Rose, Feminism, Mike Tyson and God

OUR LIVES, OUR TIMES
By the Rolling Stone Readers

TIM ROBBINS
Behind 'Bob Roberts'

Can CLINTON Prevent Economic Collapse?
By William Greider

IZZY STRADLIN
Life After Guns n' Roses

525

# Rolling Stone

HOT 1992
Starring SHARON STONE

with
TEENAGE FANCLUB
BRAD PITT
JULIETTE LEWIS
PM DAWN

526

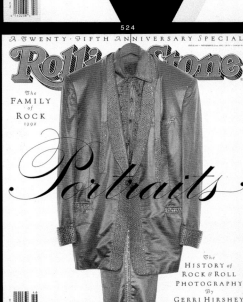

# Rolling Stone

The FAMILY of ROCK 1992

*Portraits*

THE HISTORY of ROCK & ROLL PHOTOGRAPHY By GERRI HIRSHEY

527

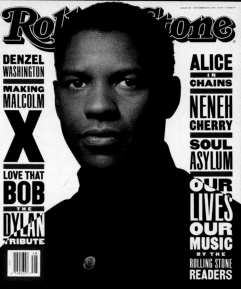

# Rolling Stone

DENZEL WASHINGTON
MAKING MALCOLM X

LOVE THAT BOB
THE DYLAN TRIBUTE

ALICE IN CHAINS
NENEH CHERRY
SOUL ASYLUM

OUR LIVES OUR MUSIC
BY THE ROLLING STONE READERS

528

# JIMI

*The Man and the Music*

Photographs by Herb Ritts

THE *Bats*

AS IT WAS LAID OUT in her fat, annotated script, Michelle Pfeiffer's first day before the camera as Cat-woman looked to be an easy one. She just had to stand silhouetted in the frame and deliver one line:

Catwoman Michelle Pfeiffer · By Gerri Hirshey

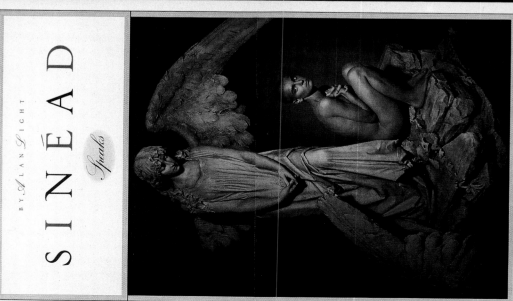

BY ALAN LIGHT

# SINÉAD *Speaks*

■ (PREVIOUS SPREAD) **518-528** ART DIRECTOR: FRED WOODWARD DESIGNERS: DEBRA BISHOP (518), FRED WOODWARD (519, 521, 522, 523-528), GAIL ANDERSON (520) PHOTOGRAPHERS: MARK SELIGER (518, 523), ALBERT WATSON (519, 520, 521, 522, 525, 526-528), DIRECTOR OF PHOTOGRAPHY: LAURIE KRATOCHVIL PUBLISHER: STRAIGHT ARROW PUBLISHERS COUNTRY: USA ■ **518-528** SPREADS AND COVERS FROM *ROLLING STONE*: ICE T WHO BECAME NOTORIOUS FOR HIS SONG "COP KILLER"; ACTOR TOM CRUISE, A FILM ON MALCOLM X, CLINT EASTWOOD, WHOSE PORTRAIT IS PAINTED ON A HUGE SCREEN AT EURO DISNEY; FILM DIRECTOR DAVID CRONENBERG. ● (VORANGEHENDE DOPPELSEITE) **518-528** DOPPELSEITEN UND UMSCHLÄGE AUS DER ZEITSCHRIFT *ROLLING STONE*: ICE T, DESSEN SONG «COP KILLER» ZUM SKANDAL WURDE; SCHAU-SPIELER TOM CRUISE; EIN FILM ÜBER MALCOM X; CLINT EASTWOOD, DESSEN PORTRÄT AUF EINER RIESENLEINWAND IM EURO DISNEY PRANGT;

532

FILMREGISSEUR DAVID CRONENBERG. ▲ **518-528** (DOUBLE PAGE PRÉCÉDENTE) QUELQUES EXEMPLES DE DOUBLES PAGES ET COUVERTURES DU MAGAZINE *ROLLING STONE*: ICE T, DONT LA CHANSON «COP KILLER» A FAIT SCANDALE; L'ACTEUR TOM CRUISE; LE FILM SUR MALCOM X; ACTEUR CLINT EASTWOOD DONT LE PORTRAIT, PEINT SUR PANNEAU GÉANT, DÉCORE EURO DISNEY; LE RÉALISATEUR DAVID CRONENBERG.

■ **529-532** ART DIRECTOR: FRED WOODWARD DESIGNERS: CATHERINE GILMORE-BARNES(529), FRED WOODWARD(530), ANGELA SKOURAS (531) PHO-TOGRAPHERS: GERED MANKOWITZ (529), HERB RITTS (530, 532), ALBERT WATSON (531) DIRECTOR OF PHOTOGRAPHY: LAURIE KRATOCHVIL PUB-LISHER: STRAIGHT ARROW PUBLISHERS COUNTRY: USA ■ **529-532** SPREADS AND COVER OF *ROLLING STONE*: THE JIMI HENDRIX STORY; CAT-WOMAN MICHELLE PFEIFFER, AN INTERVIEW WITH SINÉAD O'CONNOR; BATMAN. ● **529-532** SEITEN UND UMSCHLAG VON *ROLLING STONE*: DIE JIMI-HENDRIX-STORY; KATZENFRAU MICHELLE PFEIFFER; EIN INTERVIEW MIT SINÉAD O'CONNOR; BATMAN. ▲ **529-532** DOUBLES PAGES ET UNE COUVERTURE DE *ROLLING STONE*: JIMI HENDRIX; MICHELLE PFEIFFER, LA FEMME-CHAT; UNE INTERVIEW DE SINÉAD O'CONNOR; BATMAN.

■ 533-535 ART DIRECTOR/DESIGNER: CLAUDE MAGGIORI DESIGNERS: MARTIN FONQUERNIE (533), CLAUDE MAGGIORI (534, 535) PHOTOGRAPHERS: PATRICE LOIEZ (533), ALAIN GUILLOU (535) AGENCY: EDITORIAL PUBLISHER: *LIBÉRATION* COUNTRY: FRANCE ■ 533-535 COVERS OF FRENCH MAGAZINE *LIBÉRATION*. THE SPECIAL ISSUES ARE ON SCIENTIFIC ISSUES, THE RUSSIAN REVOLUTION AND SAILING. ● 533-535 UMSCHLÄGE DER FRANZÖSISCHEN ZEITSCHRIFT *LIBÉRATION*. SPEZIALTHEMEN: WISSENSCHAFT, DIE RUSSISCHE REVOLUTION, SEGELN. ▲ 533-535 COUVERTURES DE HORS-SÉRIE DE *LIBÉRATION*: UN NUMÉRO CONSACRÉ AUX INFORMATIONS SCIENTIFIQUES, LES ÉVÉNEMENTS DE RUSSIE, LES VOILIERS.

533

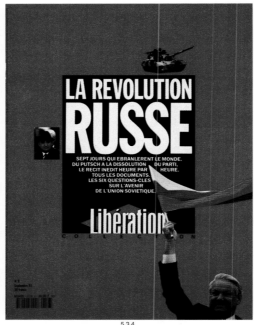

534

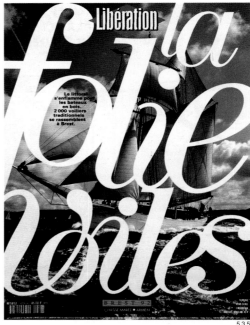

535

■ 536-542 ART DIRECTORS: KARL LEHMANN-HAUPT, NANCY COHEN PHOTOGRAPHERS: DAVID STETSON (536), VITRA MUSEUM (537, 540) KRISTINE LARSEN (538), TIM STREET-PORTER (541), WYATT TROLL (542) PUBLISHER: BELLEROPHON PUBLICATIONS, INC. COUNTRY: USA ■ 536-542 SPREADS AND COVERS OF *METROPOLIS* MAGAZINE: RARE, EXQUISITE TEXTILES BY JUNICHI ARAI; CZECH CUBISM; JULY/AUGUST COVER; CZECH CUBISM; FRANK GEHRY; ARCHITECT RICHARD NEUTRA. ● 536-542 DOPPELSEITEN UND UMSCHLÄGE VON *METROPOLIS*: UNGEWÖHNLICHE, EXQUISITE TEXTILIEN VON JUNICHI ARAI, TSCHECHISCHER KUBISMUS, DIE JULI/AUGUST AUSGABE, TSCHECHISCHER KUBISMUS, FRANK GEHRY, ARCHITECT RICHARD NEUTRA. ▲ 536-542 DOUBLES PAGES ET COUVERTURES DU MAGAZINE *METROPOLIS*: LES TISSUS ÉTRANGES ET RAFFINÉS DE JUNICHI ARAI, LE CUBISME TCHÈQUE, LE NUMÉRO JUILLET/AOÛT, LE CUBISME TCHÈQUE, FRANK GEHRY, L'ARCHITECTE RICHARD NEUTRA.

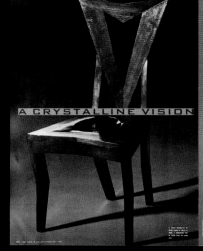

A CRYSTALLINE VISION

NEARLY LOST AMIDST THE DUST AND DRABNESS OF COMMUNIST RULE, CZECHOSLOVAKIA'S CUBIST ARCHITECTURE AND FURNISHINGS HAVE BEEN REDISCOVERED. VIBRANT, AUDACIOUS, EVEN VERTIGINOUS, CZECH CUBISM MAY BE AMONG THIS CENTURY'S MOST STARTLING, BEAUTIFUL, AND INFLUENTIAL DESIGN MOVEMENTS. BY EMMA DENT COAD

# METROPOLIS

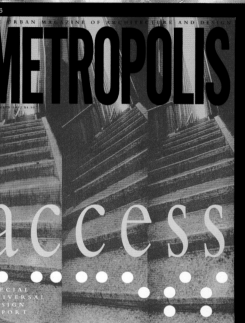

access

● ● ● ●
● ● ● ●
● ● ● ●

SPECIAL
UNIVERSAL
DESIGN
REPORT

# METROPOLIS

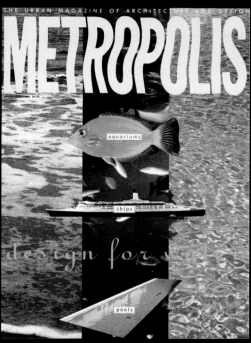

aquariums

ships

design for w...

pools

# METROPOLIS

czech cubism

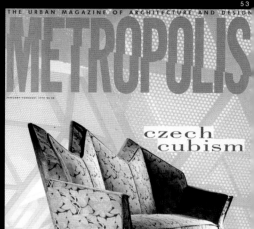

A woman builds a new Japan ▲ Can a museum save a town? ▲ Designing for disassembly

he acts out. he's famous for his lowlife materials. now, brash architect frank gehry turns lyrical.

why we love frank

by akiko busch

SURVIVAL AND DESIGN: ON THE 100TH ANNIVERSARY OF HIS BIRTH, RICHARD NEUTRA, IS REMEMBERED FOR HIS MISSION: CREATING MODERN ARCHITECTURE IN HARMONY WITH SOUTHERN CALIFORNIA'S LIFESTYLE.

BY ELIZABETH HARTMAN CANNELL

544

## Il design manifesto
### *Design on Display*

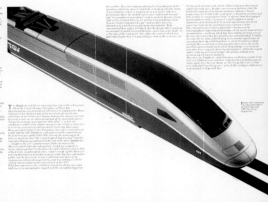

65

## l'ARCA

545

543

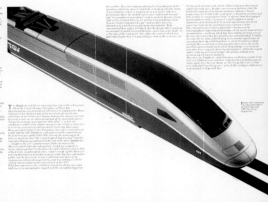

546

## Ethos, nuova *concept car*

■ **543-547** ART DIRECTOR: BOB NOORDA PHOTOGRAPHERS: RICHARD BRYANT (543), FEDERICO BRUNETTI (544, 546) PUBLISHER: L'ARCA EDIZIONI COUNTRY: ITALY ■ **543-547** THE CONIC TOWERS OF THE KUNST UND AUSSTELLUNGSHALLE (ART MUSEUM) IN BONN, DESIGNED BY GUSTAV PEICHL, ARE SHOWN ON THE COVER OF ARCHITECTURAL MAGAZINE *L'ARCA*. THE SPREADS SHOW A NIGHTTIME VIEW OF THE GALERIA CRISPI IN VENICE FROM INSIDE AND OUTSIDE (544, 546), A MODEL OF THE TGV HIGH-SPEED TRAIN AND ETHOS, AN OPEN-TOP TWO-SEATER SPORTS CAR MADE OF RECYCLABLE, THERMOPLASTIC MATERIAL. ● **543-547** DIE KONISCHEN TÜRME DER BONNER KUNST- UND AUSSTELLUNGSHALLE, ENT-WORFEN VON GUSTAV PEICHL, AUF DEM UMSCHLAG DER ARCHITEKTURZEITSCHRIFT *L'ARCA*. DIE DOPPELSEITEN ZEIGEN DIE GALERIA CRISPI IN VENEDIG BEI NACHT, VON INNEN UND AUSSEN GESEHEN (544, 546); EIN MODEL DES HOCHGESCHWINDIGKEITSZUGES TGV UND EINEN OFFENEN ZWEISITZER AUS WIEDERVERWERTBAREM THERMOPLASTISCHEM MATERIAL. ▲ **543-547** LES TOURS CONIQUES DE LA KUNST- UND AUSSTEL

548

LUNGSHALLE (UN MUSÉE D'ART MODERNE) DE BONN, DESSINÉE PAR L'ARCHITECTE GUSTAV PEICHL, EN COUVERTURE DU MAGAZINE D'ARCHI-TECTURE *L'ARCA*. LES DOUBLES PAGES REPRÉSENTENT: LA GALERIA CRISPI DE VENISE, VUE DE NUIT, DE L'EXTÉRIEUR ET DE L'INTÉRIEUR (544, 546); UN MODELE DU TGV FRANÇAIS; UN CABRIOLET DEUX PLACES FABRIQUÉ À PARTIR DE MATÉRIAUX THERMOPLASTIQUES RECYCLABLES.

■ **548** ART DIRECTOR/DESIGNER: HELEN MCCARTY PHOTOGRAPHER: ALEKSANDR V. AGAFONOV AGENCY: HELEN MCCARTY PUBLISHER: MUSEUM OF NEW MEXICO COUNTRY: USA ■ **548** THIS SPREAD FROM A MUSEUM'S MAGAZINE IS FEATURING AN ARTICLE ON THE CURATOR'S TRIP TO THE UKRAINE. THE RODSCHENKO POSTER FROM 1925 ADVERTISES A BOOK. ● **548** DIESE DOPPELSEITE EINER MUSEUMSZEITSCHRIFT BEZIEHT SICH AUF EINE REISE DES KURATORS IN DIE UKRAINE. DAS RODSCHENKO-PLAKAT (1925) WIRBT FÜR EIN BUCH. ▲ **558** CETTE DOUBLE PAGE D'UN MAGAZINE DE MUSÉE SE RAPPORTE À UN VOYAGE DU CONSERVATEUR EN UKRAINE. L'AFFICHE DE RODSCHENKO (1925) EST UNE PUBLICITÉ POUR UN LIVRE.

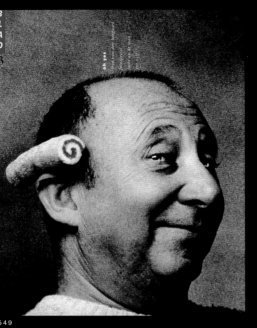

nominaties 1991

the image of imagination

fabulous fabien

man 2002

Q

V

vrouwbeelden in het fin de siècle

bingo

■ 549-555 Art Directors: Hans Wolf, Hans van Blommestein (563 only) Designers: Bas van der Paardt, Tiny Laarakker (553 only) Photographers: John Claridge (549), Ger Wierdsma (550), Dana Lixenberg (552), Rene van Haeften (553), Reinier Gerritsen (564, 555) Illustrators: Peret (551), Toon Michiels (553) Publisher: VNU/Admedia, De Geillustreerde Pers BV (553 only) Country: Netherlands ■ 549-555 The covers of BLAD magazines are marked by simple, expressive pictures delicately supported by typography. The portrait of a young man in 2002 (553) was done in cooperation with AVENUE. ● 549-555 Die Umschläge von BLAD sind durch ausdrucksvolle Bilder geprägt, die durch sparsam eingesetzte Typographie ergänzt werden. Das Bild des jungen Mannes im Jahr 2002 (553) entstand in Zusammenarbeit mit AVENUE. ▲ 549-555 Les couvertures de BLAD présentent la plupart du temps des images spectaculaires accompagnées d'une typographie originale, mais discrète. Les thèmes des doubles pages:

556

557

Une interview du directeur artistique Fabien Baron, l'homme de l'an 2002 (en collaboration avec AVENUE), l'interview d'une experte en marketing hollandaise sur la femme contemporaine, une interview du concepteur de magazines Jan van Halm.

■ 556, 557 Art Directors/Designers: Todd Hart, Shawn Freeman Photographer: Phil Hollenbeck Agency: Focus 2 Publisher: Dallas Society of Visual Communication Country: USA ■ 556, 557 Spreads from ROUGH, the large-format newsletter of the Dallas Society of Visual Communication. ● 556, 557 Doppelseiten aus ROUGH, dem Newsletter der Dallas Society of Visual Communication. ▲ 556, 557 Doubles pages de ROUGH, le bulletin d'information de la Dallas Society of Visual Communication.

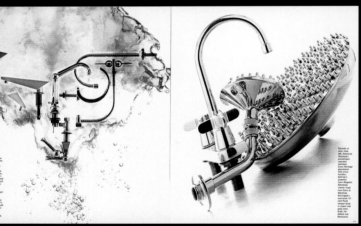

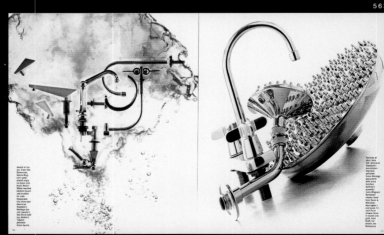

The architect of the Pirelli Tower brought his inventive wit to bear on 20th-century interiors as well as Milan skyscrapers

CHARLES BRICKER

# REMEMBERING GIO PONTI

IN AN ORGANIC MOOD

Up to our old ethno-anthro antics, we definitely dig them

PRODUCED BY JEAN-YVES LEGRAND; PHOTOGRAPHY BY JAMES WOJCIK

**CLEARLY FESTIVE**

Let it cascade, tune it needle-sharp, and say so long to shiatsu

# WATER WORKS

PRODUCED BY MARGARET RUSSELL; PHOTOGRAPHY BY RAYMOND MEIER

Miracles from Milan: sensuous Latin sensibilities are high-style again. This summer, pattern yourself a Ponti-inspired table

# NEO GIO

PRODUCED BY LINDA O'KEEFFE; PHOTOGRAPHY BY NED/GLIKO MATURA

# ALL ABOUT BLOOMS

Seeing is believing: display the cut flowers from bulbs with crystal clarity

PRODUCED BY MARGARET RUSSELL; PHOTOGRAPHY BY WES MAAS

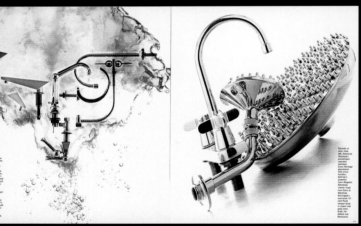

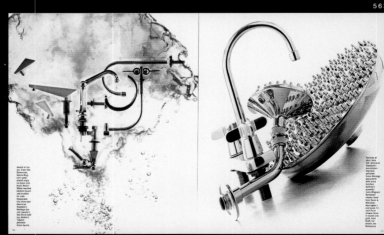

566

567

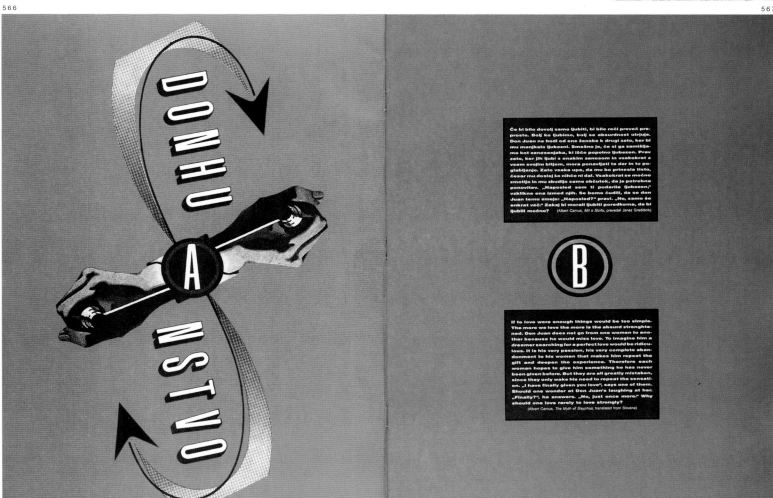

568

■ **558-566** ART DIRECTOR: CAROLINE BOWYER DESIGNER: JO HAY PHOTOGRAPHY: GIO PONTI ARCHIVES (558), JAMES WOJCIK (559), RAYMOND MEIER (560, 561, 565), NEDJELJKO MATURA (562, 563), RITA MAAS (564), FELICE FRANKEL (566) STYLISTS: CHARLES BRICKER (558), JEAN-YVES LEGRAND (559), MARGARET RUSSELL (560, 561, 564, 565), LINDA O'KEEFFE (562, 563), PUBLISHER: ELLE DECOR COUNTRY: USA ■ **558-566** SPREADS AND COVER OF ELLE DECOR. ● **558-566** DOPPELSEITEN UND UMSCHLAG VON ELLE DECOR: ▲ **558-566** DOUBLES PAGES ET COUVERTURE DE ELLE DECOR: LE DESIGNER ET ARCHITECTE GIO PONTI, DES OBJETS USUELS EXOTIQUES, LES CANDÉLABRES D'ANNE NILSSON, LES TUYAUTERIES DES SALLES DE BAIN, LES JARDINS D'HIVER, LES FLEURS DANS DES VASES DE CRISTAL, ENFIN LES PISCINES, BAINS ET DOUCHES.

■ **567, 568** ART DIRECTOR/DESIGNER/ILLUSTRATOR: PROSPECTIVES DEPT. AGENCY: PROSPECTIVES DEPT. PUBLISHER: DRAMA SNG MARIBOR COUNTRY: CROATIA ■ **567, 568** CARMEN AND DON JUAN ARE THE SUBJECTS OF THE COVER AND THE SPREAD OF DRAMA MAGAZINE. THE TECHNIQUE: XEROXED COLLAGES, HAD-APPLIED TYPOGRAPHY AND A COMBINATION OF COMPUTER AND CLASSICAL PHOTO-TYPE SETTING. ● **567, 568** CARMEN UND DON JUAN SIND DIE THEMEN DIESES UMSCHLAGS UND DER DOPPELSEITE DER THEATERZEITSCHRIFT DRAMA. TECHNIK: PHOTOKOPIERTE COLLAGEN, HANDSATZ UND EINE KOMBINATION VON COMPUTER- UND HERKÖMMLICHEM PHOTOSATZ. ▲ **567, 568** CARMEN ET DON JUAN SONT LES THÈMES DE LA COUVERTURE ET DE CETTE DOUBLE PAGE DU MAGAZINE DE THÉÂTRE DRAMA. TECHNIQUE: COLLAGES PHOTOCOPIÉS, COMPOSITION À LA MAIN, AINSI QU'UNE COMBINAISON DE COMPOSITION PHOTOGRAPHIQUE TRADITIONNELLE ET DE PAO.

569

Lo Stile di... BIANCA JAGGER

570

571

572

573

574

■ **569-576** ART DIRECTOR: LUCA STOPPINI PHOTOGRAPHERS: MICHEL COMTE (569), ELLEN VON UNWERTH (570), STEVEN MEISEL (571, 573, 575, 576), ALBERT WATSON (572), UPI/BETTMANN (574) CLIENT: *VOGUE ITALIA* PUBLISHER: EDIZIONE CONDÉ NAST S.P.A. COUNTRY: ITALY ■ **569-576** THE THEMES OF THESE SPREADS AND COVERS: MODEL CINDY CRAWFORD; THE STYLE OF BIANCA JAGGER; NEW SOFIA (LOREN) OR AVA (GARDNER); ROCK'N JEANS; ETHNO FASHION; A BOOK ABOUT THE ANN WOODWARD CASE; FASHION FOR FALL/WINTER 92/93; ACTRESS SOFIA COPPOLA. ● **569-576** DIE THEMEN DIESER DOPPELSEITEN UND UMSCHLÄGE: CINDY CRAWFORD; BIANCA JAGGERS STIL; DIE NEUE SOFIA (LOREN) ODER AVA (GARDNER); ROCK'N JEANS; ETHNO-MODE; EIN BUCH ÜBER DEN ANN-WOODWARD-FALL, MODE HERBST/WINTER 92/93, DIE SCHAUSPIELERIN SOFIA COPPOLA. ▲ **569-576** LE MANNEQUIN CINDY CRAWFORD, LE STYLE BIANCA JAGGER, LA NOUVELLE SOFIA (LOREN) OU AVA (GARDNER), LA MODE ROCKER, LE LOOK ETHNO, UN LIVRE SUR LE CAS ANN WOODWARD, LES COLLECTIONS AUTOMNE/HIVER 92/93, L'ACTRICE SOFIA COPPOLA.

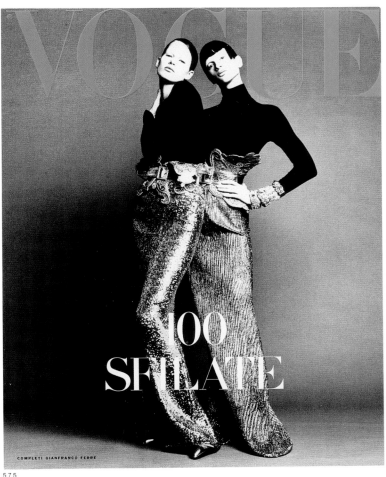

575

576

■ (FOLLOWING SPREAD) **577-586** ART DIRECTOR: LUCA STOPPINI PHOTOGRAPHERS: WALTER CHIN (577, 580, 584), ALBERT WATSON (578), STEVEN MEISEL (579, 582, 583), ALFA CASTALDI (585, 586) CLIENT: *VOGUE ITALIA* PUBLISHER: EDIZIONE CONDÉ NAST S.P.A. COUNTRY: ITALY ■ **577-586** THE SUBJECTS OF THESE SPREADS FROM *VOGUE ITALIA*: FASHION, SHOES AND GLASSES, ELEGANT UNDERWEAR; OUTFITS BY CHRISTIAN LACROIX (LEFT) AND COMME DES GARÇONS (RIGHT); FILM STAR OF THE THIRTIES DITA PARLO; ACTRESS SOFIA COPPOLA; BABY DOLL; REGULAR SPREADS OF ANNA PIAGGI. ● (FOLGENDE DOPPELSEITE) **577-586** THEMEN DIESER DOPPELSEITEN AUS *VOGUE ITALIA*: MODE, SCHUHE UND BRILLEN; ELEGANTE UNTERWÄSCHE; ENSEMBLES VON CHRISTIAN LACROIX (LINKS) UND COMME DES GARÇONS (RECHTS); DITA PARLO, FILMSTAR DER DREISSIGER JAHRE, DIE SCHAUSPIELERIN SOFIA COPPOLA; BABY DOLL UND ZWEI DER REGULÄREN, VON ANNA PIAGGI GESTALTETEN DOPPELSEITEN. ▲ (DOUBLE PAGE SUIVANTE) **577-586** LES SUJETS DE CES DOUBLES PAGES: LES NOUVEAUX DÉTAILS DE LA MODE; LES CHAUSSURES ET LES LUNETTES; L'ÉLÉGANCE SOBRE; DES COORDONNÉS DE CHRISTIAN LACROIX (À GAUCHE) ET DE COMME DES GARÇONS (À DROITE); DITA PARLO, STAR DES ANNÉES 30, LA DERNIÈRE COQUELUCHE DE MADONNA; L'ACTRICE SOFIA COPPOLA; BABY DOLL; DEUX EXEMPLES DES «DOPPIE PAGINE» D'ANNA PIAGGI, CONSACRÉES ICI AUX OBJETS USUELS ET À DES IDÉES INSPIRÉES PAR DES DRAPEAUX.

# new
*Camelie rose e margherite*
# details!

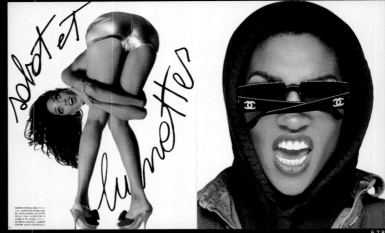

*dolcet et lunettes*

# scegliersi uno stile, indossare capi sobri e raffinati, muoversi con grande
# allure
## per sottolineare l'innato chic di capi di essenziale eleganza

132

ABITINO DI OTTOMAN CON SPACCO LATERALE SU MINI-GONNA, GIORGIO ARMANI. FA-SHION EDITOR PAUL CAVACO.

NEW YORK

Chi è **DITA PARLO** e
**nuovo mito e**
**l'ossessione di**
**MADONNA**
?

L'ha vista in un film anni '30, ed è stato coup de foudre. Ora Mrs Ciccone si ispira a lei, si identifica in lei. E in «Sex» scrive: Il mio nome è Dita...

«I miei maestri? Al Pacino, Diane Keaton. E mio padre»

ABITO DI ORGANZA A PIÙ
STRATI CON STRASS, CHLOÉ.
BIJOUX SCOOTER, SABOTS
LERRE. NELLA PAGINA AC-
CANTO, TUTÙ E SPENCER
BRODÉ, BIJOUX E SCARPE:
TUTTO CHRISTIAN LACROIX.

270
271

# DAILY USE

Giarrettiere, mollette per capelli,
manifesti strappati, cartoni ondu-
lati sono alcune tra le
materie prime dei nuovi artisti e
stilisti recuperatori.
Le seggiole-scultura di Kris
di Sam Rey? «Objets trouvés» riciclati,
strutture a vista, orli lace-
rati, «fermati» da colla-
caoutchouc (Comme des
Garçons),
da tecniche sar-
toriali (Chanel) o
sforbiciati (Issey Miya-
ke). Gilet di papier maché
(Martin Margiela), giacche
in skaï da sedile di auto-
mobile (Jean Colonna).

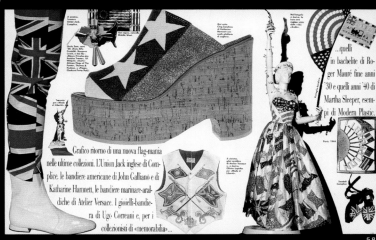

Grafico ritorno di una nuova flag-mania
nelle ultime collezioni. L'Union Jack inglese di Compli-
ce, le bandiere americane di John Galliano e di
Katharine Hamnett, le bandiere marinare-aral-
diche di Atelier Versace. I gioielli-bandie-
ra di Ugo Correani e, per i
collezionisti di «memorabilia»...

■ 587-592 Art Director: Andrea Schraml Designer: Irmgard Gabriel Photographers: William Wegman (587), Jean-Loup Sieff (588), James Balog (589), Stock, Tinting Studio Kratzig (590), Georg Riha (591), Stock (592) Publisher: KURIER, FREIZEIT Country: Austria ■ 587-592 Covers from the weekly magazine of a newspaper. The images in the top row were taken from a calendar (Harry N. Abrams,) the book YSL (Schirmer Mosel), and the book Survivors (Harry N. Abrams). The portrait of Grace Kelly comes from the archives of Prestl Verlag, the "Spirit of Autumn" shows the Schönbrunn Castle, and the portrait of Elton John is from the KURIER archives. ● 587-592 Umschläge des Wochenmagazins der Zeitung KURIER. Die Bilder in der oberen Reihe stammen aus einem Kalender (Harry N. Abrams), dem Buch YSL (Schirmer Mosel) und aus dem Buch Survivors (Harry N. Abrams). Das Porträt

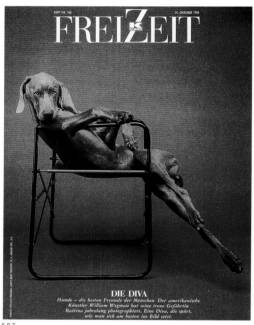

587

588

589

590

591

592

von Grace Kelly stammt aus dem Archiv des Prestl Verlags, «Herbststimmung» zeigt das Wiener Schloss Schönbrunn, das Porträt von Elton John stammt aus dem Kurier-Archiv. ▲ 587-592 Couvertures du supplément hebdomadaire du journal KURIER.

■ 593-595 Art Directors: Régis Pagniez, Olivia Badrutt-Giron Photographers: Gilles Bensimon (593, 595), Mike Reinhardt (594) Stylists: Fanny Pagniez (593, 595), Jackie Frank (594) Publisher: Hachette Magazines Inc. Country: USA ■ 593-595 Spreads from ELLE magazine: red, hot and wild fashion; all the right moves; swim wear. ● 593-595 Doppelseiten aus der amerikanischen Ausgabe der Zeitschrift ELLE: heisse, aufregende Mode in Rot; die richtigen Bewegungen; Bademode. ▲ 593-595 Doubles pages de l'édition américaine de ELLE: le rouge cramoisi, une couleur sexy; les nouveaux maillots de bain en pleine action; le rouge chocking.

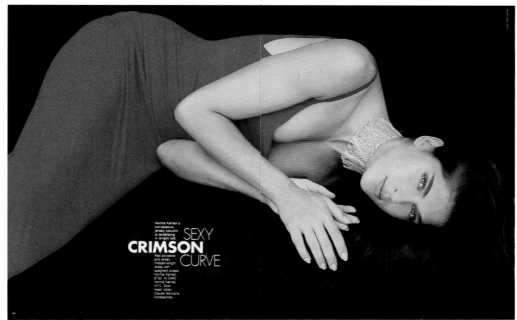

Norma Kamali's
curvaceous
jersey column
is tantalizing
in bright red.

SEXY
**CRIMSON**
CURVE

Red polyester
and jersey
midcalf-length
dress with
spaghetti straps,
Norma Kamali,
$150. At OMO
Norma Kamali
NYC. Gold
mesh collar,
Claude Montana
Accessories.

593

**BRIGHTLY
COLORED
SUITS
ROLL INTO
ACTION**

Left: Color-
blocked Supplex
and Lycra tank
suit. Swimwear
by Adrienne
Vittadini. At Lord
& Taylor.
Turquoise and
black wrist
guards, Roller-
blade, $22.
Right: Chartreuse
sequined tank
suit, Harriet Sel-
ling. Sunglasses,
Oakley $106.
Cycling gloves,
Descente, $25.
In-line skates,
Rollerblade, $330.
For details, see
Retail Guide.

594

Scarlet flashes
from Yohji
Yamamoto and
Rei Kawakubo.

FULL-
THROTTLE
**COLOR**

Left: Red long
wool shirt,
knotted in front,
Yohji Yamamoto
$990. At
Alan Bilzerian,
Boston; Maxfield,
Los Angeles.
Right: Red paper
top with zippered
collar, Comme
des Garçons
by Rei Kawakubo.
Star earrings,
Lee Brevard, $190
a pair. For
more details, see
Retail Guide.

595

# LOVE AND HATE AT TEXAS A&M

BY MIMI SWARTZ

FACING ACCUSATIONS RANGING FROM RAPE TO BAD MANNERS, TRADITION-BOUND
AGGIE CORPSMEN CAN'T DECIDE WHETHER TO WELCOME WOMEN OR DRIVE THEM OFF.

# RODEO TEXAS U ★ S ★ A PHOTOGRAPHY MARY ELLEN MARK

*fig. 2* TROPICAL OX BEETLE
*Strategus aloeus*

*fig. 3* GIANT WALKINGSTICK
*Megaphasma dentricus*

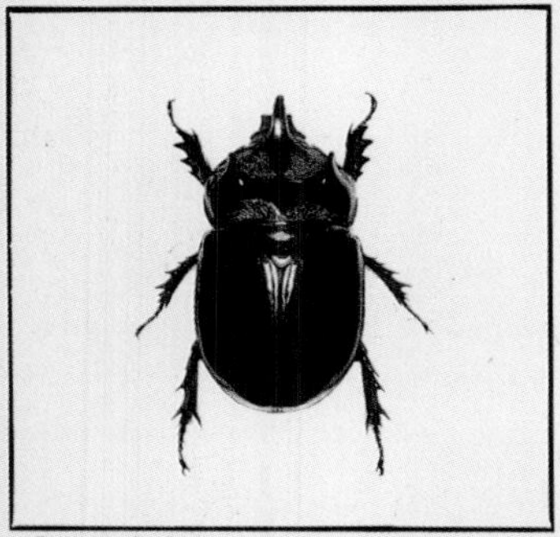

*fig. 6* VINE SPHINX
*Eumorpha vitis*

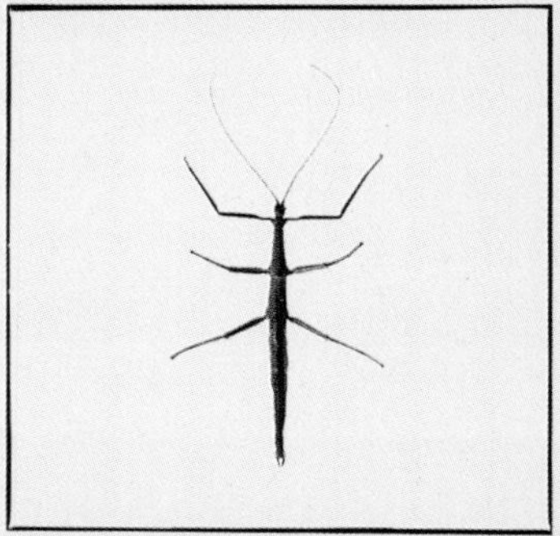

*fig. 7* GROUND BEETLE
*Pasimachus sublaevis*

*fig. 8* EYED CLICK BEETLE
*Alaus oculatus*

*fig. 9* CICADA KILLER
*Sphecius speciosus*

*fig. 10* TWO-TAILED TIGER SWALLOWTAIL
*Papilio multicaudata*

■ **596-599** Art Director/Designer: D.J. Stout Photographers: Dan Winters (596, 598, 599), Mary Ellen Mark (597) Publisher: *Texas Monthly* Country: USA ■ **596-599** The themes of these spreads: the problems involved with having women in the Texas A&M Corps; small town rodeos in Texas; "Meet the Beetles". ● **596-599** Doppelseiten aus *Texas Monthly*: Probleme durch die Aufnahme von Frauen in das A&M-Corps von Texas; Kleinstadt-Rodeos in Texas; Käfer und Insekten. ▲ **596-599** Les problèmes que posent l'enrôlement de femmes dans le corps A&M du Texas; les rodéos dans les petites villes du Texas; les insectes.

■ **600-604** Art Director: Claude Maggiori Designers: Claude Maggiori, Marc Belli (604) Photographers: Wayne Maser (600), Steven Meisel (601), Denis Malerbi (602), Dahmane (603), Serge Guérand (604) Agency: Editorial Client: *Lui* Publisher: Editions des Savanes Country: France ■ **600-604** Covers and spreads from *Lui* magazine: "The phenomenal body of Brigitte Nielsen;"

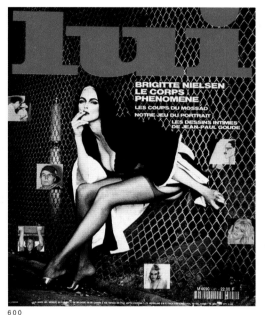

600

601

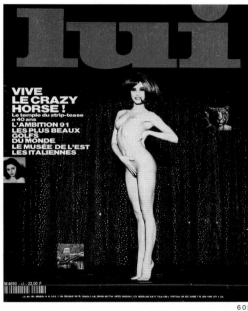

602

603

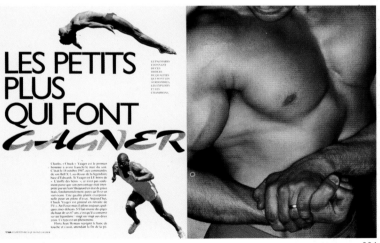

604

"Madonna finally nude;" "The temple of strip tease is 40 years old;" the intimate portfolio of a photographer showing the loves of his life; "The little things that make you win". ● **600-604** Umschläge und Doppelseiten aus *Lui*: «Der phänomenale Körper von Brigitte Nielsen»; «Madonna endlich nackt»; «Der Tempel des Strip-tease wird 40»; ein Photograph zeigt intime Bilder seiner Geliebten; «Die kleinen Extras, die zum Gewinn führen». ▲ **600-604** Couvertures et doubles pages du magazine mensuel *Lui*: Brigitte Nielsen; la couverture du numéro comportant les photos de Madonna nue; l'une des danseuses du Crazy Horse à Paris; les images intimes de l'album d'un photographe; ouverture d'un article sur ce qui fait «l'étoffe des héros».

ARREDAMENTO
# DEKORASYON

ÖZEL FOTO-RÖPORTAJ:
**VENEDİK'TE**
**ÇİFTE SARAYLAR**

PROFİL:
**LOUIS KAHN**

**POZİTİF'LE**
**POZİTİF BİR**
**SÖYLEŞİ**

DOSYA:
**ÇAY VE ÇAYDANLIK**

**AĞA HAN ÖDÜLLERİ**

**BARCELONA**
**1980-1992**

**BİENAL/DANS/FOTOĞRAF**

**MEGA BEYMEN-ANKARA**
**ÇİMENTAŞ-İZMİR**
**ASİTANE-İSTANBUL**

604

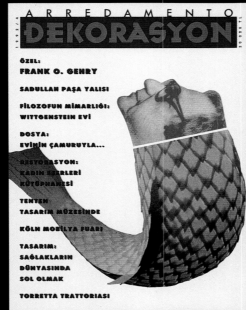

ARREDAMENTO
# DEKORASYON

ÖZEL:
**FRANK O. GEHRY**

**SADULLAH PAŞA YALISI**

FİLOZOFUN MİMARLIĞI:
**WITTGENSTEIN EVİ**

DOSYA:
**EVİNİN ÇAMURUYLA...**

RESTORASYON:
**KADIN ESERLERİ**
**KÜTÜPHANESİ**

**TENTEN**
**TASARIM MÜZESİNDE**

**KÖLN MOBİLYA FUARI**

TASARIM:
**SAĞLAKLARIN**
**DÜNYASINDA**
**SOL OLMAK**

**TORRETTA TRATTORIASI**

605

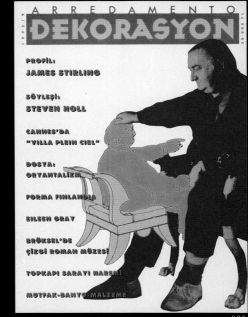

ARREDAMENTO
# DEKORASYON

PROFİL:
**JAMES STIRLING**

SÖYLEŞİ:
**STEVEN HOLL**

CANNES'DA
**"VILLA PLEIN CIEL"**

DOSYA:
**ORYANTALİZM**

**FORMA FINLANDIA**

**EILEEN GRAY**

BRÜKSEL'DE
**ÇİZGİ ROMAN MÜZESİ**

**TOPKAPI SARAYI HAREMİ**

**MUTFAK-BANYO-MALZEME**

606

*Design+*

607

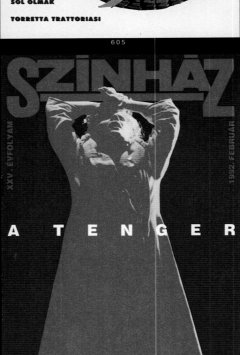

# SZINHAZ

XXV. ÉVFOLYAM
1992. FEBRUÁR

A TENGER

ASSZONYA

608

Hausmagazin der Lindner Unternehmensgruppe

nennl *Ansichten*

2/92

609

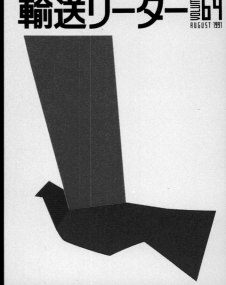

トラック輸送の明日に向かって発信

輸送リーダー VOLUME 63
JUNE 1991

610

OCTOBER 1992/$2.95

# LIFE

## CAN WE STOP AGING?

There are
scientists who
believe we can and
will—but would
we really want to?

Sally Woodbridge of Berkeley,
California, in 1992 and 1944.

611

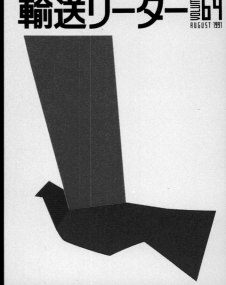

トラック輸送の明日に向かって発信

輸送リーダー VOLUME 64
AUGUST 1991

612

■ 604-606 Art Director/Designer: BÜLENT ERKMEN Publisher: BOYUT PUBLICATION GROUP Country: TURKEY ■ 604-606 COVERS OF A MAGAZINE ON ARCHITECTURE AND DESIGN. THE COVER STORIES ARE ON ARCHITECTS LOUIS KAHN, FRANK O. GEHRY, JAMES STIRLING. ● 604-606 UMSCHLÄGE EINER ZEITSCHRIFT FÜR ARCHITEKTUR UND DESIGN. DIE TITEL-STORIES BETREFFEN LOUIS KAHN, FRANK O. GEHRY UND JAMES STIRLING. ▲ 604-606 COUVERTURES D'UN MAGAZINE D'ARCHITECTURE ET DE DESIGN. LES THÈMES: LOUIS KAHN, FRANK O. GEHRY, JAMES STIRLING.

■ 607 Art Director: MIKE SKINNER Designers: NORTHBROOK COLLEGE STUDENTS Photographers: COLLEGE DIPLOMA STUDENTS Client: NORTHBROOK COLLEGE Country: GREAT BRITAIN ■ 607 COVER OF A 'STYLE DOCUMENT' FOR TEXTILE COURSES. ● 607 UMSCHLAG EINES 'STIL-DOKUMENTS' FÜR TEXTIL-DESIGN. ▲ 607 COUVERTURE D'UN 'EXERCICE DE STYLE' DE LA SECTION TEXTILE DU NORTHBROOK COLLEGE.

■ 608 Art Director: GYÖRGY KEMÉNY Publisher: SZINHAZ Country: HUNGARY ■ 608 A THEATER MAGAZINE: "THE WOMAN OF THE SEA" (IBSEN) ● 608 THEATERZEITSCHRIFT: IBSENS »DIE FRAU VOM MEER«. ▲ 608 COUVERTURE D'UN MAGAZINE DE THÉÂTRE: «LA FEMME DU MER» PAR IBSEN.

■ 609 Art Directors: STEFAN NOWAK, KLAUS HESSE Designers: STEFAN NOWAK, ERIKA HILLEMACHER Photographer: GERD GEORGE Agency: HESSE DESIGNAGENTUR Client: LINDNER UNTERNEHMENSGRUPPE Country: GERMANY ■ 609 "INTERIOR VIEWS," COVER OF A HOUSE MAGAZINE. ● 609 »INNENANSICHTEN«, UMSCHLAG EINER MITARBEITERZEITSCHRIFT. ▲ 609 «INTÉRIEURS», COUVERTURE D'UNE REVUE D'ENTREPRISE.

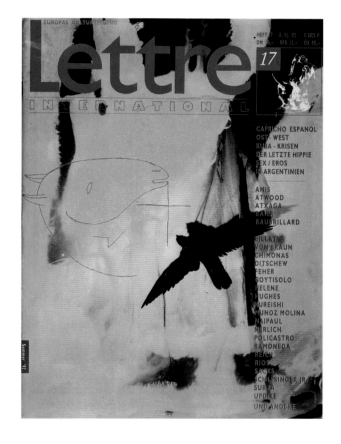

■ 610, 612 Art Director: TOSHIYUKI USUI Designer/Illustrator: ZENJI FUNABASHI Agency: COA PLANNING CORP. Client: ISUZU TRUCK COMPANY Country: JAPAN ■ 610, 612 HOUSE MAGAZINE. ● 610, 612 HAUSZEITSCHRIFT. ▲ 610, 612 LE MAGAZINE D'UNE FIRME DE TRANSPORT.

■ 611 Art Director/Designer: TOM BENTKOWSKI Photographer: BOBBY ADAMS Publisher: *LIFE* MAGAZINE, TIME INC. Country: USA ■ 611 SALLY WOODBRIDGE, 1992 AND 1944. ● 611 EIN GESICHT IN DEN JAHREN 1992 UND 1944 - «KANN MAN DAS ALTERN STOPPEN?». MANCHE WISSENSCHAFTLER BEHAUPTEN, DASS ES MÖGLICH SEI. ▲ 611 LE MÊME VISAGE EN 1992 ET EN 1944 – «PEUT-ON EMPÊCHER LE VIEILLISSEMENT?»

■ 613 Art Director: JÖRG KOHN Designer: STEPHAN SCHWARDMANN Illustrator: MIMMO PALADINO Publisher: LETTRE INTERNATIONAL Country: GERMANY ■ 613 COVER OF A EUROPEAN CULTURAL MAGAZINE. THIS ISSUE IS ON THE SUBJECTS OF EROTICS AND SPAIN. EACH ISSUE CONTAINS ILLUSTRATIONS OF A DIFFERENT EUROPEAN ARTIST, IN THIS CASE MIMMO PALADINO. ● 613 UMSCHLAG EINER EUROPÄISCHEN KULTURZEITUNG. DIE THEMEN IN DIESER AUSGABE SIND EROTIK UND SPANIEN. ▲ 613 COUVERTURE D'UN MAGAZINE CULTUREL EUROPÉEN.

学習評価研究
Journal of Learning & Evaluation
No.7 1991 Fall

Test & Evaluation          Curriculum & Guidance

Learning & Instruction          Information & Technology

C.S.L.
The Center for the Study of Learning

614

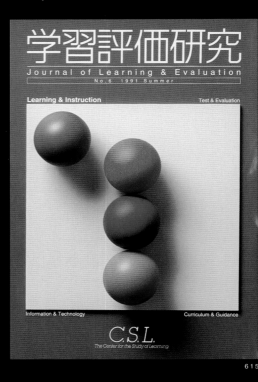

学習評価研究
Journal of Learning & Evaluation
No.6 1991 Summer

Learning & Instruction          Test & Evaluation

Information & Technology          Curriculum & Guidance

C.S.L.
The Center for the Study of Learning

615

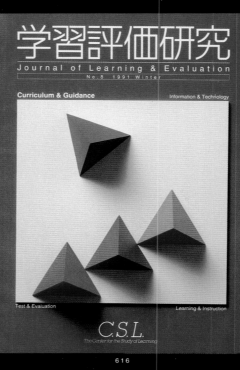
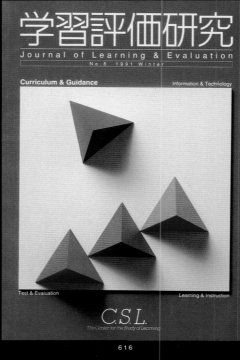

学習評価研究
Journal of Learning & Evaluation
No.8 1991 Winter

Curriculum & Guidance          Information & Technology

Test & Evaluation          Learning & Instruction

C.S.L.
The Center for the Study of Learning

616

学習評価研究
Journal of Learning & Evaluation
Special Issue Ⅲ 1991
特集 不安と学習

Learning & Instruction          Test & Evaluation

Information & Technology          Curriculum & Guidance

C.S.L.
The Center for the Study of Learning

617

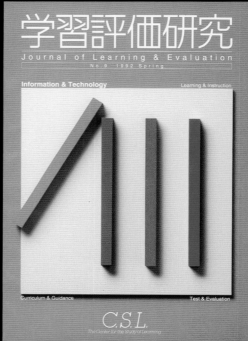

学習評価研究
Journal of Learning & Evaluation
No.9 1992 Spring

Information & Technology          Learning & Instruction

Curriculum & Guidance          Test & Evaluation

C.S.L.
The Center for the Study of Learning

618

■ **614-618** Aʀᴛ Dɪʀᴇᴄᴛᴏʀ: HIROYUKI HAYASHI Dᴇsɪɢɴᴇʀs: ETSUYA HATTORI, YOSHIKO CHUJO Pʜᴏᴛᴏɢʀᴀᴘʜᴇʀ: HARUO KOISHIZAWA Aɢᴇɴᴄʏ: GRAPHICS AND DESIGNING INC. Pᴜʙʟɪsʜᴇʀ: HICHI NOKEN Cᴏᴜɴᴛʀʏ: JAPAN ■ **614-618** BASIC SHAPES SERVE AS ILLUSTRATION OF THE COVERS OF *THE JOURNAL OF LEARNIGN & EVALUATION* PUBLISHED BY THE C.S.L. RESEARCH INSTITUTE. ● **614-618** GRUNDFORMEN ALS ILLUSTRATIONS-ELEMENTE DER UMSCHLÄGE EINES VON EINER FORSCHUNGSANSTALT HERAUSGEGEBENEN MAZGAZINS. ▲ **614-618** DES FORMES ÉLÉMENTAIRES UTILISÉES COMME ÉLÉMENTS DÉCORATIFS SUR LES COUVERTURES DU MAGAZINE D'INSTRUCTION PUBLIÉ PAR UN INSTITUT DE RECHERCHE.

■ **619** Aʀᴛ Dɪʀᴇᴄᴛᴏʀ: KIT HINRICHS Dᴇsɪɢɴᴇʀ: JACKIE FOSHAUG Iʟʟᴜsᴛʀᴀᴛᴏʀ: IKKO TANAKA Aɢᴇɴᴄʏ: PENTAGRAM DESIGN, SAN FRANCISCO Pᴜʙʟɪsʜᴇʀ: PACE COMMUNICATIONS Cᴏᴜɴᴛʀʏ: USA ■ **619** COVER OF UNITED AIRLINES' INFLIGHT MAGAZINE. ● **619** UMSCHLAG DES KUN-DENMAGAZINS DER FLUGGESELLSCHAFT UNITED AIRLINES. ▲ **619** COUVERTURE DU MAGAZINE DE BORD DE LA COMPAGNIE UNITED AIRLINES.

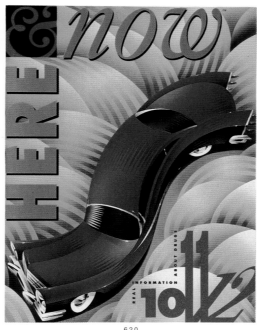

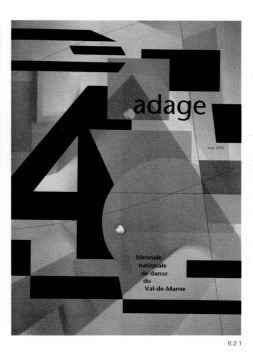

619

620

621

■ **620** Aʀᴛ Dɪʀᴇᴄᴛᴏʀs: JULIA LAPINE, JOHN HORNALL Dᴇsɪɢɴᴇʀs: JULIA LAPINE, JOHN HORNALL, HEIDI HATLESTAD, DAVID BATES, LIAN NG, BRUCE BRANSON-MEYER. Iʟʟᴜsᴛʀᴀᴛᴏʀ: DAN PICASSO Aɢᴇɴᴄʏ: HORNALL ANDERSON DESIGN WORKS Cʟɪᴇɴᴛ: CHEF/RF&A Cᴏᴜɴᴛʀʏ: USA ■ **620** THIS MAGAZINE ADDRESSES ISSUES LIKE DRUGS AND OTHER DEPENDENCIES. ● **620** DIESE ZEITSCHRIFT BEFASST SICH MIT DROGEN UND ANDEREN SUCHTMITTELN. ▲ **620** CE MAGAZINE DESTINÉ AUX ÉCOLIERS TRAITE DES PROBLÈMES DE LA DROGUE ET DES AUTRES DÉPENDANCES.

■ **621** Dᴇsɪɢɴᴇʀ: SEVAN DEMIRDJIAN Aɢᴇɴᴄʏ: SEVAN DESIGN COMMUNICATION Cʟɪᴇɴᴛ: BIENNALE NATIONALE DE DANSE DU VAL DE MARNE Cᴏᴜɴᴛʀʏ: FRANCE ■ **621** COVER OF A MAGAZINE ON CONTEMPORARY DANSE IN FRANCE. ● **621** UMSCHLAG EINER ZEITSCHRIFT ÜBER ZEITGE-NÖSSISCHEN TANZ IN FRANKREICH. ▲ **621** COUVERTURE D'UNE REVUE TRIMESTRIELLE SUR LA DANSE CONTEMPORAINE EN FRANCE.

■ 622, 623 ART DIRECTOR: ULRICH VOSSNACKE ILLUSTRATOR: PETER KRÄMER CLIENT: DEUTSCHE LUFTHANSA AG COUNTRY: GERMANY ■ 622, 623 THE "CHECK LIST" PAGES OF LUFTHANSA'S INFLIGHT MAGAZINE. THE SUBJECT IS MODERN FLIGHT TECHNIQUES. ● 622, 623 DIE RUBRIK «CHECK LIST» (THEMA FLUGTECHNIK) AUS DEM LUFTHANSA BORDBUCH. ▲ 622, 623 LA RUBRIQUE «CHECK LIST» DU MAGAZINE DE BORD DE LA LUFTHANSA.

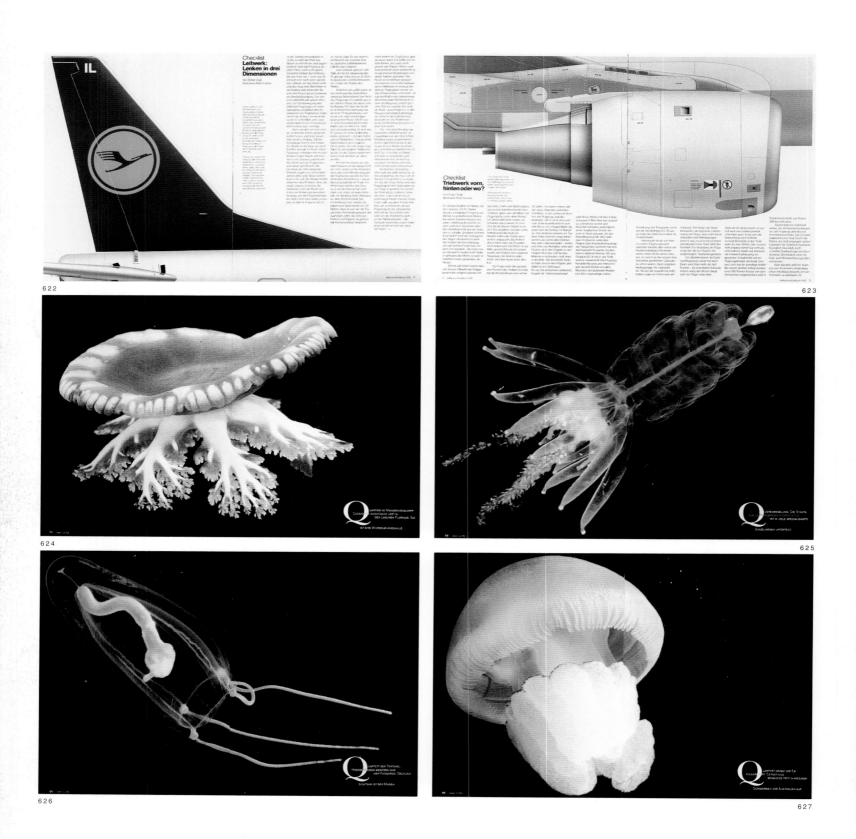

622

623

624

625

626

627

■ 624-627 ART DIRECTORS/DESIGNERS: CHRISTOF GASSNER, FABIAN NICOLAY PHOTOGRAPHERS: E. R. DEGGINGET/ANIMALS ANIMALS (624), NORBERT WU/PETER ARNOLD INC. (625, 626), KEITH GILLETT/ANIMALS ANIMALS (627) PUBLISHER: RINGIER VERLAG GMBH COUNTRY: GERMANY ■ 624-627 FROM THE DARKNESS OF THE SEA: JELLYFISH. SPREADS FROM NATUR. ● 624-627 AUS DER TIEFE DES MEERES: QUALLEN. SEITEN AUS NATUR. ▲ 624-627 PAGES DU MAGAZINE NATUR CONSACRÉES AUX MÉDUSES, CES ÉTRANGES ANIMAUX QUI HANTENT LES PROFONDEURS DE L'OCÉAN.

ILLUSTRATION

ILLUSTRATIONEN

ILLUSTRATION

628

■ **628** ILLUSTRATOR: MICHAEL MAU COUNTRY: GERMANY ■ **628** THIS IMAGE OF THE LONDON BAKERLOO LINE, THE OLDEST SUBWAY OF THE WORLD, SERVED AS SELF-PROMOTION. TECHNIQUE: OIL ON CANVAS. ● **628** DIESES BILD DER ÄLTESTEN LONDONER U-BAHN WURDE ALS EIGENWERBUNG VERWENDET. TECHNIK: ÖL AUF LEINWAND. ▲ **628** CETTE ILLUSTRATION A ÉTÉ UTILISÉE COMME AUTOPROMOTION. TECHNIQUE: HUILE SUR TOILE.

■ **629** ILLUSTRATOR: ARATA ISOZAKI ART DIRECTOR: TADANORI ITAKURA CLIENT: THE DAIMARU INC. COUNTRY: JAPAN ■ **629** A BUILDING COMPLEX OF JAPANESE ARCHITECT ARATA ISOZAKI. THE ILLUSTRATION WAS USED FOR AN EXHIBITION POSTER. ● **629** EIN GEBÄUDEKOMPLEX DES JAPANI-SCHEN ARCHITEKTEN ARATA ISOZAKI IST GEGENSTAND DER ILLUSTRATION, DIE FÜR EIN AUSSTELLUNGSPLAKAT VERWENDET WURDE. ▲ UN COM-PLÉXE DE BÂTIMENTS CRÉÉS PAR L'ARCHITECTE JAPONAIS ARATA ISOZAKI. L'ILLUSTRATION A SERVI COMME AFFICHE POUR UNE EXPOSITION.

The Museum of Contemporary Art, Los Angeles

630

631

632

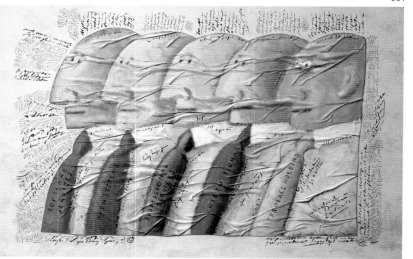

633

■ **630** ILLUSTRATOR: EDMUND GUY ART DIRECTOR: FRED WOODWARD PUBLISHER: STRAIGHT ARROW PUBLISHERS COUNTRY: USA ■ **630** A PORTRAIT OF ROCK SINGER NENEH CHERRY, USED BY *ROLLING STONE* IN A DISCUSSION OF HER SECOND ALBUM ENTITLED "HOMEBREW." ● **630** EIN PORTRÄT DER ROCKSÄNGERIN NENEH CHERRY FÜR EINE BESPRECHUNG IHRER ZWEITEN PLATTE («HOMEBREW») IM MAGAZIN *ROLLING STONE*. ▲ **630** UN PORTRAIT DE LA CHANTEUSE ROCK NENEH CHERRY POUR UN ARTICLE SUR SON DEUXIEME DISQUE, PARU DANS LE MAGAZINE *ROLLING STONE*.

■ **631** ILLUSTRATOR: MARK RYDEN COUNTRY: USA ■ **631** "THE FETCHING BONES MONSTER" USED AS SELF-PROMOTION. ● **631** «THE FETCHING BONES MONSTER» DIENTE ALS EIGENWERBUNG. ▲ **631** «THE FETCHING BONES MONSTER» A ÉTÉ UTILISÉE COMME AUTOPROMOTION DE L'ILLUSTRATEUR.

■ **632** ILLUSTRATOR: ROLF JANSSON PUBLISHER: BINDESTREKEN BOOK MAGAZIN COUNTRY: NORWAY ■ **632** ILLUSTRATION FOR A NOVEL DEALING WITH A SKINNY AND A FAT GIRL. THE SKINNY ONE DOES NOT ACCEPT HERSELF. ● **632** ILLUSTRATION FÜR EIN BUCH, IN DEM ES UM EIN MAGERES UND EIN DICKES MÄDCHEN GEHT. DAS MAGERE AKZEPTIERT IHREN KÖRPER NICHT. ▲ **632** ILLUSTRATION POUR UN LIVRE DANS LEQUEL IL EST QUESTION D'UNE PETITE FILLE MAIGRE ET D'UNE PETITE FILLE GROSSE. LA MAIGRE NE S'ACCEPTE PAS TELLE QU'ELLE EST.

634

635

■ **633** ILLUSTRATOR: WALTER VAN LOTHRINGEN REPRESENTATIVE: MARGARETHE HUBAUER CLIENT: PROFACE COUNTRY: NETHERLANDS ■ **633** IILLUSTRATION FOR THE BROCHURE OF A COMPUTER CONSULTING FIRM. MIXED MEDIA. ● **633** ILLUSTRATION FÜR DIE BROSCHÜRE EINER COM-PUTER-BERATUNGSFIRMA. ▲ **633** ILLUSTRATION POUR LA BROCHURE D'UNE FIRME DE CONSULTANCE EN INFORMATIQUE. TECHNIQUE MIXTE.

■ **634** ILLUSTRATOR: VIRGINIA HALSTEAD CLIENT: VIRGINIA HALSTEAD COUNTRY: USA ■ **634** "WIFE, CAREER OR MOTHER?"—THE ANGST, EMOTIONS AND UNCERTAINTY OF WOMEN TRYING TO DO IT ALL. TECHNIQUE: OIL PASTEL ON PAPER. ● **634** «EHEFRAU, KARRIERE ODER MUTTER?» – DIE ANGST, GEFÜHLE UND UNSICHERHEIT VON FRAUEN, DIE ALLES SCHAFFEN WOLLEN. TECHNIK: ÖLKREIDE AUF PAPIER. ▲ **634** «EPOUSE, FEMME D'AFFAIRE OU MÈRE?» – LA PEUR, LES SENTIMENTS ET L'INCERTITUDE DE FEMMES QUI VEULENT ÊTRE TOUT CELA À LA FOIS. PASTEL À HUILE.

■ **635** ILLUSTRATOR: CATHLEEN TOELKE ART DIRECTOR: JULIE DUQUET PUBLISHER: DOUBLEDAY COUNTRY: USA ■ **635** COVER ILLUSTRATION FOR A NOVEL ABOUT A TURN-OF-THE-CENTURY MEXICAN FAMILY. ● **635** UMSCHLAG EINES ROMANS ÜBER DAS LEBEN EINER MEXIKANISCHEN FAMILIE UM DIE JAHRHUNDERTWENDE. ▲ **635** COUVERTURE D'UN ROMAN QUI PARLE DE LA VIE D'UNE FAMILLE MEXICAINE AU DÉBUT DU SIÈCLE.

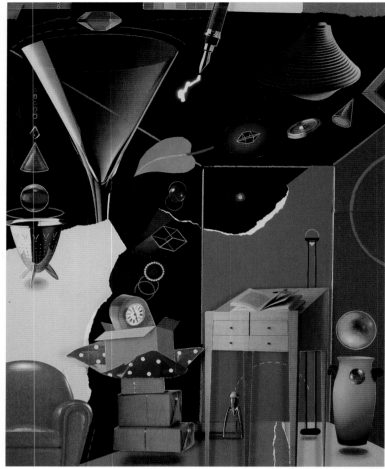

636

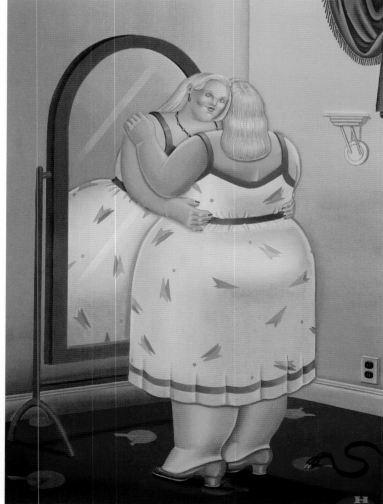

637

638

639

■ **636** Illustrator: DENNIS CORRIGAN Client: REVIVAL GRAPHICS Country: USA ■ **636** "PUNK CHILD IN A RURAL SETTING" IS THE TITLE OF THIS ILLUSTRATION WHICH WAS USED FOR SELF-PROMOTION. ● **636** «PUNK IN LÄNDLICHER UMGEBUNG». DIESE ILLUSTRATION WURDE ALS EIGEN-WERBUNG VERWENDET. TECHNIK: ÖL AUF HARTFASERPLATTE. ▲ **636** «PUNK DANS UN PAYSAGE CHAMPÊTRE» – HUILE SUR BOIS AGGLOMÉRÉ.

■ **637** Illustrator: ANDRZEJ DUDZINSKI Representative: MARGARETHE HUBAUER Agency: BEITHAN, HESSLER, MÄTTIG Client: MESSE FRANKFURT Country: GERMANY ■ **637** COLLAGE AND PASTEL DRAWING ON THE SUBJECT OF HOME FURNISHINGS OF THE AUTUMN FAIR IN FRANKFURT. ● **637** COLLAGE/PASTELL FÜR DIE FRANKFURTER HERBSTMESSE. ▲ **637** COLLAGE DE PASTELS POUR LA FOIRE DE FRANCFORT.

■ **638, 639** Illustrator: SANDRA HENDLER Art Directors: RICK PRACHER (638), JOANNE DUZASTROW (639) Publisher: ATLANTIC MONTHLY PRESS (650), *RUTERS MAGAZINE* (651) Country: USA ■ **638, 639** OIL PAINTINGS AS COVER ILLUSTRATION FOR A BOOK ENTITLED *COCK AND BULL* DEALING WITH MEN AND WOMEN (LEFT) AND AS ILLUSTRATION OF AN ARTICLE DEALING WITH THE DISCRIMINATION OF OVERWEIGHT PEOPLE (RIGHT). ● **638, 639** ILLUSTRATIONEN FÜR EINEN BUCHUMSCHLAG UND EINEN ARTIKEL ÜBER DIE DISKRIMINIERUNG ÜBERGEWICHTIGER MENSCHEN. ▲ **638, 639** DES PEINTURES À L'HUILE QUI ONT SERVI D'ILLUSTRATIONS: À GAUCHE, POUR LA COUVERTURE D'UN LIVRE SUR LES HOMMES ET LES FEMMES; À DROITE, POUR UN ARTICLE DANS LEQUEL IL ÉTAIT QUESTION DE LA DISCRIMINATION DES HOMMES TROP GROS.

■ **640** Illustrator: PETER KRÄMER Art Director: ULRICH VOSSNACKE Client: DEUTSCHE LUFTHANSA AG Country: GERMANY ■ **640** AIRBRUSH ILLUSTRATION FOR LUFTHANSA'S INFLIGHT MAGAZINE. ● **640** AIRBRUSH-ILLUSTRATION FÜR DIE «RUBRIK CHECK LIST» IM «BORDBUCH» DER DEUTSCHEN LUFTHANSA. ▲ **640** ILLUSTRATION À L'AÉROGRAPHE POUR LA RUBRIQUE «CHECK LIST» DU MAGAZINE DE BORD DE LA LUFTHANSA.

640

641

642

643

644

■ **641-644** Illustrator: HANS HILLMANN Art Director: HANS-GEORG POSPISCHIL Publisher: FRANKFURTER ALLGEMEINE ZEITUNG Country: GERMANY ■ **641-644** ILLUSTRATIONS FOR TWO LOVE STORIES IN THE *FAZ MAGAZIN*. THE PROTAGONISTS ARE THE POET GUILLAUME APOLLINAIRE AND ANNIE PLAYDEN, AS WELL AS PAINTER PHILIPP OTTO RUNGE AND PAULINE BASSENGE. ● **641-644** ILLUSTRATIONEN FÜR ZWEI LIEBESGESCHICHTEN IM *FRANKFURTER ALLGEMEINE MAGAZIN*: DER DICHTER GUILLAUME APOLLINAIRE UND ANNE PLAYDEN SOWIE DER MALER PHILIPP OTTO RUNGE UND PAULINE BASSENGE. ▲ **641-644** ILLUSTRATIONS POUR DEUX HISTOIRES D'AMOUR DANS LE *FAZ MAGAZIN*. LES PROTAGONISTES SONT LE POÈTE GUILLAUME APOLLINAIRE ET ANNE PLAYDEN, AINSI QUE LE PEINTRE PHILIPP OTTO RUNGE ET PAULINE BASSENGE.

■ **645** Illustrator: JANE MOLLER KRETZ Client: SCHOOL OF VISUAL ARTS Country: USA ■ **645** COVER FOR THE BULLETIN OF THE SCHOOL OF VISUAL ARTS. ● **645** UMSCHLAG FÜR DAS BULLETIN DER SCHOOL OF VISUAL ARTS. ▲ **645** COUVERTURE DU BULLETIN DE LA SCHOOL OF VISUAL ARTS.

646

647

648

*Le bassin*

649

650

■ **646** ILLUSTRATOR: SEYMOUR CHWAST ART DIRECTOR: HANS-GEORG POSPISCHIL AGENCY: THE PUSHPIN GROUP PUBLISHER: FRANKFURTER ALLGEMEINE MAGAZIN COUNTRY: GERMANY ■ **646** "MUSEUMS" WERE THE SUBJECT OF AN ARTICLE IN THE *FAZ MAGAZINE*. ● **646** «MUSEEN» WAREN GEGENSTAND EINES ARTIKELS IM *FAZ MAGAZIN*. ▲ **646** «LES MUSÉES» ÉTAIENT LE SUJET D'UN ARTICLE PARU DANS *FAZ MAGAZIN*.

■ **647** ILLUSTRATOR: JEFF KOEGEL ART DIRECTOR: RICK VAUGHN AGENCY: VAUGHN WEDEEN CREATIVE CLIENT: PECOS RIVER LEARNING CENTER COUNTRY: USA ■ **647** THIS ILLUSTRATION SUGGESTS THAT YOU WILL GAIN GREATER VISION BY CHANGING YOUR PERSPECTIVE. IT WAS USED IN A HANDBOOK FOR A LEARNING CENTER PROMOTING CREATIVE PROBLEM SOLVING. ● **647** UM EINE GROSSZÜGIGERE SICHT DER DINGE ZU ERLANGEN, VERÄNDERE MAN SEINEN STANDPUNKT. DIE ILLUSTRATION STAMMT AUS DEM HANDBUCH EINES LERNZENTRUMS, BEI DEM ES UM KREATIVE PROBLEMLÖSUNGEN GEHT. ▲ **647** L'ILLUSTRATION SUGGÈRE QUE POUR AVOIR UNE VISION PLUS AMPLE DES CHOSES, IL FAUT SAVOIR CHANGER DE POINT DE VUE. ELLE PROVIENT D'UN MANUEL DANS LEQUEL IL EST QUESTION DE RÉSOUDRE DES PROBLÈMES DE MANIÈRE CRÉATIVE.

■ **648** ILLUSTRATOR: MICHIKO STEHRENBERGER ART DIRECTOR: TROY MCQUILLEN AGENCY: USC IN-HOUSE PUBLISHER: USC BUSINESS MAGAZINE COUNTRY: USA ■ **648** IMAGE FOR THE OPENING SPREAD OF AN ARTICLE ENTITLED "MANAGEMENT BY NOSING AROUND." ● **648** TITEL DES DAZUGEHÖRIGEN ARTIKELS: "MANAGEMENT DURCH HERUMSCHNÜFFELN". ▲ **648** POUR UN ARTICLE INTITULÉ «LES MANAGERS INQUISITEURS».

■ **649** ILLUSTRATOR: PIERRE LE-TAN COUNTRY: FRANCE ■ **649** "LE BASSIN"—ILLUSTRATION FROM A SERIES OF URBAN LANDSCAPES. ● **649** »LE BASSIN« – BEISPIEL AUS EINER REIHE VON STADTLANDSCHAFTEN. ▲ **649** «LE BASSIN» – EXEMPLE TIRÉ D'UNE SÉRIE DE PAYSAGES URBAINS.

■ **650** ILLUSTRATOR: DENNIS CORRIGAN CLIENT: REVIVAL GRAPHICS COUNTRY: USA ■ **650** SELF-PROMOTIONAL ITEM FOR THE ILLUSTRATOR. TECHNIQUE: OIL ON CANVAS. ● **650** EIGENWERBUNG. TECHNIK: ÖL AUF LEINWAND. ▲ **650** AUTOPROMOTION. TECHNIQUE: HUILE SUR TOILE.

651

■ **651** ILLUSTRATOR: BRALDT BRALDS ART DIRECTOR: FRED WOODWARD PUBLISHER: STRAIGHT ARROW PUBLISHERS COUNTRY: USA ■ **651** PORTRAIT OF JOHN LENNON, THE WAY THE ILLUSTRATOR REMEMBERS HIM: AS AN ADVOCATE OF PEACE. IT WAS USED IN AN INTERVIEW FOR *ROLLING STONE* MAGAZINE. ● **651** PORTRÄT VON JOHN LENNON, SO WIE DER ILLUSTRATOR IHN ERINNERT: ALS ANWALT DES FRIEDENS. ES WURDE FÜR EIN INTERVIEW IN DER ZEITSCHRIFT *ROLLING STONE* VERWENDET. ▲ **651** PORTRAIT DE JOHN LENNON, TEL QUE L'ILLUSTRATEUR L'A GARDÉ EN MÉMOIRE, À SAVOIR COMME UN APÔTRE DE LA PAIX. L'IMAGE A ÉTÉ REPRODUITE DANS UNE INTERVIEW DU MAGAZINE *ROLLING STONE*.

■ **652** ILLUSTRATOR: MCRAY MAGLEBY SILKSCREENER: RORY ROBINSON COUNTRY: USA ■ **652** THIS IMAGE WAS USED IN A POSTER WITH A SPACE FOR IMPRINTS ON THE BOTTOM. THE THEME: THE FRENCH REVOLUTION. ● **652** DIESE ILLUSTRATION WURDE FÜR EIN PLAKAT VERWENDET. DAS THEMA: DIE FRANZÖSISCHE REVOLUTION. ▲ **652** CETTE IMAGE A ÉTÉ UTILISÉE COMME AFFICHE. LE SUJET: LA RÉVOLUTION FRANÇAISE.

652

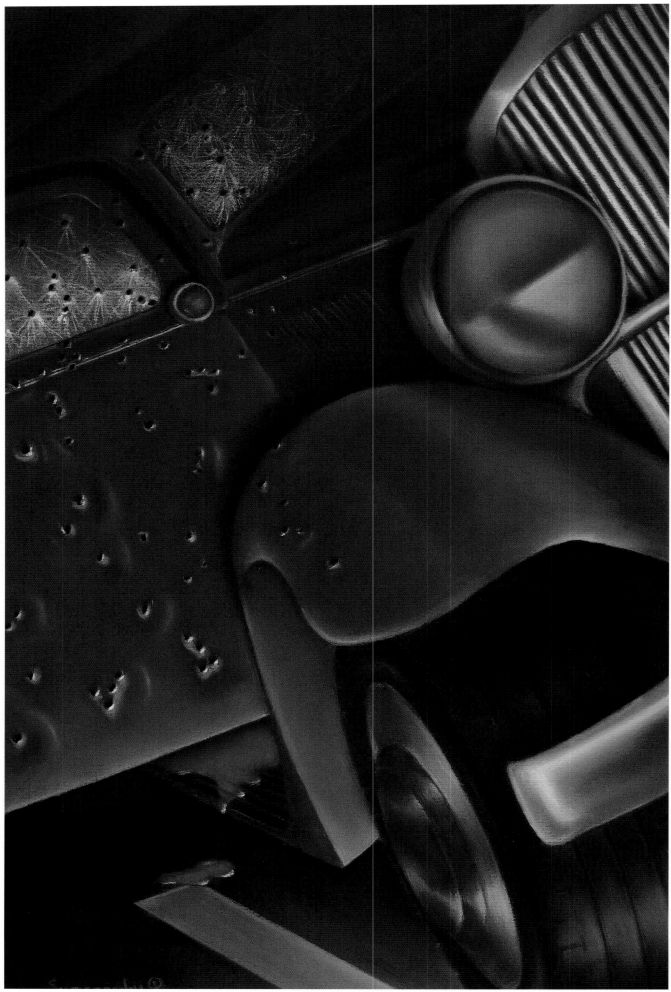

654

655

656

657

■ **653** Illustrator: ELENI CANE Publisher: SCHOOL OF VISUAL ARTS Country: USA ■ **653** "GANGS OF NEW YORK"—ASSIGNMENT FOR THE SOCIETY OF ILLUSTRATORS ANNUAL SCHOLARSHIP COMPETITION. ● **653** ARBEIT EINER STUDENTIN FÜR DEN JÄHRLICHEN STIPENDIENWETTBEWERB DER SOCIETY OF ILLUSTRATORS. ▲ **653** PROJET D'UNE ÉTUDIANTE FIGURANT DANS LE *PORTFOLIO THIRTEEN* DE LA SCHOOL OF VISUAL ARTS.

■ **654-657** Illustrator: MARZENA DOMAGALA Country: GERMANY ■ **654-657** GRADUATE WORK OF A STUDENT. THE FICTITIOUS CLIENT WAS THE BODY SHOP CHAIN. ● **654-657** DIPLOMARBEIT EINER STUDENTIN. DER ANGENOMMENE AUFTRAGGEBER WAR THE BODY SHOP, EINE LADENKETTE, DIE VOR ALLEM NATURKOSMETIK ANBIETET. ▲ **654-657** TRAVAIL DE DIPLÔME D'UNE ÉTUDIANTE. LE CLIENT FICTIF ÉTAIT THE BODY SHOP.

■ **658** Illustrator: PHILLIP BURKE Art Director: FRED WOODWARD Publisher: STRAIGHT ARROW PUBLISHERS Country: USA ■ **658** PORTRAIT OF KURT COBAIN OF THE ROCK GROUP NIRVANA, PUBLISHED IN *ROLLING STONE* MAGAZINE. ● **658** PORTRÄT VON KURT COBAIN VON DER ROCKGRUPPE NIRVANA, AUS *ROLLING STONE*. ▲ **658** PORTRAIT DE KURT COBAIN, DU GROUPE NIRVANA, PUBLIÉ DANS LE MAGAZINE *ROLLING STONE*.

■ (FOLLOWING SPREAD) **659** Illustrator: JEFF KOEGEL Art Director: STEVE FORBES Client: INGRAM MICRO Country: USA ■ **659** "FORGED OF STRONGER STUFF"—ILLUSTRATION FOR AN ADVERTISEMENT HIGHLIGHTING THE CLIENT'S SIZE AND STRENGTH IN THE COMPUTER RESELLING INDUSTRY. ● (NÄCHSTE DOPPELSEITE) **659** «AUS STÄRKEREM STOFF GESCHMIEDET» – ILLUSTRATION FÜR EINE ANZEIGE, IN DER DIE BEDEUTUNG UND STÄRKE DES KUNDEN ALS WIEDERVERKÄUFER VON COMPUTERN HERAUSGESTELLT WIRD. ▲ (DOUBLE PAGE SUIVANTE) **659** ILLUSTRATION POUR UNE ANNONCE DANS LAQUELLE ON SUGGÈRE LA TAILLE ET L'IMPORTANCE DU CLIENT DANS LE SECTEUR DE LA REVENTE D'ORDINATEURS.

658

CORPORATE IDENTITY

FIRMENERSCHEINUNGSBILDER

IDENTITÉ CORPORATE

PACKAGING

PACKUNGEN

PACKAGING

# Logos

■ **660** Art Director: SHARON WERNER Designer: JOHN SORGAARD Client: JOE DUFFY DESIGN Country: USA ■ **661** Art Director/Designer: DOUGLAS MAY Agency: MAY & CO. Client: INTEX SOFTWARE Country: USA ■ **662** Art Director: JOHN SWIETER Designers: JIM VOGEL, PAUL MUNSTERMAN, JOHN SWIETER Agency: SWIETER DESIGN Client: OMNI SWITCH Country: USA ■ **663** Art Director/Designer: THOMAS VASQUEZ Client: INTERNATIONAL PRODUCTS FOR MEN Country: USA ■ **664** Art Director/Designer: RÜDIGER GÖTZ Agency: STUBENRAUCH&SIMON Client: MERCATOR AUTOLEASING Country: GERMANY ■ **665** Art Director: MICHEL RABY Designer: NOELLE PRINZ Agency: ICI DESIGN Client: SHIZUKA Country: FRANCE ■ **666** Art Director/Designer: RÜDIGER GÖTZ Agency: STUBENRAUCH&SIMON, WERBEAGENTUR Client: PROF. DR. WEISMANN Country: GERMANY ■ **667** Art Director/Designer/Illustrator: DAVID ZAUHAR Agency: ZAUHAR DESIGN Client: BLACK DOG – JEFF ZAUHAR Country: USA ■ **668** Art Director: THOMAS VASQUEZ Designers/Illustrators: MIKE GOULD, THOMAS VASQUEZ Agency: BRAINSTORM INC. Client: LEGENDS Country: USA ■ **669** Art Director/Designer: MICHAEL VANDERBYL Agency: VANDERBYL DESIGN Client: BEDFORD PROPERTIES Country: USA ■ **670** Art Director/Designer/Illustrator: DIANA MCKNIGHT Agency: SIBLEY PETEET DESIGN Client: LULLABY Country: USA ■ **671** Art Directors/Designers: C.S. ANDERSON, DAN OLSON Illustrator: RANDALL DAHLK Agency: ANDERSON OLSON DESIGN CO. Client: Z-PIX Country: USA ■ **672** Designers: THOMAS HOFMANN, HANKA POLKEHN Studio: ARTCONEPT BERLIN Client: SCHWERTRANSPORT EISENHÜTTENSTADT

661  662  663  664  665  666

667  668  669  670  671  672

673  674  675  676  677  678

679  680  681  682  683  684

Country: GERMANY ■ **673** Art Director/Designer: JOE VERA Agency: JOE VERA DESIGN Client: LITTLE TOKYO DENTAL GROUP Country: USA ■ **674** Art Director/Designer: WILLIAM SCOTT Agency: FORWARD PUBLISHING Client: THE SCRUTINY COMPANY Country: GREAT BRITAIN ■ **675** Art Director: GORDON GILL Designer: DAWN LILLINGTON Agency: MARKETPLACE DESIGN GROUP Client: ROVER COMPANY Country: GREAT BRITAIN ■ **676** Art Director/Designer: DAN HOWARD Agency: DESIGNSENSE Client: ERIC MCNULTY Country: USA ■ **677** Art Directors: DITI KATONA, JOHN PYLYPCZAK Designer: JOHN PYLYPCZAK Agency: CONCRETE DESIGN Client: DESIGN EXCHANGE Country: CANADA ■ **678** Art Director: JOSE SERRANO Designer: JOSE SERRANO Illustrator: NANCY STAHL Agency: MIRES DESIGN Client: DELEO CLAY TILE CO. Country: USA ■ **679** Art Director: EARL GEE Designers: EARL GEE, FANI CHUNG Studio: EARL GEE DESIGN Client: SAN FRANCISCO ARTS COMMISSION Country: USA ■ **680** Art Director/Designer: ROMAN ROSYK Client: UNIVERSITY OF WROCLAW Country: POLAND ■ **681** Art Director: JACK ANDERSON Designers: JACK ANDERSON, BRIAN O'NEILL Agency: HORNALL ANDERSON DESIGN Client: GANG OF SEVEN Country: USA ■ **682** Designer/Illustrator: BÜLENT ERKMEN Client: FRIENDS OF CUISINE Country: TURKEY ■ **683** Art Directors: ROLAND MEISSNER, CLIVE GAY Designer: ROLAND MEISSNER Agency: TRADEMARK DESIGN Client: MERCEDES BENZ Country: SOUTH AFRICA ■ **684** Art Director: CHRIS BEATTY Designer: CHRIS BEATTY Creative Directors: YOUNG + LARAMORE Agency: YOUNG + LARAMORE Client: VANDERVELDE INDUSTRIAL EDUCATION Country: USA

■ **685** Art Director: GARRY EMERY Studio: EMERY VINCENT ASSOCIATES Client: AEROSPACE TECHNOLOGIES OF AUSTRALIA Country: AUSTRALIA ■ **686** Designer: KAZUMASA NAGAI Studio: NIPPON DESIGN CENTER, INC. Client: YASUDA MUTUAL LIFE INSURANCE CO. Country: JAPAN ■ **687** Art Director: LANA RIGSBY Designer: LANA RIGSBY Illustrator: ANDY DEARWATER Agency: RIGSBY DESIGN INC. Client: PRESENTATION TECHNOLOGIES Country: USA ■ **688** Designer: ADRIENNE POLLARD Agency: POLLARD DESIGN Client: CLIMBING GUIDE Country: USA ■ **689** Art Director/Designer: THOMAS VASQUEZ Agency: BRAINSTORM INC. Client: MECCA Country: USA ■ **690** Designer: CALVIN L. NG Agency: THE CRICKET CO. Client: STATIC FREE Country: USA ■ **691** Art Director: KIT HINRICHS Designer: MARK SELF Agency: PENTAGRAM DESIGN Client: PACIFIC DESIGN CENTER Country: USA ■ **692** Art Director: TODD HAUSWIRTH Designer: TODD HAUSWIRTH Agency: CHARLES S. ANDERSON DESIGN CO. Client: TODD HAUSWIRTH Country: USA ■ **693, 694** Art Director: MAKOTO SAITO Designer: MAKOTO SAITO Client: CITY OF TOKYO Country: JAPAN ■ **695** Designer: SABINE POTTHAST Client: SPV GMBH Country: GERMANY ■ **696** Art Directors: KEN WHITE, TRINA CARTER NUOVO Designer: TRINA CARTER NUOVO Agency: WHITE & ASSOCIATES Client: AJAX MEDIA COMPANY Country: USA ■ **697** Art Director: DUNG D. HOANG Designer: DUNG D. HOANG Client: ASIAN FILM FESTIVAL Country: USA ■ **698** Art Director: FREDERICK KNAPP

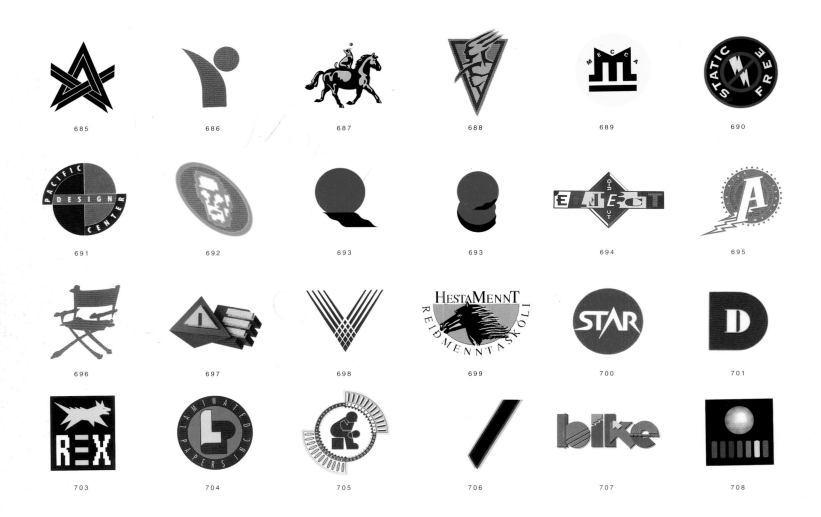

685    686    687    688    689    690

691    692    693    693    694    695

696    697    698    699    700    701

703    704    705    706    707    708

Designer: FREDIRICK KNAPP Agency: FUSION DESIGN Client: AVENUE EDIT Country: USA ■ **699** Art Director: BYRON JACOBS Designer: BYRON JACOBS Agency: PPA DESIGN LTD. Client: VALUATION SERVICES LTD. Country: HONG KONG ■ **700** Art Director: GISLI B. BJÖRNSSON Designer: GISLI B. BJÖRNSSON Client: HESTAMENNT Country: ICELAND ■ **701** Art Directors: KAN TAI-KEUNG, FREEMAN LAU SIU HONG, EDDY YU CHI KONG Designers: CLEMENT YICK TAT WA, BARRY WONG ON MING Agency: KAN TAI-KEUNG DESIGN & ASSOCIATES LTD. Client: STAR PAGING (HOLDING) LTD. Country: HONG KONG ■ **702** Designer: ANDY DEARWATER Client: ANDY DEARWATER DESIGN Country: USA ■ **703** Art Director: JOEL FULLEN Designers: LISA ASHNERTH, JOEL FULTEN Illustrator: RALF SCHUETZ Agency: PINKHAUS DESIGN CORPORATION Client: REX III Country: USA ■ **704** Art Director/Designer: ROBERT CIPRIANI Agency: CIPRIANI KREMER DESIGN Client: LAMINATED PAPERS, INC. Country: USA ■ **705** Art Director: ALEXANDER JAMES MUSSON Agency: ENDEAVOUR CORPORATE DESIGN Client: PAP, PROGRESSIVE ALLIANCE OF PHILOSOPHERS Country: AUSTRALIA ■ **706** Art Director: KLAUS HESSE Designer: STEFAN CAESAR, MARCUS DORAU Agency: HESSE DESIGNAGENTUR Client: VOSS TV ATELIERS Country: GERMANY ■ **707** Art Director: JAN RASMUS MAHLER Designer: JAN RASMUS MAHLER Client: BIKE Country: GERMANY ■ **708** Art Director: MICHAEL MEADE Designer: MICHAEL MEADE Client: GTE CORPORATION Country: USA

709

710

711

712

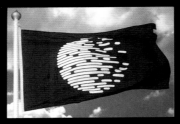

713

714

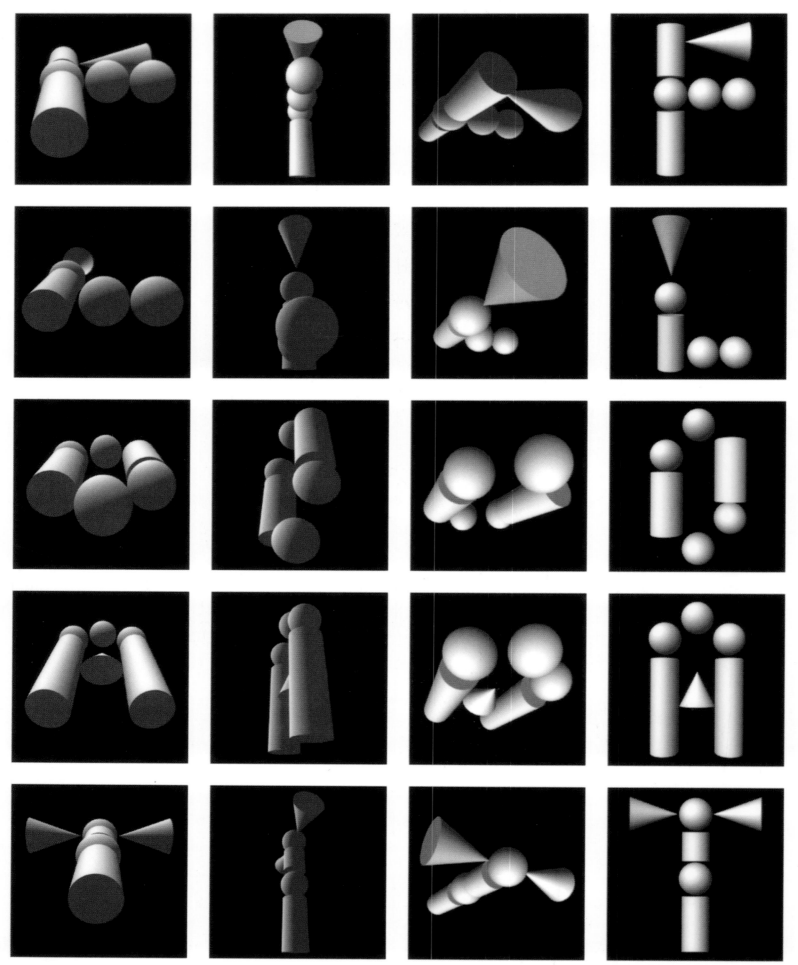

■ (PREVIOUS SPREAD) **708** Art Director: MICHAEL MEADE Designer: MICHAEL MEADE Client: GTE CORPORATION Country: USA ■ **709** Art Director: SHIN MATSUNAGA Designer: SHIN MATSUNAGA Client: SHIN MATSUNAGA DESIGN Country: JAPAN ■ **710** Art Director: PAULA SCHER Designer: PAULA SCHER Agency: PENTAGRAM DESIGN Client: THOMSON CONSUMER ELECTRONICS/RCA Country: USA ■ **711** Art Director: LANA RIGSBY, LOWELL WILLIAMS Designer: LANA RIGSBY Studio: LOWELL WILLIAMS DESIGN Client: THE CONTEMPORARY ARTS MUSEUM OF HOUSTON Country: USA ■ **712** Art Directors: ERIC RICKABAUGH, MARK KRUMEL Designer: MICHAEL TENNYSON SMITH Client: OHIO STATE UNIVERSITY Country: USA ■ **713** Art Directors: TOR PETTERSEN, PAUL MANN Designers: PAUL MANN, SANJAY PATEL Photographer:

716

717

718

JULIA WISEMAN Agency: PETTERSEN & PARTNERS LTD. Client: CABLE AND WIRELESS PLC Country: GREAT BRITAIN ■ **714** Art Director: JAMES SKILES Designer/Illustrator: KATHRYN KLEIN Agency: MIDNIGHT OIL STUDIOS Client: THE ORIGINAL SPORTS SALOON Country: USA

■ (THIS SPREAD) **715** Art Director: AKIO OKOMURA Designer: EMI KAJIHARA Agency: PACKAGING CREATE INCORPORATED Client: INOUE YOSHITEN COMPANY, LTD. Country: JAPAN ■ **716** Designer: MARK RYDEN Client: MARK RYDEN Country: USA ■ **717** Art Director: MICHAEL BIERUT Designer: MICHAEL BIERUT Agency: PENTAGRAM DESIGN Client: THE COUNCIL OF FASHION DESIGNERS OF AMERICA Country: USA ■ **718** Art Director: KELLY O'KEEFE Illustrator: SCOTT WRIGHT Agency: O'KEEFE MARKETING Client: PUBLICITY HOUNDS Country: USA

719

720

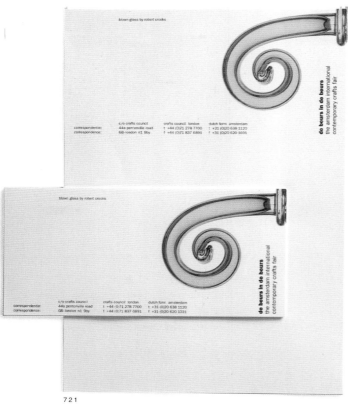

721

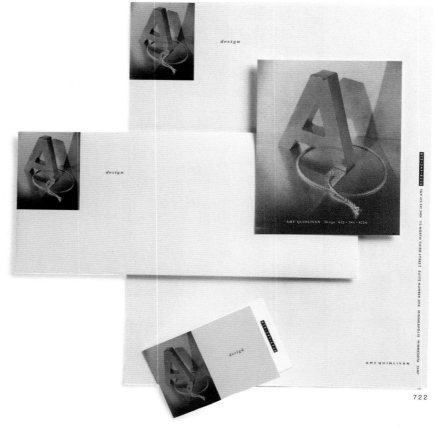

722

723

■ **719** Designer: Ron van der Vlugt Illustrator: Ron van der Vlugt Client: Marcel van der Vlugt Country: Netherlands ■ **720** Art Director: John Coy Designer: Laurie Handler Signage: Sean Alatorre Agency: Coy Client: San Diego Design Center Country: USA ■ **721** Art Director: John Rushworth Designers: John Rushworth, Nick Finney Agency: Pentagram Design Ltd. Client: Crafts Council Country: Great Britain ■ **722** Art Director: Amy Quinlivan Photographer: Daniel Arsenault Country: USA ■ **723** Art Director: Sharon M. Werner Illustrators: Sharon M. Werner, Lynn Schulte Agency: Werner Design Werks Inc. Client: Joanie Bernstein Country: USA

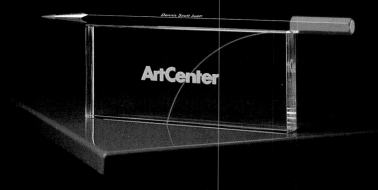

724

725

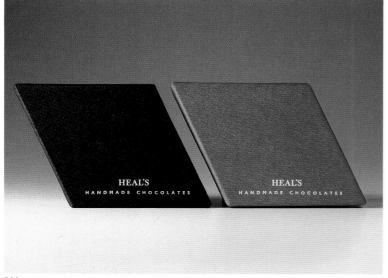

726

727

■ **724** ART DIRECTOR/DESIGNER: DENNIS SCOTT JUETT AGENCY: THE GRAPHICS SHOP CLIENT: ART CENTER COLLEGE OF DESIGN COUNTRY: USA ■ **724** A GIFT GIVEN TO MAJOR DONORS TO THE ART CENTER COLLEGE OF DESIGN. THE PENCIL, A BASIC TOOL OF THE SCHOOL, WAS CHOSEN AS SYMBOL. IT IS INSCRIBED WITH THE DONOR'S NAME. ● **724** EIN GESCHENK FÜR SPONSOREN DES ART CENTER COLLEGE OF DESIGN. DER BLEI-STIFT, EINES DER ELEMENTAREN ARBEITSINSTRUMENTE DER SCHULE, DIENTE ALS SYMBOL. ▲ **724** UN CADEAU DESTINÉ AUX SPONSORS DU ART CENTER COLLEGE OF DESIGN, PASADENA. LE CRAYON, INSTRUMENT CLASSIQUE DE L'ÉCOLE PRIMAIRE, A ÉTÉ CHOISI COMME SYMBOLE.

■ **725** ART DIRECTOR: MARY LEWIS DESIGNERS: PETER KAY, MARY LEWIS, MARGARET NOLAN PHOTOGRAPHER: ROBIN BROADBENT AGENCY: LEWIS MOBERLY CLIENT: PARFUMS ICARDI EGAN COUNTRY: GREAT BRITAIN ■ **725** "JOURNEY" IS A NEW MALE FRAGRANCE AIMED AT YOUNG, ASPIRING MEN. ITS IDENTITY WAS TO BE CLEAR AND SIMPLE. THE FROSTED AQUAMARINE BOTTLE IS DESIGNED TO FEEL SLIM IN THE HAND AND COOL TO THE TOUCH. ● **725** "JOURNEY" IST EIN NEUES PARFUM FÜR DEN JUNGEN, AUFSTREBENDEN MANN. ES SOLLTE SICH KLAR UND SCHLICHT PRÄSENTIEREN. DIE FLASCHE AUS OPAKEM GLAS IN AQUAMARIN FÜHLT SICH SCHLANK UND KÜHL AN. ▲ **725** "JOURNEY" EST UN NOUVEAU PAR-FUM POUR LES HOMMES JEUNES ET DYNAMIQUES. IL DEVAIT ÊTRE PRÉSENTÉ DE MANIÈRE CLAIRE, AVEC SIMPLICITÉ. LA BOUTEILLE DE VERRE OPAQUE DE COULEUR AIGUE-MARINE EST AGRÉABLE ET FRAÎCHE AU TOUCHER. L'EMBALLAGE EN CARTON EST CONSTITUÉ DE DEUX PARTIES.

■ **726, 727** ART DIRECTOR: MARY LEWIS DESIGNER: JIMMY YANG AGENCY: LEWIS MOBERLY CLIENT: HEAL'S COUNTRY: GREAT BRITAIN ■ **726, 727** THE PACKAGING FOR HEAL'S HOMEMADE CHOCOLATES STANDS FOR PURE FORM AND ATTENTION TO DETAIL. THE DISTINCTIVE ANGLED SHAPE CRE-ATES STRIKING IN-STORE DISPLAYS, WHICH WAS AN ESSENTIAL PART OF THE ASSIGNMENT. ● **726, 727** DIE VERPACKUNG FÜR HAUSGEMACHTE SCHOKOLADE STEHT FÜR KLARE FORMEN UND LIEBE ZUM DETAIL. DIE FORM ERLAUBT EINE ATTRAKTIVE PRÄSENTATION IM LADEN, WAS EIN WICHTIGER PUNKT DES AUFTRAGS WAR. ▲ **726, 727** L'EMBALLAGE DE CE CHOCOLAT MAISON DE HEALS REFLÈTE LA TRADITION DE CE FABRICANT AIMANT LA SIMPLICITÉ ET SOUCIEUX DU DÉTAIL. LA FORME PARTICULIÈRE PERMET UNE PRÉSENTATION SPECTACULAIRE DANS LES MAGASINS

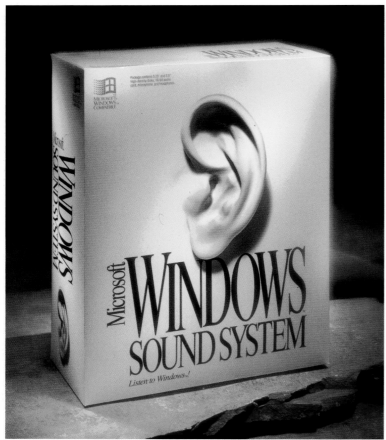

728

729

■ **728** ART DIRECTOR/DESIGNER: ROSS PATRICK CREATIVE DIRECTOR: KEN ORVIDAS PHOTOGRAPHER: DAN LANGLEY CLIENT: MICROSOFT CORPORATE COMMUNICATIONS COUNTRY: USA ■ **728** PACKAGING FOR MICROSOFT'S WINDOWS SOUND SYSTEM. THE HUMAN EAR, THE BEST PIECE OF "SOUND" EQUIPMENT, WAS CHOSEN AS A SYMBOL. ● **728** VERPACKUNG FÜR DAS WINDOWS TONSYSTEM VON MICROSOFT. DAS MENSCHLICHE OHR DIENT ALS SYMBOL. ▲ **728** EMBALLAGE DU SYSTÉME SONORE WINDOWS DE MICROSOFT. L'OREILLE HUMAINE SYMBOLISE LE CONTENU.

■ **729** ART DIRECTOR: EARL GEE DESIGNERS: EARL GEE, FANI CHUNG ILLUSTRATORS: EARL GEE, DAVID BOTTOMS AGENCY: EARL GEE DESIGN CLIENT: PENSOFT CORPORATION COUNTRY: USA ■ **729** SOFTWARE PACKAGE. ● **729** VERPACKUNG FÜR SOFTWARE. ▲ **729** EMBALLAGE DE LOGICIEL.

■ **730** ART DIRECTOR/DESIGNER: TODD WATERBURY CLIENT: AVANT COUNTRY: USA ■ **730** PACKAGING FOR A PRIVATE-LABEL LINE OF SALON PRODUCTS. THE MATERIALUSED IS INEXPENSIVE AND RECYCLABLE, AND ECHOES THE INDUSTRIAL MOTIF OF THE SALON'S INTERIOR. ● **730** VERPACKUNG FÜR DIE PRODUKTE EINES COIFFEUR-SALONS. DAS VERWENDETE MATERIAL IST BILLIG UND WIEDERVERWERTBAR. GLEICHZEITIG ENTSPRICHT ES DEM INDUSTRIELLEN TOUCH DER EINRICHTUNG DES SALONS. ▲ **730** CONDITIONNEMENT POUR LES PRODUITS D'UN SALON DE COIFFURE. LE MATÉRIEL UTILISÉ EST ÉCONOMIQUE ET RECYCLABLE. EN MÊME TEMPS, IL CORRESPOND AU LOOK INDUSTRIEL DE CE SALON.

■ **731** ART DIRECTORS: ERIK BOLTON, CALVIN L. NG DESIGNER: CALVIN L. NG AGENCY: WEST COAST BEAUTY SUPPLY CO., IN-HOUSE CLIENT: THE CRICKET COMPANY COUNTRY: USA ■ **731** PACKAGING FOR A SERIES OF SPECIALTY COMBS FOR PROFESSIONAL HAIRSTYLISTS. ● **731** VERPACKUNG FÜR SPEZIALKÄMME FÜR COIFFEURSALONS. ▲ **731** EMBALLAGE POUR DES PEIGNES SPÉCIAUX VENDUS DANS DES SALONS DE COIFFURE.

■ **732** ART DIRECTOR: NORA VAIVADS ILLUSTRATOR: MICHAEL SAMUEL AGENCY: GOLDSMITH/JEFFREY CLIENT: BODYSLIMMERS COUNTRY: USA ■ **732** THESE JARS CONTAIN BODY ENHANCING GARMENTS FOR WOMEN. EACH PRODUCT LABEL IS DISTINGUISHED BY COLOR. ● **732** DIESE GLÄSER ENTHALTEN TEXTILIEN WIE BODIES, LEGGINGS ETC. ▲ **732** PROJET D'ÉTIQUETTE POUR DES VÊTEMENTS POUR FEMMES METTANT EN VALEUR LE CORPS.

730

731

732

733

■ 733 Art Director/Designer: JAN LEPAIR Agency: LEPAIR DESIGN Client: DRUKKERIJ SLINGER BV Country: NETHERLANDS ■ 733 THE HOLIDAY SEASON PRESENT OF A PRINTER, ACTUALLY A 3-DIMENSIONAL COLOR FAN, IS PRINTED IN 30 COLORS (PMS). THE COLORS CAN BE TAKEN OUT OF THE FRAME FOR COMPARISON. CHANGING THE CUBES ALLOWS FOR NUMEROUS DESIGN VARIATIONS. ● 733 NEUJAHRSGESCHENK EINES DRUCKERS. ES IST EINE DREIDIMENSIONALE FARBSKALA, DIE AUS 30 (PMS)FARBEN BESTEHT. DIE FARBEN LASSEN SICH ZU VERGLEICHS-ZWECKEN AUS DEM RAHMEN NEHMEN. DIE VERÄNDERUNG DER KUBEN ERMÖGLICHT ZAHLREICHE VARIATIONEN DES DESIGNS. ▲ 733 CADEAU DE NOUVEL AN ENVOYÉ AUX CLIENTS D'UN IMPRIMEUR. IL S'AGIT D'UN DÉGRADÉ TRIDIMENSIONNEL COMPOSÉ DE 30 COULEURS (PMS). ON PEUT LES RETIRER DU CADRE AFIN DE LES COMPARER. LA MODIFICATION DES CUBES PERMET D'INNOMBRABLES VARIATIONS AU NIVEAU DU DESIGN.

■ 734 Art Director: PAUL CURTIN Designer: PETER LOCKE Agency: PAUL CURTIN DESIGN LTD. Client: KEENA Country: USA ■ 734 REDESIGN OF THE PACKAGING FOR A PROMOTIONAL ITEM, A PLASTIC CAMERA WHICH CAN TAKE 4 SHOTS IN ONE FRAME. THE CHALLENGE WAS TO RAISE THE PRODUCT'S PERCEIVED VALUE AND TO CREATE A HUMOROUS INSTRUCTION BOOKLET. ● 734 NEUGESTALTUNG DER VERPACKUNG FÜR EINEN

734

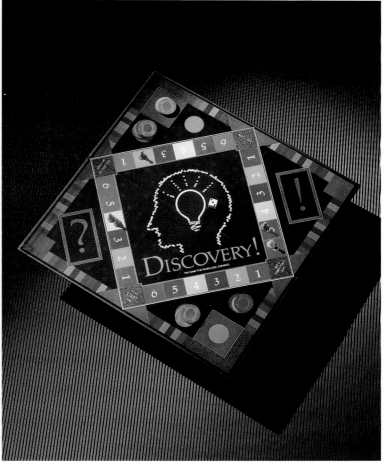

735

WERBEARTIKEL, EINE PLASTIKKAMERA, DIE VIER AUFNAHMEN IN EINEM RAHMEN MACHEN KANN. DIE HERAUSFORDERUNG LAG IN DER AUFWERTUNG DES PRODUKTS UND IN DER GESTALTUNG EINER HUMORVOLLEN GEBRAUCHSANWEISUNG. ▲ 734 RÉACTUALISATION DE L'EMBAL-LAGE D'UN ARTICLE PUBLICITAIRE, UNE CAMÉRA EN PLASTIQUE BON MARCHÉ QUI PEUT PRENDRE QUATRE CLICHÉS DANS UN CADRE. L'OBJEC-TIF ÉTAIT DE METTRE EN VALEUR LE PRODUIT ET DE CRÉER UN MODE D'EMPLOI SI POSSIBLE HUMORISTIQUE DANS SA PRÉSENTATION.

■ 735 Art Directors: SANDY HILL, TOM ANTREASIAN Designer: SANDY HILL Agency: A-HILL DESIGN LTD. Client: AMERICAN SOCIETY OF RADIOLOGIC TECHNOLOGISTS Country: USA ■ 735 GRAPHIC DESIGN AND PACKAGING FOR AN EDUCATIONAL BOARD GAME FOR ENTRY-LEVEL RADIOLOGY STUDENTS. ● 735 GRAPHISCHE GESTALTUNG UND VERPACKUNG FÜR EIN BRETTSPIEL, DAS DER AUSBILDUNG VON RADIOLOGIE-STU-DENTEN DIENT. ▲ 735 UN JEU DE SOCIÉTÉ QUI EST UTILISÉ DANS LA FORMATION DES ÉLÈVES EN RADIOLOGIE DES ÉTUDIANTS EN MÉDECINE.

736

737

738

739

740

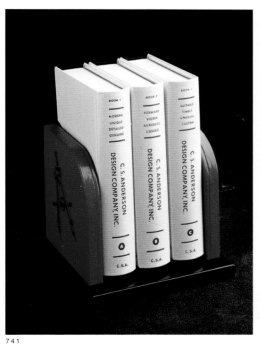

741

742

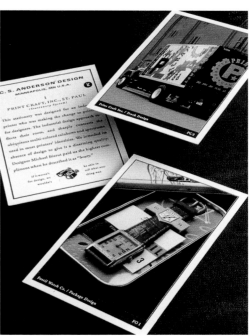

743

■ **736-739** ART DIRECTOR: CHARLES S. ANDERSON DESIGNERS: CHARLES S. ANDERSON, DANIEL OLSON ILLUSTRATORS: CHARLES S. ANDERSON, RANDALL DAHLK AGENCY: C.S. ANDERSON DESIGN CO. CLIENT: C.S. ANDERSON DESIGN CO. COUNTRY: USA ■ **736-739** MANUFACTURED BY THE FOSSIL WATCH COMPANY, THESE CHARLES S. ANDERSON DESIGN COMPANY WATCHES ARE SOLD IN MUSEUMS AND TO DESIGNERS. IT IS THE COMPANY'S FIRST ATTEMPT AT MARKETING A PRODUCT OF ITS OWN DESIGN DIRECTY TO THE PUBLIC. ● **736-739** DIESE VON DER CHARLES S. ANDERSON DESING COMPANY ENTWORFENEN UHREN WERDEN AN MUSEEN UND DESIGNER VERKAUFT. DAMIT BIETET DIE FIRMA ZUM ERSTEN MAL EIN EIGENES PRODUKT DIREKT ZUM VERKAUF AN. HERSTELLER IST DIE FOSSIL WATCH COMPANY. ▲ **736-739** CES MONTRES CRÉÉES PAR LE STUDIO DE DESIGN CHARLES S. ANDERSON SONT VENDUES À DES MUSÉES ET À DES DESIGNERS. IL S'AGIT DE LA PREMIÈRE TENTATIVE DE CETTE FIRME DE COMMERCIALISER DIRECTEMENT L'UN DE SES PRODUITS. ELLES ONT ÉTÉ FABRIQUÉES PAR LA FOSSIL WATCH COMPANY.

744

■ (PREVIOUS SPREAD) **740** ART DIRECTORS: SCOTT MEDNICK, CHERYL RUDICH, LOID DER DESIGNER: LOID DER PHOTOGRAPHERS: CHRIS WIMPEY, SUSAN WERNER AGENCY: THE MEDNICK GROUP CLIENT: BELL SPORTS COUNTRY: USA ■ **740** PACKAGES THAT HAD TO BE A STRONG AND STRIKING FOR THE BEST IMPACT IN BIKING SPECIALTY STORES. IN ADDITION THEY HAD TO REFLECT THE TECHNICAL AND DESIGN ADVANCEMENTS OF THE NEW LINE OF BICYCLING HELMETS. ● (VORANGEHENDE DOPPELSEITE) **740** DIESE VERPACKUNGEN FÜR FAHRRADHELME MUSSTEN AUFFÄL-LIG SEIN, UM AUCH AUF DEM FUSSBODEN VON FAHRRADSPEZIALGESCHÄFTEN ZU WIRKEN. ▲ (DOUBLE PAGE PRÉCÉDENTE) **740** CES EMBAL-LAGES DEVAIENT ÊTRE SOLIDES ET VOYANTS AFIN DE FAIRE ÉGALEMENT DE L'EFFET SUR LES SOLS DES MAGASINS DE CYCLES SPÉCIALISÉS.

■ (PREVIOUS SPREAD) **741-743** ART DIRECTOR: CHARLES S. ANDERSON DESIGNERS: CHARLES S. ANDERSON, DANIEL OLSON ILLUSTRATORS: CHARLES S. ANDERSON, RANDALL DAHLK AGENCY: CHARLES S. ANDERSON DESIGN CO. CLIENT: CHARLES S. ANDERSON DESIGN CO. COUNTRY: USA ■ **741-743** METAL BOOKS HOLDING CARDS WITH THE WORK OF THE CHARLES S. ANDERSON DESIGN COMPANY. THE FLEXIBLE DESIGN ALLOWS THEM TO BE TAILOR-MADE FOR EACH PROSPECTIVE CLIENT. ● (VORANGEHENDE DOPPELSEITE) **741-743** METALLBÜCHER, DIE KARTEN MIT PHO-TOS UND BESCHREIBUNGEN DER ARBEITEN DER ANDERSON DESIGN COMPANY ENTHALTEN. DAS SYSTEM ERMÖGLICHT EINE MASSGESCHNEI-DERTE ZUSAMMENSTELLUNG DER KARTEN FÜR JEDEN EINZELNEN KUNDEN. ▲ (DOUBLE PAGE PRÉCÉDENTE) **741-743** UNE SÉRIE DE LIVRES EN MÉTAL QUI RENFERMENT LES CARTES ILLUSTRÉES DE PHOTOS ET DE DESCRIPTIONS DES TRAVAUX DU STUDIO ANDERSON DESIGN COMPANY.

745

746

747

748

■ **744** ART DIRECTOR/DESIGNER: TAKU SATOH AGENCY: TAKU SATOH DESIGN OFFICE INC. CLIENT: THE CALPIS FOOD INDUSTRY COUNTRY: JAPAN ■ **744** CAN DESIGN FOR A SOFT DRINK. ● **744** DOSENGESTALTUNG FÜR EIN ERFRISCHUNGSGETRÄNK. ▲ **744** POUR UNE BOISSON RAFRAÎCHISSANTE.

■ **745** ART DIRECTORS: LANNY SOMMESE, KRISTIN SOMMESE DESIGNER: KRISTIN SOMMESE ILLUSTRATOR: KRISTIN SOMMESE AGENCY: SOMMESE DESIGN CLIENT: AQUAPENN SPRING WATER CO. COUNTRY: USA ■ **745** LABEL AND PACKAGE DESIGN FOR A SERIES OF BOTTLED FRUIT DRINKS. A BLACK BACKGROUND WAS CHOSEN FOR THE LABELS TO SET OFF THE BRILLIANT COLORS. ● **745** FRUCHSAFTGETRÄNKE. UM DIE LEUCHTENDEN FARBEN OPTIMAL ZUR GELTUNG ZU BRINGEN, WURDE FÜR DIE ETIKETTEN EIN SCHWARZER HINTERGRUND GEWÄHLT. ▲ **745** DES BOISSONS AUX FRUITS. AFIN DE METTRE LE MIEUX POSSIBLE EN VALEUR LES COULEURS LUMINEUSES, ON A ADOPTÉ UN FOND NOIR POUR LES ÉTIQUETTES.

■ **746-748** ART DIRECTOR/DESIGNER/ILLUSTRATOR: RÜDIGER ERTEL AGENCY: E DESIGN COUNTRY: GERMANY ■ **746-748** A SERIES OF LABELS FOR EXCLU-SIVE, HIGH-QUALITY WINES. THEY WERE NOT USED. ● **746-748** ETIKETTEN FÜR EXKLUSIVE, HOCHWERTIGE WEINE. SIE WURDEN NICHT VER-WENDET. ▲ **746-748** UNE SÉRIE D'ÉTIQUETTES POUR DES VINS EXCLUSIFS, DE QUALITÉ SUPÉRIEURE. ELLE N'A TOUTEFOIS PAS ÉTÉ UTILISÉE.

■ 749 ART DIRECTOR: TAKU SATOH DESIGNER: TAKU SATOH AGENCY: TAKU SATOH DESIGN OFFICE CLIENT: TAKARA SHUZO CO., LTD. COUNTRY: JAPAN
■ 749 BOTTLE LEVERY FOR JAPANESE LIQUOR. ● 749 AUSSTATTUNG FÜR JAPANISCHEN SCHNAPS. ▲ 749 POUR UNE EAU-DE-VIE JAPONAISE.

■ 750 ART DIRECTOR: EBERHARD RAPP DESIGNER: JOERG BAUER AGENCY: LEONHARDT + KERN CLIENT: SCHWABEN BRÄU ROB. LEICHT KG COUNTRY: GERMANY ■ 750 BOTTLE AND LABEL DESIGN FOR A SPECIAL BEER MARKETED EACH YEAR AT CHRISTMAS TIME. ● 750 AUSSTATTUNG FÜR DAS WEIHNACHTSBIER VON SCHWABENBRÄU. ▲ 750 BOUTEILLES ET ÉTIQUETTES POUR UNE BIÈRE QUI EST DISTRIBUÉE CHAQUE ANNÉE À NOËL.

■ 751 ART DIRECTOR: STEVE SANDSTROM DESIGNERS: STEVE SANDSTROM, GEORGE VOGT AGENCY: WIEDEN & KENNEDY CLIENT: MCKENZIE RIVER CORPORATION/BLACK STAR BEER COUNTRY: USA ■ 751 HISTORICAL PACKAGING FOR A BRAND NEW BEER TO BE USED IN AN ADVERTISING CAMPAIGN ABOUT THE BEER'S FABULOUS (BUT FICTITIOUS) PAST. THE DESIGNERS HAD TO WORK BACKWARDS FROM THE PRESENT PACKAGING. THE BOTTLES ARE ACTUAL ANTIQUES WITH NEW "ANTIQUED" LABELS APPLIED. ● 751 HISTORISCHE FLASCHENGESTALTUNG FÜR EIN NEUES BIER. SIE WAR FÜR ANZEIGEN ÜBER DIE GROSSE (ERDACHTE) VERGANGENHEIT DES BIERS BESTIMMT. DIE GESTALTER GINGEN VON DER GEGENWÄRTIGEN VERPACKUNG AUS. DIE FLASCHEN SIND ANTIK, DIE ETIKETTS ANTIK GETRIMMT. ▲ 751 DES BOUTEILLES CONÇUES À L'ANCIENNE POUR UNE NOUVELLE MARQUE DE BIÈRE. CE DÉCOR FUT DANS UN PREMIER TEMPS CONÇU EN VUE D'UNE CAMPAGNE D'ANNONCES SUR LE PASSÉ PRESTIGIEUX (OU DU MOINS CONSIDÉRÉ COMME TEL) DE CETTE BIERE. LES DESIGNERS FURENT OBLIGÉS DE PARTIR DE L'EMBALLAGE EXISTANT. LES BOUTEILLES SONT VÉRITABLEMENT ANCIENNES, TANDIS QUE LES ÉTIQUETTES ONT ÉTÉ CONÇUES DANS UN STYLE RÉTRO.

749

■ 752 ART DIRECTORS: JOE DUFFY, TODD WATERBURY DESIGNER: TODD WATERBURY AGENCY: JOE DUFFY DESIGN CLIENT: JIM BEAM BRANDS CO. COUNTRY: USA ■ 752 THE GOAL OF THIS PACKAGE DESIGN WAS TO COMMUNICATE THE COOL PEPPERMINT FLAVOR OF FROSTBITE LIQUOR. ● 752 FLASCHENAUSSTATTUNG FÜR EIN ERFRISCHENDES GETRÄNK MIT PFEFFERMINZGESCHMACK. ▲ 752 POUR UNE BOISSON RAFRAÎCHISSANTE.

■ 753 ART DIRECTOR/DESIGNER: SHARON WERNER AGENCY: JOE DUFFY DESIGN CLIENT: JIM BEAM BRANDS CO. COUNTRY: USA ■ 753 THIS BOTTLE BELONGS TO A LINE OF "KENTUCKY SMALL BATCH" BOURBONS, EACH OF WHICH HAS ITS OWN IDENTITY. KNOB CREEK DRAWS ITS AUTHENTIC IMAGE FROM THE LABEL FEATURING A NEWSPAPER ARTICLE ABOUT DISTILLING BOURBON. ● 753 DIESE FLASCHE GEHÖRT ZU EINER SERIE VON KENTUCKY BOURBON WHISKEYS IN KLEINER AUFLAGE, VON DENEN JEDE IHRE EIGENE IDENTITÄT HAT. KNOB CREEK ERHÄLT SEIN AUTHENTISCHES IMAGE DURCH DAS ETIKETT MIT DEM AUSSCHNITT EINES ZEITUNGSARTIKELS FÜR DIE HERSTELLUNG DES BOURBON. ■ 753 CETTE BOUTEILLE APPARTIENT À UNE SÉRIE DE WHISKEYS PRODUITS EN QUANTITÉ ARTISANALE. CHAQUE MODÈLE DE BOUTEILLE POSSÈDE SA PROPRE PERSONNALITÉ.

750

751

752

753

754

755

756

757

758

759

■ **754** Art Director: DAWN WOLF Designers: DAWN WOLF, MICHAEL WILDMAN Agency: WOLF DESIGN² Client: FANNY MAY CANDY SHOPS Country: USA ■ **754** PACKAGE DESIGN FOR A CLASSIC LINE OF CANDIES. ● **754** ART-DECO-VERPACKUNG FÜR PRALINEN. ▲ **754** EMBALLAGE DE PRALINÉS.

■ **755** Art Director/Designer: KRISTIN KONIAREK Agency: ATELIER FÜR KUNST UND DESIGN ERWIN SCHMÖLZER Client: WEINGUT HILLINGER Country: AUSTRIA ■ **755** LABEL DESIGN CREATED FOR AN AUSTRIAN VINEYARD. ● **755** ENTWICKLUNG EINER WEINETIKETTENSERIE, EINGEBUNDEN IN DAS CORPORATE DESIGN DIESES ÖSTERREICHISCHEN WEINGUTES. ▲ **755** PROJET D'ÉTIQUETTE POUR UN DOMAINE VITICOLE AUTRICHIEN.

■ **756** Art Director: JACK ANDERSON Designers: JACK ANDERSON, JULIE TANAGI-LOCK, MARY HERMES, LIAN NG Illustrator: JULIA LAPINE Agency: HORNALL ANDERSON DESIGN WORKS Client: STARBUCKS COFFEE COMPANY Country: USA ■ **756** IMAGES OF STEAMING COFFEE AND THE COFFEE ROASTER ARE THE CENTRAL ELEMENTS OF A LINE OF PACKAGING FOR STARBUCKS COFFEE. ● **756** DARSTELLUNGEN VON DAMP-FENDEM KAFFEE UND DEM KAFFEERÖSTEN STEHEN IM MITTELPUNKT EINER PACKUNGSREIHE FÜR STARBUCK-KAFFEE. ▲ **756** DES IMAGES D'UNE TASSE DE CAFÉ FUMANT ET DES GRAINS DE CAFÉ SERVENT DE LEITMOTIV À CETTE GAMME DE PACKAGING POUR LE CAFÉ STARBUCKS.

■ **757** Art Director: PRIMO ANGELI Designer: PHILIPPE BECKER Agency: PRIMO ANGELI INC. Client: JUST DESSERTS Country: USA ■ **757** WARM GOLDEN AND BROWN SHADES ASSOCIATED WITH BAKED GOODS WERE USED ON THIS PACKAGE FOR BISCUITS. ● **757** WARME GOLD- UND BRAUN-TÖNE, DIE AN FRISCHE BACKWAREN DENKEN LASSEN, WURDEN FÜR VERPACKUNG DIESER BISKUITS VERWENDET. ▲ **757** ON A UTILISÉ DES ORS ET DES BRUNS CHALEUREUX, QUI FONT PENSER À DES GÂTEAUX TOUT FRAIS SORTIS DU FOUR, POUR LES EMBALLAGES DE CES BISCUITS.

■ **758** Art Director/Designer: IRMGARD JANSSEN Country: GERMANY ■ **758** A STUDENT'S PROJECT: BRAND CONCEPT FOR SPICES. ● **758** STUDENTENPROJEKT: ENTWICKLUNG EINES MARKENKONZEPTES FÜR GEWÜRZE. ▲ **758** PROJET D'ÉTUDIANT: EMBALLAGE POUR DES ÉPICES.

■ **759** Designer/Illustrator: DAVID LANCASHIRE Client: EUREKA FARM PRODUCE Country: AUSTRALIA ■ **759** PACKAGING FOR A PRODUCER OF QUALITY JAMS, MUSTARDS, OILS AND VINEGARS. A CLEAN, SPECIAL LOOK WAS DESIRED, ONE THAT EMPHASIZED NATURALNESS OF THE PROD-UCTS. ● **759** PACKUNGSGESTALTUNG FÜR EINEN HERSTELLER VON QUALITÄTS-KONFITÜREN, SENF, ESSIG UND ÖL. GEFRAGT WAR EIN KLARER, SPEZIELLER LOOK MIT BETONUNG DER NATÜRLICHKEIT DER PRODUKTE. ▲ **759** CRÉATION D'EMBALLAGES POUR UN FABRICANT DE CONFITURES, DE MOUTARDE, DE VINAIGRE ET D'HUILE D'UNE QUALITÉ EXCEPTIONNELLE. IL AVAIT ÉTÉ EXIGÉ UN LOOK QUI SOULIGNE LE NATUREL DU PRODUIT.

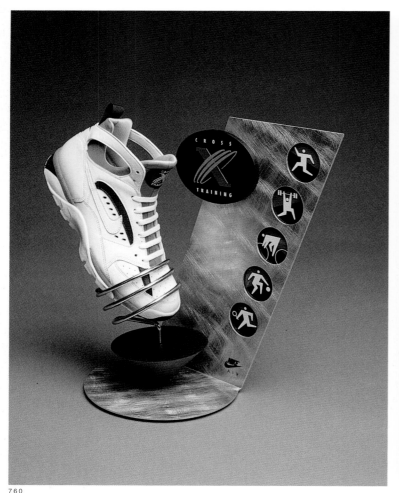

760

761

■ **760** ART DIRECTOR/DESIGNER: ALAN COLVIN ILLUSTRATORS: ALAN COLVIN, LENA JAMES AGENCY: NIKE GRAPHIC DESIGN CLIENT: NIKE, INC. COUNTRY: USA ■ **760** A CROSS-TRAINING FOOTWEAR DISPLAY THAT SHOWCASES A SINGLE SHOE. IT USES PICTOGRAMS REPRESENTING OF A VARIETY OF ATHLETIC ACTIVITIES TO EXPLAIN THE EXPRESSION "CROSS-TRAINING." ● **760** LADENDISPLAY FÜR EINEN EINZELNEN «CROSS-TRAINING» TURNSCHUH VON NIKE, DER SICH FÜR VERSCHIEDENE SPORTARTEN EIGNET. DIE PIKTOGRAMME VERSCHIEDENER ATHLETISCHER DISZIPLINEN ERKLÄREN DEN BEGRIFF «CROSS-TRAINING». ▲ **760** PRÉSENTATION DE CHAUSSURES POUR LE CROSS, CONVENANT ÉGALEMENT À D'AUTRES SPORTS. LES PICTOGRAMMES REPRÉSENTANT DIVERSES DISCIPLINES ATHLÉTIQUES EXPLIQUENT LE TERME DE «CROSS-TRAINING».

■ **761** ART DIRECTOR: KEN BRIDGER DESIGNER: LISA FARMER AGENCY: BRIDGER & BRIDGER GRAPHIC COMMUNICATION CLIENT: ALPI COUNTRY: ITALY ■ **761** THIS BOTTLE OF OLIVE OIL WAS A CHRISTMAS GIFT TO CLIENTS. ● **761** DIESE FLASCHE GEFÜLLT MIT OLIVENÖL WURDE AN WEIHNACHTEN AN DIE KUNDEN VERSCHENKT. ▲ **761** CETTE BOUTEILLE CONTENANT DE L'HUILE D'OLIVE ÉTAIT UN CADEAU DE NOËL DESTINÉ AUX CLIENTS.

RECORD COVERS, BOOKS, CALENDARS


SCHALLPLATTEN, BÜCHER, KALENDER


DISQUES, LIVRES, CALENDRIERS

■ 762 ART DIRECTOR: MARIANNE VON ALLESCH DESIGNER: MARIANNE VON ALLESCH PUBLISHER: SPV GMBH COUNTRY: GERMANY ■ 763-770 ART DIRECTOR: KEISUKE UNOSAWA DESIGNER: KEISUKE UNOSAWA PHOTOGRAPHERS: EIICHIRO SAKATA (763, 764) CLIFF WATTS (765, 766), EDWARD M. HAMES (767, 768) STYLIST: MIHO KINOMURA (763, 764, 767, 768) STUDIO: KEISUKE UNOSAWA DESIGN CLIENT: VIDEOARTS JAPAN COUNTRY: JAPAN

762

763

764

765

766

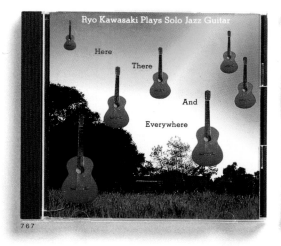

767

768

769

770

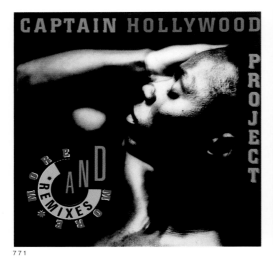

771

772

773

774

775

776

777

778

779

■ **771, 773** ART DIRECTORS/DESIGNERS: SUSANNE WACKER, WOLFGANG SCHÄFFER PHOTOGRAPHERS: ESSER & STRAUSS AGENCY: DESIGN 3 PUBLISHER: INTERCORD TON COUNTRY: GERMANY ■ **771, 773** COVERS FOR MAXI CDS. ● **771, 773** HÜLLEN FÜR MAXI-CDS. ▲ **771, 773** CASSETTES DE CD GÉANTS.

■ **772** ART DIRECTOR/DESIGNER: ALEXANDER BARTEL AGENCY: HEYE + PARTNER CLIENT: ARIOLA CLASSIC MEDIA COUNTRY: GERMANY ■ **772** LP COVER WITH A STYLIZED HEAD OF HITLER FOR THE ORIGINAL SOUNDTRACK OF THE GERMAN MOVIE "SCHTONK". (SCHTONK IS THE WORD WITH WHICH CHARLIE CHAPLIN CULMINATED EACH SPEECH IN THE FILM "THE GREAT DICTATOR"). THE FILM IS ABOUT THE "DISCOVERY" OF HITLER'S DIARIES. ● **772** LP-HÜLLE MIT STILISIERTEM HITLERKOPF FÜR DIE FILMMUSIK ZUM SPIELFILM «SCHTONK». (IN DEM FILM «DER GROSSE DIKTATOR» VERWENDETE CHARLIE CHAPLIN DIESES PHANTASIEWORT ALS SCHLUSS- BZW. HÖHEPUNKT SEINER JEWEILIGEN REDE.) ▲ **772** UNE TÊTE STYLISÉE D'HITLER SUR LA POCHETTE DU 33 TOURS DE LA MUSIQUE DU FILM SCHTONK. (DANS LE FILM «LE DICTATEUR», CHARLIE CHAPLIN TERMINAIT CHACUN DE SES DISCOURS PAR LE MOT «SCHTONK».) CE FILM TRAITE DE LA «DÉCOUVERTE» DU JOURNAL D'HITLER.

■ **774, 777-779** ART DIRECTOR: MASUMI OHASHI DESIGNERS: NAONOBU NAKAMURA (774, 777, 778), KEISHI MATSOKA (779) ILLUSTRATOR: NAONOBU NAKAMURA (774) PHOTOGRAPHER: YUTAKA SAKANO (777-779) AGENCY: ROUND TABLE ASSOCIATES CLIENT: AVEX D.D. INC. COUNTRY: JAPAN ■ **774, 777-779** COVERS FOR CDS WITH MUSIC BY DIFFERENT ARTISTS. ● **774, 777-779** HÜLLEN FÜR IN JAPAN VERTRIEBENE CDS MIT MUSIK VERSCHIEDENER INTERPRETEN. ▲ **774, 777-779** COUVERTURES DE CD RASSEMBLANT PLUSIEURS INTERPRÈTES, DESTINÉS AU MARCHÉ JAPONAIS.

780

■ **775** ART DIRECTOR/DESIGNER: MARGO CHASE PHOTOGRAPHER: HERB RITTS AGENCY: MARGO CHASE DESIGN CLIENT: EMI RECORDS GROUP COUNTRY: USA ■ **775** COVER EVOKING THE CONCEPT OF THE TITLE. ● **775** INTERPRETATION DES CD-TITELS. ▲ **775** UNE INTERPRÉTATION DU TITRE DU CD.

■ **776** ART DIRECTOR/DESIGNER: MARGO CHASE PHOTOGRAPHER: MERLYN ROSENBERG, HERB RITTS AGENCY: MARGO CHASE DESIGN CLIENT: GEFFEN RECORDS COUNTRY: USA ■ **776** RECORD ALBUM BY CHER: "LOVE HURTS." ● **776** «LOVE HURTS» CD VON CHER. ▲ **776** CD DE CHER «LOVE HURTS».

■ **780** ART DIRECTOR: PAUL CURTIN DESIGNER: PETER LOCKE ILLUSTRATOR: TIM CLARK AGENCY: PAUL CURTIN DESIGN LTD. CLIENT: ECLAT COUNTRY: USA ■ **780** CD SOFTWARE PACKAGING INTRODUCING ARCHITECTS, ENGINEERS AND CONSTRUCTION PROFESSIONALS TO PRODUCT INFORMATION ON COMPACT DISC. IT HAD TO APPEAR ACCESSIBLE WHILE AVOIDING THE POP MUSIC CD PACKAGING LOOK. ● **780** CD SOFTWARE-VERPACKUNG, DIE BAUFACHLEUTE MIT PRODUKTINFORMATION AUF CD VERTRAUT MACHEN SOLL. SIE SOLLTE EINLADEND AUSSEHEN, OHNE ZU SEHR AN EINE POP-CD ERINNERN. ▲ **780** UN EMBALLAGE DE LOGICIEL QUI DOIT FAMILIARISER LES ARCHITECTES, INGÉNIEURS ET PROFESSIONNELS DE LA CONSTRUCTION AVEC DES INFORMATIONS SUR CD. IL DEVAIT ÊTRE MODERNE, SANS POUR AUTANT RESSEMBLER À UN CD DE MUSIQUE POP.

■ **781-786** ART DIRECTOR/DESIGNER: MARCO GANZ PHOTOGRAPHERS: HOLGER NEU (785), A.N. SIMMEN (781-784, 786) PUBLISHER: WIESE VERLAG COUNTRY: SWITZERLAND ■ **781-786** SPREADS FROM A BOOK PRESENTING THE LIGHT SCULPTURES BY SWISS ARTIST CHRISTIAN HERDEG. ● **781-786** DOPPELSEITEN AUS EINEM BUCH MIT DEN LICHTSKULPTUREN, FARBLICHTFELDERN UND LICHTINSTALLATIONEN DES KÜNSTLERS CHRISTIAN HERDEG. ▲ **781-786** DOUBLES PAGES D'UN LIVRE PRÉSENTANT LES SCULPTURES LUMINEUSES DE L'ARTISTE SUISSE CHRISTIAN HERDEG.

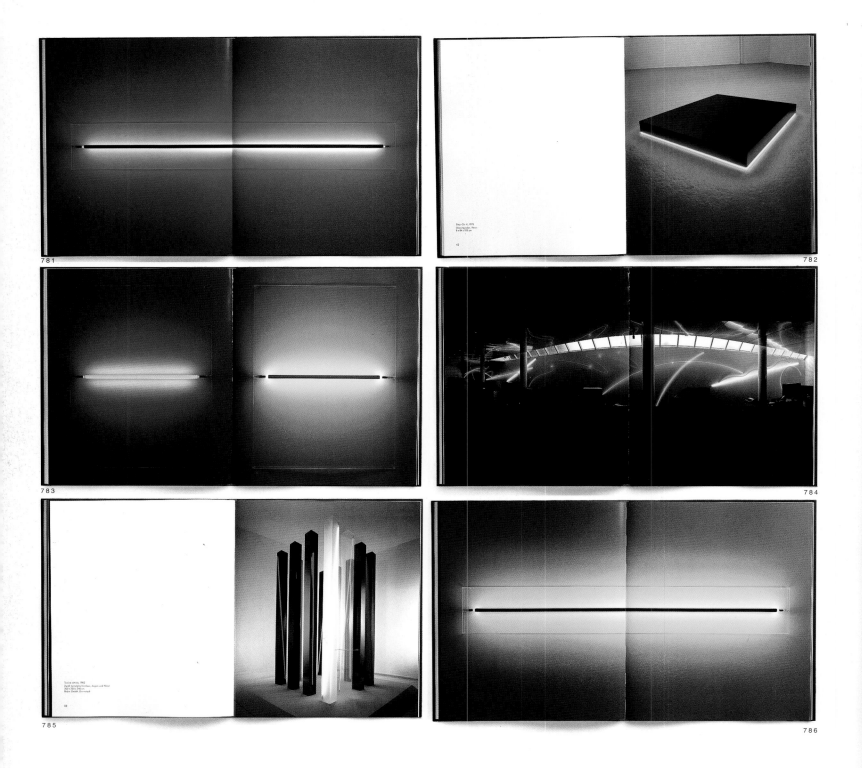

781

782

783

784

785

786

■ **787-794** ART DIRECTOR: KEIZU MATSUI DESIGNER: YUKO ARAKI PHOTOGRAPHER: YASUNORI SAITO AGENCY: TOTAL MEDIA DEVELOPMENT INSTITUTE CO., INC. PUBLISHER: TAKENAKA CARPENTRY TOOLS MUSEUM COUNTRY: JAPAN ■ **787-794** TRADITIONAL EUROPEAN WOODWORKING TOOLS ARE THE SUBJECT OF THIS MUSEUM CATALOG. ● **787-794** EUROPÄISCHE WERKZEUGE FÜR DIE HOLZBEARBEITUNG SIND DAS THEMA DIESES

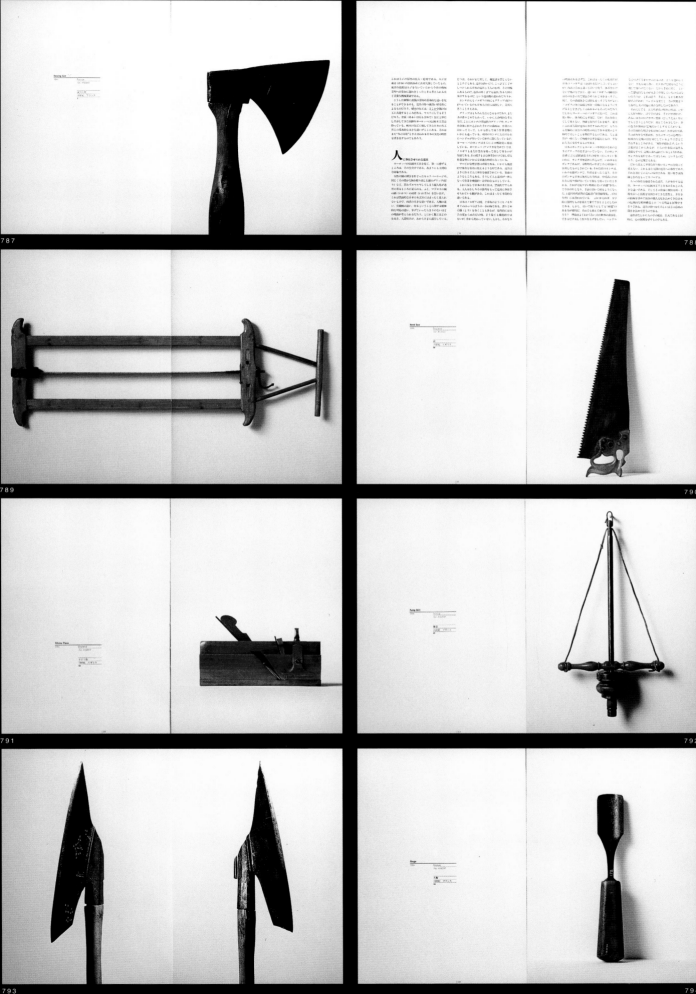

795

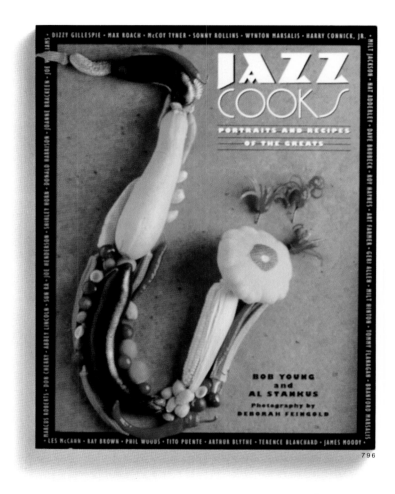

796

■ 795 ART DIRECTOR: MICHAEL BIERUT DESIGNER: AGNETHE GLATVED PHOTOGRAPHER: ALBERT WATSON AGENCY: PENTAGRAM DESIGN CLIENT: AMERICAN PHOTOGRAPHY COUNTRY: USA ■ 795 JACKET OF THE ANNUAL *AMERICAN PHOTOGRAPHY.* ● 795 SCHUTZUMSCHLAG EINES JAHRBUCHES ÜBER ANGEWANDTE UND FREIE PHOTOGRAPHIE AUS USA UND KANADA. ▲ 795 COUVERTURE DE L'ANNUAIRE DE LA PHOTOGRAPHIE AMÉRICAINE.

■ 796 ART DIRECTOR/DESIGNER: JIM WAGEMAN PHOTOGRAPHER: MARTIN JACOBS PUBLISHER: STEWART TABORI + CHANG, INC. COUNTRY: USA ■ 796 COVER FOR A BOOK WITH PORTRAITS AND RECIPES OF FAMOUS JAZZ MUSICIANS. ● 796 UMSCHLAG EINES BUCHES MIT PORTRÄTS UND REZEPTEN BERÜHMTER JAZZMUSIKER. ▲ 796 COUVERTURE D'UN LIVRE RENFERMANT LES PORTRAITS ET LES RECETTES DES MUSICIENS DE JAZZ.

■ 797 ART DIRECTOR: LUTZ MENZE DESIGNERS: LUTZ MENZE, KLAUS UNTIET PHOTOGRAPHER: CICO HEUKAMP AGENCY: LUTZ MENZE DESIGN PUBLISHER: SEKRETARIAT FÜR GEMEINSAME KULTURARBEIT IN NRW COUNTRY: GERMANY ■ 797 COVER OF A REGULAR PUBLICATION PRESENTING

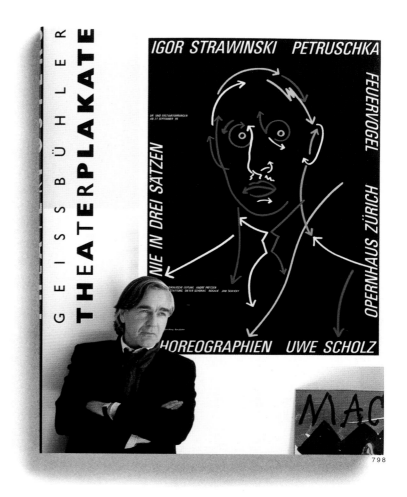

TALENTED BUT YET UNKNOWN AUTHORS. ● 797 UMSCHLAG EINER REGELMÄSSIG ERSCHEINENDEN PUBLIKATION, IN DER TALENTIERTE, NOCH UNBEKANNTE AUTORINNEN UND AUTOREN MIT TEXTEN, REZENSIONEN UND KURZBIOGRAPHIEN VORGESTELLT WERDEN. ▲ 797 COUVERTURE D'UNE PUBLICATION PARAISSANT RÉGULIÉREMENT, DANS LAQUELLE DES AUTEURS TALENTUEUX, MAIS ENCORE INCONNUS, SONT PRÉSENTÉS.

■ 798 ART DIRECTOR/DESIGNER: KARL DOMENIC GEISSBÜHLER PHOTOGRAPHER: NICK OLONETZKY PUBLISHER: GRAPHIS VERLAG AG COUNTRY: SWITZERLAND ■ 798 JACKET FOR A BOOK PRESENTING THE COMPLETE RANGE OF K.D. GEISSBÜHLER'S POSTERS FOR THE ZURICH OPERA HOUSE (1976-1992) AND OTHER THEATERS, AS WELL AS HIS STAGE SETS. ● 798 SCHUTZUMSCHLAG EINES BUCHES, DAS ALLE VON K.D. GEISSBÜHLER VON 1976 BIS 1992 GESTALTETEN PLAKATE FÜR DAS OPERNHAUS ZÜRICH, SOWIE BÜHNENBILDER UND PLAKATE FÜR ANDERE KULTURELLE ANLÄSSE UND FÜR «700 JAHRE SCHWEIZ» PRÄSENTIERT. ▲ 798 JAQUETTE D'UN LIVRE QUI RENFERME TOUTES LES AFFICHES CRÉÉES PAR K.D. GEISSBÜHLER POUR L'OPÉRA DE ZURICH, AINSI QUE SES DÉCORS ET SES AFFICHES POUR D'AUTRES MANIFESTATIONS CULTURELLES.

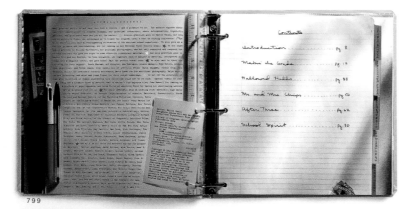

799

800

801

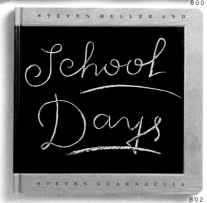

802

803

804

805

806

807

808

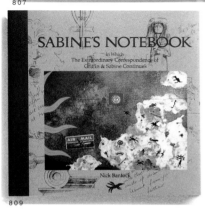

809

810

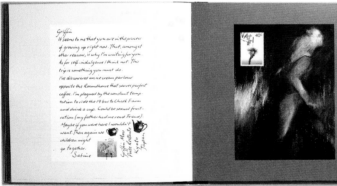

811

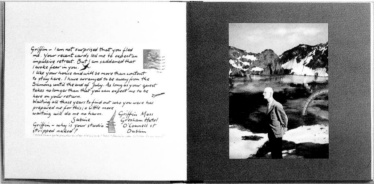

812

■ **799-806** ART DIRECTOR: RÉNÉE KHATAMI DESIGNER: LOUISE FILI PUBLISHER: ABBEVILLE PRESS COUNTRY: USA ■ **799-806** SPREADS AND COVER OF *SCHOOL DAYS*, A SCRAPBOOK OF TREASURES FROM THE GOOD OLD DAYS. THE ARTEFACTS ARE MEMENTOS OF COUNTLESS AMERICAN SCHOOL CHILDREN SPANNING AN ENTIRE CENTURY ● **799-806** DOPPELSEITEN UND UMSCHLAG VON *SCHOOL DAYS*, EINEM BUCH VOLL VON SCHÄTZEN AUS DER GUTEN ALTEN SCHULZEIT. ES SIND DIE BEHÜTETEN ERINNERUNGSSTÜCKE ZAHLLOSER AMERIKANISCHER SCHULKINDER AUS EINEM GANZEN JAHRHUNDERT. ▲ **799-806** DOUBLES PAGES ET COUVERTURE DE *SCHOOL DAYS*, UN LIVRE QUI REGORGE DE TRÉSORS DU BON VIEUX TEMPS DE L'ÉCOLE. IL S'AGIT DE SOUVENIRS QUI ONT ÉTÉ CONSERVÉS PAR D'INNOMBRABLES ÉCOLIERS AMÉRICAINS PENDANT UN SIÈCLE.

■ **807-812** ART DIRECTOR: KAREN PIKE DESIGNERS: KAREN PIKE, JULIE NOYES LONG ILLUSTRATOR: NICK BANTOCK PUBLISHER: CHRONICLE BOOKS COUNTRY: USA ■ **807-812** THE MYSTERIOUS STORY OF GRIFFIN AND SABINE IS TOLD IN POSTCARDS AND RICHLY DECORATED LETTERS THAT MUST BE REMOVED FROM THEIR ENVELOPES TO BE READ. ● **807-812** DIE SELTSAME, ROMANTISCHE GESCHICHTE VON GRIFFIN UND SABINE WIRD IN POSTKARTEN UND REICH GESCHMÜCKTEN BRIEFEN ERZÄHLT, DIE MAN AUS EINGEKLEBTEN UMSCHLÄGEN HERAUSNEHMEN MUSS, UM SIE ZU LESEN. ▲ **807-812** L'ÉTRANGE HISTOIRE DE GRIFFIN ET SABINE EST RACONTÉE SUR CES CARTES POSTALES ET CES LETTRES MAGNIFIQUEMENT DÉCORÉES: LE LECTEUR DU LIVRE DOIT EXTRAIRE CES MISSIVES DE LEURS ENVELOPPES AFIN D'EN PRENDRE CONNAISSANCE.

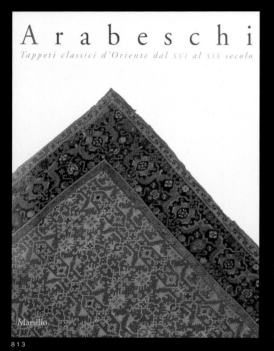

# A r a b e s c h i

*Tappeti classici d'Oriente dal XVI al XIX secolo*

Marsilio

813

# Ignazio Gardella

*progetti e architetture 1933 - 1990*

Marsilio

814

# L'arte del vetro

*silice e fuoco: vetri del XIX e XX secolo*

Marsilio

815

■ 813-815 ART DIRECTORS/DESIGNERS: E. CAMPLANI, G. PESCOLDERUNG PHOTOGRAPHER: GABRIELE BASILICO (814) AGENCY: TAPIRO S.N.C. PUBLISHER: MARSILIO EDITORI, VENEZIA COUNTRY: ITALY ■ 816 ART DIRECTOR: MICHAEL CARABETTA DESIGNERS: EARL GEE, FANI CHUNG PUBLISHER: CHRONICLE BOOKS COUNTRY: USA ■ 817 DESIGNER: PAUL ZAKRIS ILLUSTRATOR: MARYJO KOCH PUBLISHER: STEWART, TABORI + CHANG COUNTRY: USA ■ 818 ART DIRECTOR: MICHAEL CARABETTA DESIGNER: KAREN PIKE DESIGN PHOTOGRAPHER: COOKIE KINKEAD PUBLISHER: CHRONICLE BOOKS COUNTRY: USA ■ 819 ART DIRECTOR: NORBERT HEROLD PHOTOGRAPHER: JACQUES SCHUMACHER CLIENT: BUND FREISCHAFFENDER FOTOGRAFEN (BFF) COUNTRY: GERMANY ■ 820 ART DIRECTOR: HARA DESIGNER: TOM LEWIS PHOTOGRAPHER: HARA PUBLISHER: HARRY N. ABRAMS, COUNTRY: USA ■ 821 DESIGNER: SEAN PERKINS PUBLISHERS: LYNTON PLC, NATIONALE-NEDERLANDEN COUNTRY: GREAT BRITAIN, NETHERLANDS

■ **822** Art Director/Designer: Oswaldo Miranda Agency: Case de Ideas Client: "33 Paper Shop" Country: Brazil ■ **823** Designer: Michael Cronan Photographer: Penina Meisels Studio: Cronan Design Publisher: Collins Publishers Country: USA ■ **824** Designer/Illustrator: Pamela Chang Agency: RBMM/The Richards Group Publisher: Putnam's Sons Country: USA ■ **825** Art Director: Steven Brower Designer: James Victori Design Works Publisher: Carol Publishing Group Country: USA ■ **826** Art Director/Designer/Illustrator: Steven Brower Publisher: Carol Publishing Group Country: USA ■ **827** Art Director/Designer: Steven Brower Publisher: Carol Publishing Group

822

823

Country: USA ■ **828** Art Director: Suzanne Noli Illustrator: Javier Romero Publisher: HarperCollins Publishers Country: USA ■ **829** Art Director: Suzanne Noli Illustrator: Nancy Stahl Publisher: HarperCollins Publishers Country: USA ■ **830** Art Director/Designer: Steven Brower Photographer: Joanie Schwarz (Hand Tinting) Illustration: Bernard Maisner (Hand Lettering) Publisher: Carol Publishing Group Country: USA ■ **831** Art Director: Wendy Bass Designer: Gloria Adelson Photographer: Neal Peter Collection Publisher: Macmillan Publishing Co. Country: USA ■ **832** Illustrator: Rolf Jansson Publisher: Ascehoug Forlag Country: Norway

824

825

826

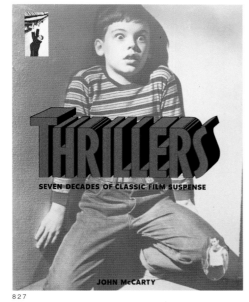

827

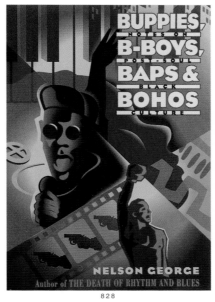

828

829

830

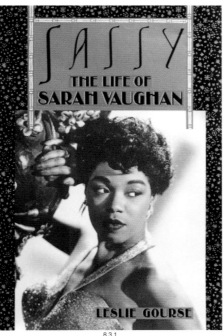

831

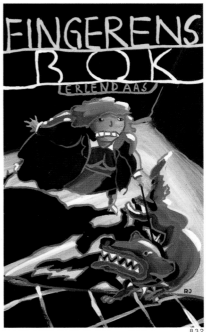

832

833

834

835

836

837

■ **833-837** Art Director: MICHAEL CARABETTA Designer: KAREN SMIDTH Photographer: LOIS GREENFIELD Publisher: CHRONICLE BOOKS Country: USA ■ **833-837** *BREAKING BOUNDS*—THE DANCE PHOTOGRAPHY OF LOIS GREENFIELD. THIS BOOK PRESENTS A COLLECTION OF STUDIO IMAGES THAT SHOW DANCERS UNFETTERED BY CHOREOGRAPHY. ● **833-837** *BREAKING BOUNDS* – DIE TANZPHOTOGRAPHIEN VON LOIS GREENFIELD. SIE PHOTOGRAPHIERTE DIE TÄNZERINNEN UND TÄNZER IN IHREM STUDIO, UM SIE BEFREIT VON DER CHOREOGRAPHIE ZEIGEN ZU KÖNNEN, UM «GRENZEN ZU SPRENGEN». ▲ **833-837** *BREAKING BOUNDS* – LES PHOTOS DE DANSE DE LOIS GREENFIELD. CE LIVRE RENFERME DES PHOTOS RÉALISÉES EN STUDIO SUR LESQUELLES LES DANSEURS ÉVOLUENT, LIBÉRÉS DES CONTINGENCES DE LA CHORÉGRAPHIE.

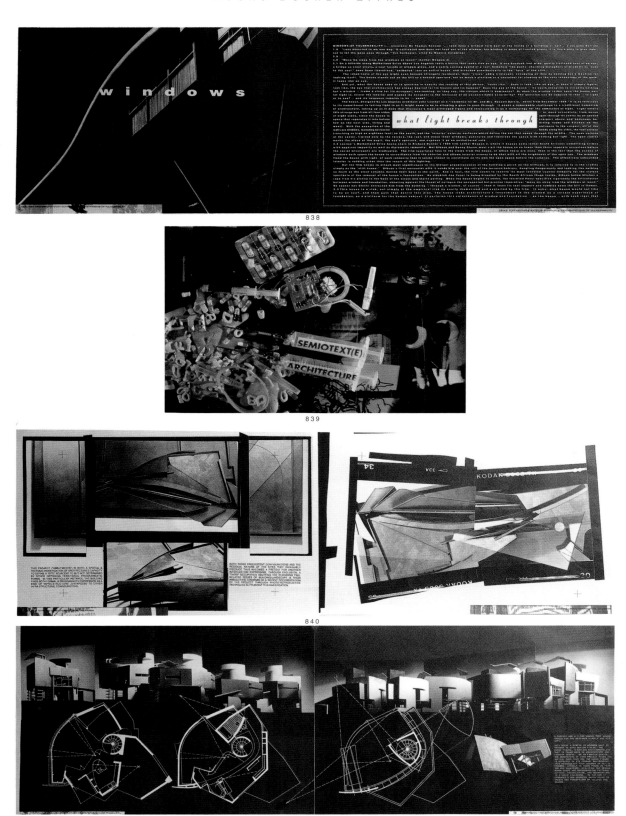

838

839

840

841

■ **838-841** ART DIRECTOR: HRAZTAN ZEITLIAN DESIGNER: TOM BONAURO (838), SHAYNE O'NEIL (840), STUDIO LOS ANGELES (841) PHOTOGRAPHER: BRIAN BOIGON (839) PUBLISHER: SEMIOTEXT(E) COUNTRY: USA ■ **838-841** THIS ISSUE OF *SEMIOTEXT(E) REVIEW* IS DEDICATED TO ADVANCED ARCHITECTURE, GRAPHIC DESIGN AND DESIGN THEORY. EACH GROUP WAS GIVEN ITS OWN SECTION TO DESIGN SO THAT THE BOOK IS ACTU-ALLY A COMPILATION OF 30 DIFFERENT PROJECTS. ● **838-841** DIESE AUSGABE DES *SEMIOTEXT(E) REVIEW* IST FORTSCHRITTLICHER ARCHITEKTUR, GRAPHIK-DESIGN UND DESIGN-THEORIE GEWIDMET. JEDE GRUPPE HAT IHRE SEITEN SELBST GESTALTET, SO DASS DAS BUCH EINE SAMMLUNG VON DREISSIG VERSCHIEDENEN PROJEKTEN ENTHÄLT. ▲ **838-841** CE NUMÉRODE *SEMIOTEXT(E) REVIEW* EST CONSACRÉ À L'ARCHITECTURE, AU DESIGN GRAPHIQUE ET À LA THÉORIE DU DESIGN CONTEMPORAIN. CHAQUE GROUPE ÉTAIT RESPONSABLE DE SA PAGE.

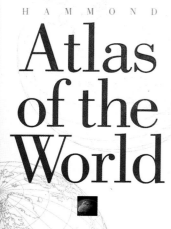

842

843

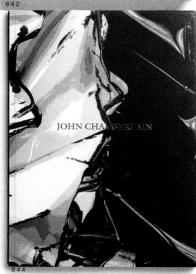

844

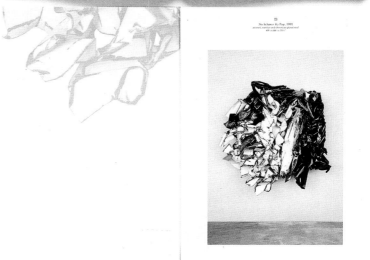

845

846

847

DAS APOKALYPTISCHE MENÜ

848

849

■ 842, 843 ART DIRECTORS: MICHAEL GERICKE, COLIN FORBES DESIGNERS: MICHAEL GERICKE, DONNA CHING, SHARRON HAREL AGENCY: PENTAGRAM DESIGN PUBLISHER: HAMMOND INC. COUNTRY: USA ■ 842, 843 THIS IS THE FIRST ATLAS TO BE CREATED ENTIRELY FROM A DIGITAL DATABASE. IT CONTAINS MAPS, CHARTS AND GRAPHS. ● 842, 843 DIES IST DER ERSTE ATLAS, DER VOLLSTÄNDIG AUF DIGITALER BASIS HERGESTELLT WURDE. ▲ 842, 843 IL S'AGIT DU PREMIER ATLAS À AVOIR ÉTÉ RÉALISÉ ENTIÈREMENT SUR LA BASE DE DONNÉES DIGITALISÉES.

■ 844-847 CREATIVE DIRECTOR: MARC GLIMCHER DESIGNERS: TOMOKO MAKIURA, PAUL POLLARD PHOTOGRAPHER: PETER FOE (844, 845), ELLEN PAGE WILSON (846, 847) PUBLISHER: THE PACE GALLERY COUNTRY: USA ■ 844-847 EXHIBITION CATALOGS ON THE WORKS OF AMERICAN ARTISTS JOHN CHAMBERLAIN AND CLAES OLDENBURG. ● 844-847 AUSSTELLUNGSKATALOGE MIT WERKEN DER AMERIKANISCHEN KÜNSTLER JOHN CHAMBERLAIN UND CLAES OLDENBURG. ▲ 844-847 DEUX CATALOGUES D'EXPOSITION DES ARTISTES AMÉRICAINS JOHN CHAMBERLAIN ET CLAES OLDENBURG.

■ 848, 849 DESIGNER: PETER SCHMIDT, THOMAS NECHLEBA PHOTOGRAPHER: CHRISTIAN VON ALVENSLEBEN PUBLISHER: EDITION CHRISTIAN BRANDSTÄTTER COUNTRY: GERMANY/AUSTRIA ■ 848, 849 THIS BOOK CONTAINS PHOTOGRAPHS OF A SPECIAL MENU AND TEXTS THAT URGE READERS TO CHANGE THEIR EATING/COOKING HABITS FOR THE SAKE OF THE ENVIRONMENT. ● 848, 849 DIESES BUCH ENTHÄLT PHOTOS EINES SPE-

850

851

ZIELLEN MENUS SOWIE TEXTE, DIE DEN LESER AUFFORDERN, SEINE ESS- UND KOCHGEWOHNHEITEN ZU ÄNDERN, UM DIE UMWELT ZU RETTEN. ▲ 848, 849 CE LIVRE RENFERME DES PHOTOS D'UN MENU PARTICULIER, AINSI QUE DES TEXTES QUI DEVRAIENT ENCOURAGER LE LECTEUR À CHANGER SES HABITUDES EN MATIÈRE D'ALIMENTATION ET DE CUISINE, AFIN DE CONTRIBUER À LA PROTECTION DE L'ENVIRONNEMENT.

■ 850 ART DIRECTORS/DESIGNERS: RAFAEL JIMÉNEZ, CLAUDIA CASAGRANDE AGENCY: JIMÉNEZ & CASAGRANDE PUBLISHER: BENEDIKT TASCHEN VERLAG COUNTRY: GERMANY ■ 850 FRONT AND BACK OF A SOFT COVER BOOK ON JAPANESE DESIGN. ● 850 VOLLSTÄNDIGER UMSCHLAG EINES BROSCHIERTEN BUCHES ÜBER JAPANISCHES DESIGN. ▲ 850 COUVERTURE COMPLÈTE D'UN LIVRE BROCHÉ SUR LE DESIGN JAPONAIS.

■ 851 DESIGNERS: RANDY BRAATEN, LEIF ÅÅBJÖRNSSON PUBLISHER: SWEDEN POST STAMPS COUNTRY: SWEDEN ■ 851 HARD-COVER BOOK WITH A BANDEROLE PRESENTING SWEDISH ART AND STAMPS. ● 851 EIN GEBUNDENES BUCH MIT BANDEROLE: EINE SAMMLUNG SCHWEDISCHER KUNST UND BRIEFMARKEN. ▲ 851 UN LIVRE RELIÉ AVEC UN BANDEAU RÉPÉTANT LE TITRE. L'OUVRAGE PRÉSENTE DES ŒUVRES D'ART ET DES TIMBRE SUÉDOIS.

852

853

854

855

856

857

858

■ **852-854** ART DIRECTOR/DESIGNER: JEFF LARSON ILLUSTRATOR: RHONDA NASS STUDIO: LARSON DESIGN ASSOC. CLIENT: LITHO PRODUCTIONS COUNTRY: USA ■ **852-854** QUARTERLY POSTER CALENDAR FOR A PRINTING COMPANY. EACH HAS A SPECIAL SLOGAN: "KEEPING COOL AS PRESSURES SNOWBALL," "BRINGING COLORFUL IDEAS TO LIFE;" "THE RIGHT TOOLS FOR CHANGING TIMES." ● **852-854** QUARTALSKALENDER EINER DRUCKEREI IN PLAKATFORMAT. JEDES KALENDERBLATT HAT EINEN BESONDEREN LEITSATZ: «WIR BEHALTEN AUCH UNTER DRUCK EINEN KÜHLEN KOPF»; «WIR BRINGEN FARBIGE IDEEN ZUM LEBEN» UND «DAS RICHTIGE WERKZEUG FÜR VERÄNDERTE ZEITEN». ▲ **852-854** CALENDRIER TRIMESTRIEL D'UNE IMPRIMERIE. CHAQUE AFFICHE A UN LEITMOTIV PARTICULIER: «NOUS GARDONS LA TÊTE FROIDE, MÊME DANS LES SITUATIONS DE STRESS», «NOUS DONNONS VIE À DES IDÉES COLORÉES», «L'OUTIL QU'IL FAUT EN CETTE ÉPOQUE DE CHANGEMENTS».

■ **855-858** ART DIRECTOR: JENNIFER MORLA DESIGNERS: JENNIFER MORLA, SHARRIE BROOKS PHOTOGRAPHER: HOLLY STEWART STYLIST: BRIGITTE HARM VAN HOLDEN FLOWER STYLIST: MICHAELE THUNEN CLIENTS: MORLA DESIGN, HOLLY STEWART PHOTOGRAPHY COUNTRY: USA ■ **855-858** TWO VERSIONS OF A CALENDAR SERVING AS PROMOTION FOR BOTH THE DESIGN STUDIO AND THE PHOTOGRAHER. THE WATCHES INDICATE THE MONTHS AND SERVE AS SYMBOL FOR THE PASSING OF TIME. IN THE PHOTOGRAPHER'S VERSION, THEY ARE SUBSTITUTED BY STILL LIFES. ● **855-858** ZWEI VERSIONEN EINES KALENDERS, DIE DEM DESIGN-STUDIO BEZIEHUNGSWEISE DER PHOTOGRAPHIN ALS EIGENWERBUNG DIENEN. DIE MONATSUHREN DIENEN ALS SYMBOL FÜR DIE VERGÄNGLICHKEIT DER ZEIT. IN DER VERSION DER PHOTOGRAPHIN FINDEN SICH AN IHRER STELLE STILLEBEN. ▲ **855-858** DEUX VERSIONS D'UN AGENDA QUI SERT DE PUBLICITÉ AU STUDIO DE DESIGN AINSI QU'À LA PHOTOGRAPHE. LES RÉVEILS SYMBOLISENT LA FUGACITÉ DU TEMPS. DANS LA VERSION DE LA PHOTOGRAPHE, ILS ONT ÉTÉ REMPLACÉS PAR DES PHOTOS.

■ **859-864** ART DIRECTOR/DESIGNER: HANS KENTIE PHOTOGRAPHER: RENÉ DE WIT CLIENT: DUROX NEDERLAND BV COUNTRY: NETHERLANDS ■ **859-864** CALENDAR FOR A MANUFACTURER OF BUILDING MATERIAL. THE TYPOGRAPHY OF THE CALENDARIUM SUGGESTS THE RHYTHM OF THE BUILDINGS SHOWN. ● **859-864** DIESER KALENDER FÜR EINEN HERSTELLER VON BAUMATERIALIEN WURDE AN ARCHITEKTEN VERSCHICKT. DIE TYPOGRAPHIE DES KALENDARIUMS NIMMT DEN RHYTHMUS DER ABGEBILDETEN GEBÄUDE AUF. ▲ **859-864** CALENDRIER POUR UN FABRICANT DE MATÉRIEL DE CONSTRUCTION. LA NUMÉROTATION DES MOIS A ÉTÉ COMPOSÉE EN FONCTION DE LA PERSPECTIVE DES BÂTIMENTS REPRÉSENTÉS.

■ 865, 866 ART DIRECTORS/DESIGNERS: KOEWEIDEN/POSTMA PHOTOGRAPHER: YANI AGENCY: KOEWEIDEN/POSTMA CLIENT: MINISTRY OF ECONOMIC AFFAIRS COUNTRY: NETHERLANDS ■ 865, 866 THE COPY OF THESE SHEETS FROM A CALENDAR FOR THE DUTCH MINISTRY OF ECONOMIC AFFAIRS READS: "VENTURE CAPITAL—STARTING COSTS MONEY. THE EA WANTS TO BE A PARTNER TO SOUND BUSINESS PLANS." "TECHNICAL EXPERTISE—TECHNOLOGY IS WITH YOU YOUR WHOLE LIFE. EA WANTS TECHNOLOGY TO FIND A BROAD BASE IN SOCIETY." ● 865, 866 BLÄTTER EINES KALENDERS DES NIEDERLÄNDISCHEN WIRTSCHAFTSMINISTERIUMS (EA): «STARTKAPITAL – EIN START KOSTET GELD. DAS EA WILL IHR PARTNER BEI GUTER UNTERNEHMENSPLANUNG SEIN.» «TECHNISCHE EXPERTISE – TECHNIK BEGLEITET SIE DURCH DAS GANZE LEBEN. DAS EA MÖCHTE, DASS TECHNIK IN DER GESELLSCHAFT EINE BREITE BASIS FINDET.» ▲ 865, 866 «CAPITAL DE DÉPART – DÉMARRER COÛTE DE L'ARGENT. L'EA VEUT ÊTRE VOTRE PARTENAIRE DANS VOS PROJETS D'ENTREPRISE»; «L'EXPERTISE TECHNIQUE – LA TECHNIQUE VOUS ACCOMPAGNE TOUTE VOTRE VIE DURANT. L'EA AIMERAIT QUE LA TECHNIQUE DISPOSE D'UNE BASE PLUS LARGE DANS LA SOCIÉTÉ».

865

866

■ 867-872 DESIGNERS: CARIE OLTMANN, ARNO LINDEMANN, SUSANNE SCHRÖDER, THOMAS HEUTER PHOTOGRAPHER: DIETER EIKELPOTH AGENCY: PRODUCT SERVICE PAUL BORNSCHEUER KG CLIENT: B.A.T. COUNTRY: GERMANY ■ 867-872 "HB. FOR PEOPLE WITH PERSPECTIVE." THE BEST MOTIFS FROM AN AD CAMPAIGN FOR HB CIGARETTES WERE USED IN THIS CALENDAR. ● 867-872 «HB. FÜR LEUTE MIT LAUNE.» DIE BESTEN MOTIVE EINER WERBEKAMPAGNE FÜR HB-ZIGARETTEN WURDEN IN DIESEM KALENDER VERWENDET. ▲ 867-872 «HB. POUR LES GENS DE BONNE HUMEUR». LES MEILLEURS SUJETS D'UNE CAMPAGNE DE PUBLICITÉ POUR LES CIGARETTES HB ONT ÉTÉ REPRIS DANS CE CALENDRIER.

■ 873, 874 ART DIRECTOR: HENRIK BARENDS PHOTOGRAPHER: TONO STANO CLIENT: SDH COUNTRY: NETHERLANDS ■ 873, 874 SPREADS FROM A DESK CALENDAR PRESENTING THE COMPANY'S STAFF MEMBERS. ● 873, 874 SEITEN AUS EINEM TISCHKALENDER, IN DEM DIE MITARBEITER DES BETRIEBES VORGESTELLT WERDEN. ▲ 873, 874 DOUBLES PAGES D'UN AGENDA: LES COLLABORATEURS DE L'ENTREPRISE Y SONT REPRÉSENTÉS.

867

868

869

870

871

872

873

874

875

876

877

878

879

880

■ 875-877 ART DIRECTORS: TOSHIO YAMAGATA, SERGE LUTENS DESIGNER: AOSHI KUDO PHOTOGRAPHER: SERGE LUTENS CLIENT: SHISEIDO COMPANY
LTD. COUNTRY: JAPAN ■ 875-877 SERGE LUTENS, WHO CREATED A SPECIAL, SURREALISTIC TYPE OF WOMEN FOR SHISEIDO, DEDICATES THIS
CALENDAR TO "BRILLANCY AND LIGHT." ● 875-877 SERGE LUTENS, DER FÜR SHISEIDO EINEN SPEZIELLEN SURREALISTISCHEN FRAUENTYP
SCHUF, WIDMET DIESEN KALENDER «DER BRILLANZ UND DEM LICHT». ▲ 875-877 SERGE LUTENS, QUI A CRÉÉ POUR CETTE FIRME DE COS-
MÉTIQUES UN TYPE DE FEMME SURRÉALISTE, MYSTÉRIEUSE, A CONSACRÉ CE CALENDRIER AU THÈMES DE L'ÉCLAT ET DE LA LUMIÈRE.

■ 878, 880 ART DIRECTOR/DESIGNER: KAZUMASA NAGAI AGENCY: NIPPON DESIGN CENTER CLIENT: ISHIBASHI KENSETSU KOGYO K.K. COUNTRY: JAPAN ■
878, 880 PROMOTIONAL CALENDAR WITH IMAGES OF ANIMALS FOR A CONSTRUCTION COMPANY. ● 878, 880 WERBEKALENDER MIT TIERDAR-
STELLUNGEN FÜR EINE BAUFIRMA. ▲ 878, 880 CALENDRIER PUBLICITAIRE ORNÉ D'ANIMAUX STYLISÉS POUR UNE ENTREPRISE DE CONSTRUCTION.

■ 879 ART DIRECTOR/DESIGNER: SIMON SERNEC CLIENT: RADECE PAPIR COUNTRY: SLOVENIA ■ 879 COVER SHEET OF A WALL CALENDAR FOR A
PAPER MILL. ● 879 WANDKALENDER EINES PAPIERHERSTELLERS AUS SLOWENIEN. ▲ 879 CALENDRIER MURAL POUR UN FABRICANT DE PAPIER.

INDEX


VERZEICHNIS


INDEX

# E N T R Y   F O R M

**I wish to enter the attached in the following Graphis competition:**

················································································

☐ **GRAPHIS PACKAGING 6**      ☐ **GRAPHIS POSTER 95**      ☐ **GRAPHIS PHOTO 95**      ☐ **GRAPHIS DESIGN 95**

(NOVEMBER 30, 1993)     (APRIL 30, 1994)     (AUGUST 31, 1994)     (NOVEMBER 30, 1993)

| CATEGORY | CATEGORY | CATEGORY | CATEGORY |
|---|---|---|---|
| CODES/KATEGORIEN/CATÉGORIES | CODES/KATEGORIEN/CATÉGORIES | CODES/KATEGORIEN/CATÉGORIES | CODES/KATEGORIEN/CATÉGORIES |
| **PA1** FOOD/NAHRUNGSMIT-TEL/ALIMENTATION | **PO1** ADVERTISING/WER-BUNG/PUBLICITÉ | **PH1** FASHION/MODE | **DE1** ADVERTISING/WER-BUNG/ PUBLICITÉ |
| **PA2** BEVERAGES/GETRÄN-KE/BOISSONS | **PO2** CULTURE/KULTUR | **PH2** JOURNALISM/ JOURNALISMUS | **DE2** BOOKS/BÜCHER/ LIVRES |
| **PA3** TOBACCO/TABAK-WAREN/TABAC | **PO3** SOCIAL/GESELL-SCHAFT/SOCIÉTÉ | **PH3** STILL LIFE/STILLEBEN/ NATURE MORTE | **DE3** BROCHURES/BRO-SCHÜREN |
| **PA4** COSMETICS/KOSMETIK/ COSMÉTIQUES | | **PH4** FOOD/LEBENSMITTEL/ CUISINE | **DE4** EDITORIAL/REDAKTIO-NELL/RÉDACTIONNEL |
| **PA5** FASHION/MODE | | **PH5** PEOPLE/MENSCHEN/ PERSONNES | **DE5** PHOTOGRAPHY/ PHOTOGRAPHIE |
| **PA6** HOUSEHOLD/HAUS-HALT/MÉNAGE | | **PH6** PRODUCTS/PRODUKTE/ PRODUITS | **DE6** ILLUSTRATION |
| **PA7** CARRIER BAGS/TRAG-TASCHEN/SACS | | **PH7** OUTDOORS/LAND-SCHAFT/EXTÉRIEURS | **DE7** CORPORATE IDENTITY |
| **PA8** INDUSTRY/INDUSTRIE | | **PH8** ARCHITECTURE/ ARCHITEKTUR/ | **DE8** PACKAGING/VER-PACKUNG |
| **PA9** PROMOTION | | **PH9** WILD LIFE/TIERE/ ANIMAUX | **DE9** CALENDARS/KALENDER/ CALENDRIERS |
| **PA10** MISCELLANEOUS/ ANDERE/AUTRES | | **PH10** SPORTS/SPORT | **DE10** MISCELLANEOUS/ ANDERE/DIVERS |
| | | **PH11** FINE ART/KUNST/ART | |

---

TAPE (DON'T GLUE) A COMPLETED COPY OF THIS FORM TO THE BACK OF EACH ENTRY

**TITLE OF ENTRY**

**CATEGORY CODE**      YEAR CREATED/PUBLISHED

**PERSON/COMPANY ENTERING WORK**

**PRINT NAME**

**TITLE**

**COMPANY**

**ADDRESS**

**CITY**      STATE

**COUNTRY**

**TELEPHONE**      FAX

I hereby grant permission for the attached material to be published in any Graphis book, article in Graphis magazine, or any advertisement, brochure or other material produced for the purpose of promoting Graphis publications.

**SIGNATURE**      DATE

Mail entries to:

**Graphis Press, Dufourstrasse 107, CH-8008 Zürich, or
Graphis US, Inc., 141 Lexington Ave, New York, NY 10016**

---

BITTE AUF DER RÜCKSEITE JEDER ARBEIT MIT KLEBBAND BEFESTIGEN
VEUILLEZ SCOTCHER (NE PAS COLLER) AU DOS DE CHAQUE ENVOI

**TITEL DER ARBEIT**
**TITRE DE L'ENVOI**

**KATEGORIENCODE**      ENTSTANDEN/PUBLIZIERT
**CODE DE CATÉGORIE**      CRÉÉ/PUBLIÉ (ANNÉE)

**NAME DES EINSENDERS**
**TRAVAIL ENVOYÉ PAR**

**TITEL/TITRE**

**FIRMA/SOCIÉTÉ**

**ADRESSE**

**PLZ/STADT/LAND**
**VILLE/CODE POSTAL/PAYS**

**TELEPHON**      FAX

Ich erteile Graphis hiermit das Recht zur Veröffentlichung meiner Arbeit in den Graphis-Büchern oder in der Zeitschrift Graphis sowie in Anzeigen oder Broschüren zu Werbezwecken der Graphis-Publikationen.

Par la présente, j'autorise les Editions Graphis à publier le travail ci-joint dans tout livre Graphis, dans tout article du magazine Graphis, ainsi que tout matériel publicitaire, brochure, dépliant ou autre, destiné à la promo-tion des publication Graphis.

**DATUM**      UNTERSCHRIFT
**DATE**      SIGNATURE

Bitte senden Sie Ihre Arbeit an/Veuillez envoyer à l'adresse suivante::

**Graphis Verlag AG, Dufourstrasse 107, CH-8008 Zürich,
Schweiz, Telephon: 01-383-82-11, Telefax: 01-383-16-43**

# CALL FOR ENTRIES

........................................................................................................................................................

**Graphis Packaging 6** · Entry Deadline: November 30, 1993

■ Food, beverages, tobacco products, cosmetics, fashion, household, industrial products, carrier bags, stationery, promotions, etc. Eligibility: All work produced between December 1989 and November 1993. ● Konsumgüter, Tabakwaren, Kosmetik, Mode, Haushaltartikel sowie Tragtaschen und Einwickelpapier, industrielle Produkte, Promotionsartikel usw. In Frage kommen: Arbeiten, die zwischen Dezember 1989 und November 1993 entstanden sind. ▲ Biens de consommation, tabac, produits cosmétiques, accessoires de mode, articles de ménage, sacs à commissions, papier cadeau, produits industriels, articles de promotion etc. Seront admis: tous travaux réalisés entre décembre 1989 et novembre 1993.

**Graphis Poster 95** · Entry Deadline: April 30, 1994

■ Advertising, cultural, and social posters. Eligibility: All work produced between May 1993 and April 1994. ● Plakate für Werbezwecke sowie kulturelle und soziale Plakate. In Frage kommen: Arbeiten, die zwischen Mai 1993 und April 1994 entstanden sind. ▲ Affiches publicitaires, culturelles et sociales. Seront admis: tous les travaux réalisés entre mai 1993 et avril 1994.

**Graphis Photo 95** · Entry Deadline: August 31, 1994

■ Ads, catalogs, invitations, announcements, record covers, and calendars on any subject.. Photographs taken for consumer or trade magazines, newspapers, books and corporate publications. Personal studies on any subject. Experimental or student work on any subject. Eligibility: All work produced between September 1993 and August 1994. ● Anzeigen, Kataloge, Plattenhüllen, Kalender. Photos für Zeitschriften, Zeitungen, Bücher und Firmenpublikationen. Persönliche Studien. Experimentelle Aufnahmen oder Studentenarbeiten. In Frage kommen: Arbeiten, die zwischen September 1993 und August 1994 entstanden sind. ▲ Publicité, catalogues, invitations, annonces, pochettes de disques, calendriers. Reportages pour magazines et journaux, livres et publications d'entreprise. Études personnelles, créations expérimentales ou projets d'étudiants. Seront admis: tous les travaux réalisés entre septembre 1993 et août 1994.

**Graphis Design 95** · Entry Deadline: November 30, 1993

■ Ads; promotion brochures, catalogs, invitations, record covers, announcements, logos, corporate campaigns, calendars, books, book covers, packaging, company magazines; newspapers, consumer or trade magazines, annual reports; illustration. Eligibility: All work produced between December 1, 1992 and November 30, 1993. ● Werbung, Broschüren, Kataloge, Plattenhüllen, Logos, Firmenkampagnen, Kalender, Bücher, Buchumschläge, Packungen. Zeitschriften, Hauszeitschriften, Jahresberichte, Illustrationen. In Frage kommen: Arbeiten, die zwischen Dezember 1992 und November 1993 entstanden sind. ▲ Publicité; brochures, catalogues, invitations, pochettes de disques, annonces, logos, identité visuelle, calendriers, livres, packaging;journaux, revues, magazines de sociétés, rapports annuels; illustration. Seront admis: les travaux réalisés entre décembre 1992 et novembre 1993.

■ **What to send:** Reproduction-quality duplicate transparencies (4x5" or 35mm). They are required for large, bulky or valuable pieces. ALL 35MM SLIDES MUST BE CARDBOARD-MOUNTED, NO GLASS SLIDE MOUNTS PLEASE! Please mark the transparencies with your name. If you do send printed pieces they should be unmounted, but well protected. WE REGRET THAT ENTRIES CANNOT BE RETURNED. ● **Was einsenden:** Wenn immer möglich, schicken Sie uns bitte reproduktionsfähige Duplikatdias. Bitte Dias mit Ihrem Namen versehen. Bitte schicken Sie auf keinen Fall Originaldias. KLEINBILDDIAS BITTE IM KARTONRAHMEN, KEIN GLAS! Falls Sie uns das gedruckte Beispiel schicken, bitten wir Sie, dieses gut geschützt aber nicht aufgezogen zu senden. WIR BEDAUERN, DASS EINSENDUNGEN NICHT ZURÜCKGESCHICKT WERDEN KÖNNEN. ■ **Que nous envoyer:** Nous vous recommandons de nous faire parvenir de préférence des duplicata de diapositives (4x5" ou 35mm. N'oubliez pas d'inscrire votre nom dessus). NE PAS ENVOYER DE DIAPOSITIVES SOUS VERRE! Si vous désirez envoyer des travaux imprimés, protégez-les, mais ne les montez pas sur carton. Nous vous signalons que les envois que vous nous aurez fait parvenir ne pourront vous être retournés.

■ **How to package your entry:** Please tape (do not glue) the completed entry form (or a copy) to the back of each piece. Please do not send anything by air freight. Write "No Commercial Value" on the package, and label it "Art for Contest." ● **Wie und wohin senden:** Bitte befestigen Sie das ausgefüllte Einsendeetikett (oder eine Kopie davon) mit Klebstreifen (nicht kleben) auf jeder Arbeit und legen Sie noch ein Doppel davon lose bei. Bitte auf keinen Fall Luft- oder Bahnfracht senden. Deklarieren Sie «Ohne jeden Handelswert» und «Arbeitsproben für Wettbewerb». ▲ **Comment préparer votre envoi:** Veuillez scotcher (ne pas coller) au dos de chaque spécimen les étiquettes dûment remplies. Nous vous prions également de faire un double de chaque étiquette, que vous joindrez à votre envoi, mais sans le coller ou le fixer. Ne nous expédiez rien en fret aérien. Indiquez «Sans aucune valeur commerciale» et «Echantillons pour concours».

■ **Entry fees** Single entries: United States U.S. $15; Germany, DM 15,00; all other countries, SFr 15.00. Three or more pieces entered in a single contest: North America, U.S. $35, Germany DM 40,00, All other countries SFr 40.00. These entry fees do not apply to countries with exchange controls or to students (please send copy of student identification). ● **Einsendegebühren:** Für jede einzelne Arbeit: Deutschland DM 15.00, alle andern Länder SFr 15.00. Für jede Kampagne oder Serie von drei oder mehr Stück: Deutschland DM 40.00, übrige Länder SFr 40.00. Für Studenten (Ausweiskopie mitschicken) und Länder mit Devisenbeschränkugen gelten diese Einsendegebühren nicht. ▲ **Droits d'admission:** Envoi d'un seul travail: pour l'Amérique du Nord, US$ 15.00; pour tous les autres pays: SFr. 15.00. Campagne ou série de trois travaux ou plus pour un seul concours: Amérique du Nord, US$ 35.00; autres pays: SFr. 40.00. Les participants de pays qui connaissent des restrictions monétaires sont dispensés des droits d'admission, au même titre que les étudiants (veuillez envoyer une photocopie de la carte d'étudiant).

■ **Where to send:** Entries from the United States and Canada should be sent to the New York office and checks should be made payable to GRAPHIS US, INC, NEW YORK. Entries from all other countries should be sent to the Zurich office and checks should be made payable to GRAPHIS PRESS CORP., ZURICH. ● **Wohin senden:** Bitte senden Sie uns Ihre Arbeiten an Graphis Zürich zusammen mit einem Scheck, ausgestellt in SFr. (auf eine Schweizer Bank ziehen oder Eurocheck) oder überweisen Sie den Betrag auf PC Luzern 60-3520-6 oder PSchK Frankfurt 3000 57-602 (BLZ 50010060). ▲ **Où envoyer:** Veuillez envoyer vos travaux à Graphis Zurich et joindre un chèque tiré sur une banque suisse ou un Eurochèque; ou verser le montant sur le compte chèque postal Lucerne 60–3520–6.

........................................................................................................................................................

**Graphis Press, Dufourstrasse 107, CH-8008 Zürich, Switzerland, telephone: 41-1-383 82 11, fax: 41-1-383 16 43**
**Graphis US, Inc., 141 Lexington Avenue, New York, NY 10016, telephone: (212) 532 9387, fax: (212) 213 3229**

# E N T R Y   F O R M

**I wish to enter the attached in the following Graphis competition:**

☐ **GRAPHIS PACKAGING 6**
(NOVEMBER 30, 1993)

CATEGORY

CODES/KATEGORIEN/CATÉGORIES

**PA1** FOOD/NAHRUNGSMITTEL/
ALIMENTATION

**PA2** BEVERAGES/GETRÄNKE/
BOISSONS

**PA3** TOBACCO/TABAK-
WAREN/TABAC

**PA4** COSMETICS/KOSMETIK/
COSMÉTIQUES

**PA5** FASHION/MODE

**PA6** HOUSEHOLD/HAUSHALT/
MÉNAGE

**PA7** CARRIER BAGS/TRAG-
TASCHEN/SACS

**PA8** INDUSTRY/INDUSTRIE

**PA9** PROMOTION

**PA10** MISCELLANEOUS/
ANDERE/AUTRES

☐ **GRAPHIS POSTER 95**
(APRIL 30, 1994)

CATEGORY

CODES/KATEGORIEN/CATÉGORIES

**PO1** ADVERTISING/WERBUNG/
PUBLICITÉ

**PO2** CULTURE/KULTUR

**PO3** SOCIAL/GESELLSCHAFT/
SOCIÉTÉ

☐ **GRAPHIS PHOTO 95**
(AUGUST 31, 1994)

CATEGORY

CODES/KATEGORIEN/CATÉGORIES

**PH1** FASHION/MODE

**PH2** JOURNALISM/
JOURNALISMUS

**PH3** STILL LIFE/STILLEBEN/
NATURE MORTE

**PH4** FOOD/LEBENSMITTEL/
CUISINE

**PH5** PEOPLE/MENSCHEN/
PERSONNES

**PH6** PRODUCTS/PRODUKTE/
PRODUITS

**PH7** OUTDOORS/LAND-
SCHAFT/EXTÉRIEURS

**PH8** ARCHITECTURE/
ARCHITEKTUR/

**PH9** WILD LIFE/TIERE/
ANIMAUX

**PH10** SPORTS/SPORT

**PH11** FINE ART/KUNST/ART

☐ **GRAPHIS DESIGN 95**
(NOVEMBER 30, 1993)

CATEGORY

CODES/KATEGORIEN/CATÉGORIES

**DE1** ADVERTISING/WERBUNG/
PUBLICITÉ

**DE2** BOOKS/BÜCHER/
LIVRES

**DE3** BROCHURES/BROSCHÜREN

**DE4** EDITORIAL/REDAKTIONELL/
RÉDACTIONNEL

**DE5** PHOTOGRAPHY/
PHOTOGRAPHIE

**DE6** ILLUSTRATION

**DE7** CORPORATE IDENTITY

**DE8** PACKAGING/VER-
PACKUNG

**DE9** CALENDARS/KALENDER/
CALENDRIERS

**DE10** MISCELLANEOUS/
ANDERE/DIVERS

TAPE (DON'T GLUE) A COMPLETED COPY OF THIS FORM TO THE BACK OF EACH ENTRY

BITTE AUF DER RÜCKSEITE JEDER ARBEIT MIT KLEBBAND BEFESTIGEN
VEUILLEZ SCOTCHER (NE PAS COLLER) AU DOS DE CHAQUE ENVOI

TITLE OF ENTRY

CATEGORY CODE          YEAR CREATED/PUBLISHED

PERSON/COMPANY ENTERING WORK

PRINT NAME

TITLE

COMPANY

ADDRESS

CITY          STATE

COUNTRY

TELEPHONE          FAX

TITEL DER ARBEIT
TITRE DE L'ENVOI

KATEGORIENCODE          ENTSTANDEN/PUBLIZIERT
CODE DE CATÉGORIE          CRÉÉ/PUBLIÉ (ANNÉE)

NAME DES EINSENDERS
TRAVAIL ENVOYÉ PAR

TITEL/TITRE

FIRMA/SOCIÉTÉ

ADRESSE

PLZ/STADT/LAND
VILLE/CODE POSTAL/PAYS

TELEPHON          FAX

I hereby grant permission for the attached material to be published in any Graphis book, article in Graphis magazine, or any advertisement, brochure or other material produced for the purpose of promoting Graphis publications.

SIGNATURE          DATE

Ich erteile Graphis hiermit das Recht zur Veröffentlichung meiner Arbeit in den Graphis-Büchern oder in der Zeitschrift Graphis sowie in Anzeigen oder Broschüren zu Werbezwecken der Graphis-Publikationen.

Par la présente, j'autorise les Editions Graphis à publier le travail ci-joint dans tout livre Graphis, dans tout article du magazine Graphis, ainsi que tout matériel publicitaire, brochure, dépliant ou autre, destiné à la promotion des publication Graphis.

DATUM          UNTERSCHRIFT
DATE          SIGNATURE

Mail entries to:
**Graphis Press, Dufourstrasse 107, CH-8008 Zürich, or
Graphis US, Inc., 141 Lexington Ave, New York, NY 10016**

Bitte senden Sie Ihre Arbeit an/Veuillez envoyer à l'adresse suivante::
**Graphis Verlag AG, Dufourstrasse 107, CH-8008 Zürich,
Schweiz, Telephon: 01-383-82-11, Telefax: 01-383-16-43**

GRAPHIS PHOTO · GRAPHIS PHOTO · GRAPHIS PHOTO · GRAPHIS PHOTO · GRAPHIS PHOTO · GRAPHIS PHOTO

GRAPHIS LETTERHEAD

GRAPHIS POSTER · GRAPHIS POSTER · GRAPHIS POSTER · GRAPHIS POSTER · GRAPHIS POSTER · GRAPHIS POSTER

88 89 90 91 92 93

GRAPHIS ANNUAL REPORTS · GRAPHIS ANNUAL REPORTS · GRAPHIS ANNUAL REPORTS

1 2 3

N U D E S

GRAPHIS DESIGN · GRAPHIS DESIGN · GRAPHIS DESIGN · GRAPHIS DESIGN · GRAPHIS DESIGN · GRAPHIS DESIGN

89 90 91 92 93

▶ AVAILABLE IN EARLY 1994

GRAPHIS TYPOGRAPHY

A B C D E
F G H I J
K L M N O
P Q R S T
U V W X Y
Z ! ? & ß

▶ AVAILABLE IN EARLY 1994

GRAPHIS T-SHIRT DESIGN

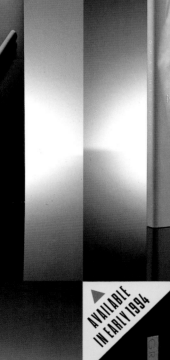

▶ AVAILABLE IN MID 1994

RECYCLED PAPERS · COATED PAPERS · UNCOATED PAPERS

3 2 1

# G R A P H I S   B O O K S

## BOOK ORDER FORM: USA, CANADA, SOUTH AMERICA, ASIA, PACIFIC

| BOOKS | ALL REGIONS |
|---|---|
| □ GRAPHIS PHOTO 93 | US$ 69.00 |
| □ GRAPHIS LOGO 2 | US$ 60.00 |
| □ GRAPHIS POSTER 93 | US$ 69.00 |
| □ GRAPHIS ANNUAL REPORTS 3 | US$ 75.00 |
| □ GRAPHIS NUDES | US$ 85.00 |
| □ GRAPHIS DESIGN 93 | US$ 69.00 |
| □ GRAPHIS LETTERHEAD 2 | US$ 69.00 |
| □ GRAPHIS LETTERHEAD 1 | US$ 69.00 |
| □ GRAPHIS LOGO 1 | US$ 50.00 |
| □ GRAPHIS PUBLICATION 1 (ENGLISH) | US$ 75.00 |
| □ GRAPHIS PACKAGING 5 | US$ 75.00 |
| □ GRAPHIS DIAGRAM 1 | US$ 65.00 |
| □ ART FOR SURVIVAL: THE ILLUSTRATOR AND THE ENVIRONMENT | US$ 40.00 |
| □ ROCK SCISSORS PAPER | US$195.00 |

□ CHECK ENCLOSED

USE CREDIT CARDS (DEBITED IN US DOLLARS)

□ AMERICAN EXPRESS    □ MASTERCARD    □ VISA

CARD NO. _____ EXP. DATE _____

CARDHOLDER NAME _____

SIGNATURE _____

□ PLEASE BILL ME (BOOK(S) WILL BE SENT WHEN PAYMENT IS RECEIVED)

(PLEASE PRINT)

NAME _____

TITLE _____

COMPANY _____

ADDRESS _____

CITY _____

STATE/PROVINCE _____ ZIP CODE _____

COUNTRY _____

SEND ORDER FORM AND MAKE CHECK PAYABLE TO:
GRAPHIS US, INC., 141 LEXINGTON AVENUE,
NEW YORK, NY 10016-8193

REQUEST FOR CALL FOR ENTRIES
PLEASE PUT ME ON YOUR "CALL FOR ENTRIES" LIST FOR THE
FOLLOWING TITLES:

□ GRAPHIS DESIGN        □ GRAPHIS ANNUAL REPORTS
□ GRAPHIS DIAGRAM       □ GRAPHIS CORPORATE IDENTITY
□ GRAPHIS POSTER        □ GRAPHIS PACKAGING
□ GRAPHIS PHOTO         □ GRAPHIS LETTERHEAD
□ GRAPHIS LOGO          □ GRAPHIS TYPOGRAPHY

SUBMITTING MATERIAL TO ANY OF THE ABOVE TITLES QUALIFIES
SENDER FOR A DISCOUNT TOWARDS PURCHASE OF THAT TITLE.

## BOOK ORDER FORM: EUROPE, AFRICA, MIDDLE EAST

| BOOKS | EUROPE/AFRICA MIDDLE EAST | GERMANY | U.K. |
|---|---|---|---|
| □ GRAPHIS PHOTO 93 | SFR.123.– | DM 149,– | £ 52.00 |
| □ GRAPHIS LOGO 2 | SFR. 92.– | DM 108,– | £ 38.00 |
| □ GRAPHIS POSTER 93 | SFR.123.– | DM 149,– | £ 52.00 |
| □ ANNUAL REPORTS 3 | SFR.137.– | DM 162,– | £ 55.00 |
| □ GRAPHIS NUDES | SFR.168.– | DM 168,– | £ 62.00 |
| □ GRAPHIS DESIGN 93 | SFR.123.– | DM 149,– | £ 52.00 |
| □ GRAPHIS LETTERHEAD 2 | SFR.123.– | DM 149,– | £ 52.00 |
| □ GRAPHIS LETTERHEAD 1 | SFR.123.– | DM 149,– | £ 52.00 |
| □ GRAPHIS LOGO 1 | SFR. 92.– | DM 108,– | £ 38.00 |
| □ GRAPHIS PUBLICATION 1 □ ENGLISH  □ GERMAN | SFR.137.– | DM 162,– | £ 55.00 |
| □ ART FOR SURVIVAL: THE ILLUSTRATOR AND THE ENVIRONMENT | SFR. 79.– | DM 89,– | £ 35.00 |

(FOR ORDERS FROM EC COUNTRIES V.A.T. WILL BE CHARGED
IN ADDITION TO ABOVE BOOK PRICES)

FOR CREDIT CARD PAYMENT (ALL CARDS DEBITED IN SWISS
FRANCS):

□ AMERICAN EXPRESS          □ DINER'S CLUB

□ VISA/BARCLAYCARD/CARTE BLEUE

CARD NO. _____ EXP. DATE _____

CARDHOLDER NAME _____

SIGNATURE _____

□ PLEASE BILL ME (ADDITIONAL MAILING COSTS WILL BE CHARGED)

(PLEASE PRINT)

LAST NAME _____ FIRST NAME _____

TITLE _____

COMPANY _____

ADDRESS _____

CITY _____ POSTAL CODE _____

COUNTRY _____

PLEASE SEND ORDER FORM TO:
GRAPHIS PRESS CORP., DUFOURSTRASSE 107
CH–8008 ZÜRICH, SWITZERLAND

REQUEST FOR CALL FOR ENTRIES
PLEASE PUT ME ON YOUR "CALL FOR ENTRIES" LIST FOR THE
FOLLOWING TITLES:

□ GRAPHIS DESIGN        □ GRAPHIS ANNUAL REPORTS
□ GRAPHIS DIAGRAM       □ GRAPHIS CORPORATE IDENTITY
□ GRAPHIS POSTER        □ GRAPHIS PACKAGING
□ GRAPHIS PHOTO         □ GRAPHIS LETTERHEAD
□ GRAPHIS LOGO          □ GRAPHIS TYPOGRAPHY

SUBMITTING MATERIAL TO ANY OF THE ABOVE TITLES QUALIFIES
SENDER FOR A DISCOUNT TOWARDS PURCHASE OF THAT TITLE.

# G R A P H I S   M A G A Z I N E